THE LION, THE ADMIRAL AND A CAT CALLED B. UMA VIJAYLAKSHMI

V. Raghunathan is an academic, author, corporate leader, columnist and hobbyist.

He has served as a professor of finance at IIM Ahmedabad, president of ING Vysya Bank, CEO of GMR Foundation and director at the Schulich School of Business, Toronto (India Campus). Additionally, he has been an adjunct professor at SDA Bocconi University in Milan, Italy, and the Schulich School of Business in Toronto, Canada.

Raghu's books include the national bestseller *Games Indians Play*, *To Every Parent, To Every School*, *Irrationally Rational*, *Return to Jammu*, *The Good Indian's Guide to Queue Jumping*, *Beyond the Call of Duty*, *Duryodhana*, *Locks, Mahabharata and Mathematics*, *Ganesha on the Dashboard*, *The Corruption Conundrum* and *Don't Sprint the Marathon*.

He also has one of the country's most varied collections of old and ancient Indian locks.

He lives in Bengaluru with his wife, Meena.

Praise for the Book

'In the best of times, it is difficult for an author to write about his own life-experiences. The question always arises: who would really care? But Raghunathan writes with such expert aplomb and confidence that one is drawn into his life wanting to know more. Some of the insights from the book are as relevant to everyday life as they may be to formal management situations. His choice of words and his sense of humour linger long after one has finished reading the book. One often smiles inwardly in sincere appreciation. A fine book to read.'

—Suresh Krishna,
Industrialist and former President, Confederation of Indian Industry

'A captivating read that draws valuable lessons from daily experiences, encouraging innovative solutions and a deep sense of fulfilment from dedicated and responsible work. Readers will connect with the author's journey and share his enthusiasm for making a meaningful impact on society, solving problems and making a difference. As a young Cadet Officer and Raghu's batchmate at INS Venduruthy in 1976, I am amazed at the authenticity of the memories he brings out in the chapter on the Good Admiral. The rest of the book is equally authentic and engaging.'

—Rear Admiral Sanatan Kulshrestha (Retd)

'Recounted in the lucid style of a consummate storyteller, the book is a collection of fascinating autobiographical stories on the unpredictability of life's experiences. I immensely enjoyed reading the stories. The book is a must read for all readers of non-fiction.'

—Samir Barua,
Former Director, IIM Ahmedabad

'This is a great book about life and various life situations the author faced as a student, teacher, officer, CEO, customer, and most of all as a citizen. The settings vary from the Indian Navy to coal mines to IIMs, banks, colleges and public places to the corporate sector. These are situations any one of us may face but few of us observe so well and respond to them the way one should, to get the best out of them and also contribute to the future of the society.'

—T.V. Rao, Former Professor, IIMA; Chairman, TVRLS; and Founder President, National HRD Network

'Absorbing account of an accomplished individual, the book is a splendid tour de force of a versatile life. Having traversed through the armed forces training, academia, corporate and higher education, and written in a candid manner, Raghu tells us how he met life on his own terms, established creditable standards and boldly confronted inequities, corruption and bureaucratic oddities without turning a Nelson's eye.'

—K. Jairaj,
Additional Chief Secretary (Retd), Government of Karnataka

'A wonderful compilation of life moments, described in such detail that I could vividly imagine and experience them as I read.'

—Hema Ravichandar,
Strategic HR Advisor and former Group Head, HRD, Infosys

'In his inimitable unputdownable style, Raghu captures some of the major happenings of his professional life in this book. Knowing him and Meena, and our common love for IIMA, the book was a sentimental journey for me. And talk of journeys. the chapter "Journey to Nowhere" captures the bus trips that Raghu and I experienced together joyfully. While "furiously typing or writing away every single day, with unvarying regularity" may be the key to success to his book writing in his own words, the beauty that he brings out of his thoughts, feelings and experiences in his eventful career lends to a great reading joy in this book.'

—G. Raghuram,
Former Director, IIM Bangalore and former Professor, IIM Ahmedabad

'I thoroughly enjoyed reading the book. It is a very authentic and relatable narrative for Indians like me who grew up in a middle-class family between the 1960s and 1980s. Raghu's memory for details is remarkable. His elegant, lucid and evocative prose laced with humour is a joy to read and many times brought a smile and even a hearty laugh. There are several nostalgic passages, none more than the reference to the *Illustrated Weekly* which in its own way had also influenced my career choice, not to forget the HMT watch!'

—Ravi Chellam,
Wildlife biologist and conservation scientist

THE LION, THE ADMIRAL AND A CAT CALLED B. UMA VIJAYLAKSHMI

Learnings from Life and Management

V. RAGHUNATHAN

Published by Westland Business, an imprint of Westland Books, a division of Nasadiya Technologies Private Limited, in 2024

No. 269/2B, First Floor, 'Irai Arul', Vimalraj Street, Nethaji Nagar, Alapakkam Main Road, Maduravoyal, Chennai 600095

ISBN: 9789360455361

10 9 8 7 6 5 4 3 2 1

Typeset by Mukul
Printed at Thomson Press (India) Ltd

To my parents and siblings, with deepest gratitude and love

Contents

CHAPTER ONE

The Good Admiral—The Glimpse of a Leader

'If there is no downside, go for it'
is a valuable strategy in navigating life's opportunities ...

1975

The Flag Office Commanding-in-Chief, or the FOC-in-C, Rear Admiral Ronald Lynsdale Pereira, AVSM (Ati Vishisht Seva Medal), was as impressive a man as the visions his name evoked. An incredibly handsome and infinitely tall man with blue eyes, his spotless white uniform with impressive golden epaulets made him even more awe-inspiring. His office was enormous and his table must once have doubled duty for billiards. Everything in the office and on the table, including half a dozen little flags, were absolutely in their place, spic and span. As we were ushered into the office by the admiral's adjutant, the admiral was in the process of signing some documents. The commander who was escorting me to the admiral clicked his heels smartly and saluted, while twenty-year-old me remained standing at attention as I had been instructed by the good commander. Almost immediately, the admiral put his pen down, got up, returned the commander's salute, and with a broad smile on his face, came around the table, shaking my hand affably, as a father would welcome a son returning from a vacation. He took me to a small round coffee table and had me seated. He took the seat opposite, while the commander remained standing.

'Ah son, you so remind me of myself, when I got my commission ...'

For the life of me I couldn't imagine what the tall, fair and handsome admiral could conceivably have had in common with me, when the admiral completed his sentence ...

On the day I stepped foot into INS Venduruthy Naval Training Academy at Willingdon Island, Cochin, the prospect of crossing paths with an admiral in the foreseeable future felt more remote than an assignation with Poseidon himself. I was just content that when I graduated from the Academy a year later, I would be an acting sub-lieutenant, which sounded good enough. A tête-à-tête with an admiral was not even in my fantasies.

My naval spell had commenced some four months earlier in June 1975. I had boarded a train to Cochin from the Delhi railway station, arriving at the Ernakulam Junction in the wee hours. I wasn't the only one arriving groggy, headed for INS Venduruthy, the well-known naval base. There were at least thirty others. There were a couple of blue navy trucks with grey canvas topping and coconut-fibre-cushioned benches laid sideways, waiting to haul us to our destination. We had a nearly twenty-minute ride in the truck, passing through the Kerala small town dawn-time landscape, before we crossed over the old Venduruthy Bridge (the new bridge today being Venduruthy-Vikranth Bridge) to enter Willingdon Island, home of INS Venduruthy. No one at the time told us the touristy titbits that the island was man-made, created in the 1930s for constructing a new port, or that it was built from the soil dredged out from Vembanad Lake (also Lake of Kochi), or that it was—and still is—the largest man-made island in India. Not that any of the information, even if supplied, would have made a difference to the collective mixed mood of the raw troop aboard the truck just then.

All that one noticed, and only just, was that as soon as we crossed the longish Venduruthy Bridge (some 700 metres long, we would learn by and by), the road turned left and almost immediately the truck entered the premises of the naval base through the wide and imposing Travancore Gate.

From here on, the rest of the day was a blur. Congregating opposite the living quarters for the officer cadets, some were allotted a room each (with a common toilet section at the end of the corridor), and others in groups of three or four were allotted a large hall (but with a toilet attached)—very clean quarters, quite 'officer-like'. A few of the quarters were already occupied as some cadets had reported the day before. Some would arrive by later trains during the day, as it was the last reporting day.

After the room allocation, breakfast at the cadets' mess, an hour to settle affairs in the room, proceed for a haircut—called the zero cut, not unlike the crop of Kim Jong Un or any number of teenagers of today—shaving, bathing, writing quick postcards home, lunch ... more formalities to be completed ... collecting basic uniform gear, caps, shoes, belts ... getting to know each other ... acting like veterans in front of the newer arrivals just as yesterday's arrivals were acting with us ... tea and snacks ... more briefings ...

The next stop was the administrative office to fill and sign myriad forms. Speaking of signing sundry forms, in one of them, one undertook to abide by all orders from one's superiors 'until one's last breath'.

Early dinner by 7 p.m. and most of us were too tired to keep our eyes open beyond 8 and crashed on our beds.

The days to follow were equally a blur. A typical day would look like this:

Rise by 5.00 or 5.15 a.m., depending on the time you required for your ablutions. Trying to get up without an alarm clock was like trying to set sail without a destination. You would be so bone-tired by the end of each day that you would hit the bed well before the 10 p.m. whistle for lights-off, and without an alarm, the danger was real that you would go on sleeping forever. No one much cared for the morning wake-up siren call, as most would be awake much earlier, lest the siren should just meld into one's dream—like a fire engine rushing past the neighbourhood—and could not be relied upon to wake you up. Most had their own mechanical alarm clocks, which would soon be supplanted by our biological ones.

Once up, you discovered that there was no luxury of performing your ablutions in any refined order. You had to learn to brush, shit, shower and shave in a random order, depending on which facility was occupied by whom at what point in time. On one occasion, being ready with a good 15 minutes to spare, I sauntered into the wing shared by three to see one of the guys sitting on the commode with a newspaper spread across his thighs in a concession to modesty, his face contorted, while another shaved in the same space 3 feet away and the third showered in the other corner. And one didn't have the luxury of hot water for a shower. This was Kerala after all, not Leh. The water in the bathrooms would come in a thin cold trickle, the overnight Kerala rains having made it nearly ice-cold.

In between the rush, you had to find the time to take in the thermos of tea or coffee left outside your door on a tray with a clean cup and saucer. The brew would arouse in you the Abraham Lincoln-like urge to shout out, 'Waiter! If this is tea, I want coffee; and if this is coffee, I want tea.' But of course, you wouldn't.

Once ready, you would rush to the parade ground by 6 a.m. for some 90 minutes of inspection and physical training. If you weren't at the parade ground at 6 sharp by the chief petty officer's moody watch, you would run a round of the huge ground as punishment—'extra drill', as it was euphemistically called.

The inspection of the parade could start with the division officer* (DO, a lieutenant, the equivalent of a captain in the army) running his palm upwards on each cadet's cheeks—left and right; and if he found a cheek rough, the proprietor of the cheek would be asked to run another round. If you were to pass the DO's muster, you had to shave running the razor both ways on the face so evenly that it would be smoother than a baby's bottom. And the punishment for giving yourself a nick while shaving (easy to get one with the 'safety blades' of that era) was beyond egregious. There was nothing more un-officer like than having a cheek with a razor snick. Or so it was drilled into us during the morning drills.

Extra drills were not the only punishment one could earn. Punishment could include push-ups, sit-ups, star jumps, pumping, standing forever at attention, running to touch a distant point and coming back, made worse when undertaken in full gear, especially during rifle training. But the worst of all was the loss of Sunday liberty.

Over half the cadets would suffer the extra drills, and worse, this was even before the parade and physical training had started for the day! About half an hour thus consumed, the subsequent parade and exercises would commence and continue under the charge of a petty officer just when the sun and the stifling humidity were rising and permeating the sky and air respectively, turning your sweat to steam. You would be convinced all energy had been squeezed out of you like the last of the toothpaste through the tube like my mother did, and you had no more reserves of energy left to muster anymore. But if you thought so, you were naïve.

* The division officer could also be replaced from time to time by the officer of the day (or OOD), of the same rank. But the difference is immaterial and the two terms, namely DO and OOD, may be used interchangeably here on.

For that's when the 7-km daily run would commence, lasting about half an hour. You would huff and you would puff all through the circuit. En route, convinced that you were on your last legs, you would stop, bent double holding your stomach, but you would not dare savour the luxury for more than a moment. The reason was that as the entire bunch of cadets, about fifty, returned to the parade ground after the 7-km run, the bunch would be divided into two groups: those who were among the first half to complete the run and those who had been the laggards. No matter how fast the entire cohort ran, some had to be in the first half and others in the second. Now each one from the second group had to carry one from the first group, back-to-back, arms locked, and run an extra round of the parade ground. Already weary beyond endurance, you would marvel that you had any reserves of energy left to perform this feat. Many would fall halfway. But there was nothing to it but to pick up your assigned load—which typically weighed a ton—again and complete the circuit. An occasional variant for the slow sloths was to walk on the gravelled road on their knees for some 100 metres, at the end of which one's knees looked like they had been worked over with the coarsest sandpaper. One could see hefty hulks and skeletal skinnies alike bawling like babies at this point.

Your salvation lay in not getting caught in the second half. But never having been a great runner, I generally finished in the second lot and must have carried many a hefty commodore- and admiral-to-be upon my back—often with bruised knees, muscle cramps, ankle twists, stomach cramps and much more.

The daily dose of the morning torture would finally end around 8 a.m. There would be some who would report sick, and if the petty officer felt inclined, you could be referred to the Sanjivani Hospital within the base premises. You were not allowed to report sick before or during the physical training. Only after.

Sundays were off only after the morning drills. However, the routine diverged from the usual 7-km run to an extended 14-km jog around the naval airport of the Willingdon base, fetching the same drills and punishment for ending among the second half of the lot.

Worse, even the liberty on Sundays depended upon how well one had performed in the parades during the week. By and by, some would learn to sneak out via the backdoors of the cabins, putting their future liberties in great peril. Not that such impudence was seriously discouraged, because a dash of such sassiness was secretly admired. Risk taking and all.

From the parade ground, one would rush to the mess for breakfast—the choices being badly toasted or raw bread with ample butter and jam, soggy cornflakes or chewy wheat porridge, sodden omelette and fruits, usually apples and bananas, all drowned with terrible tea or coffee, often weaker than sin itself.

Breakfast over, with everybody stinking equally—though each in his individual flavour—from the morning workout, one would give another shower a pass, as in any case there would be little time for it. One would get into the formal uniform (supplied three weeks after our joining) and rush to the administrative block 'on the double' (quick as you can—cadets were not supposed to walk, only jog) for the theory classes which started at 9 a.m.

The theory classes involved three sessions every day that went on until 1 p.m. They involved plenty of familiar trigonometry (related to navigation and therefore mostly hyperbolic), logistics, parts and functions of ships, categories of ships, communication, map reading, seamanship, basic marine engineering and so on. This was the best part of the day, as one was learning something cerebral and new, something which made logical sense, and best of all, didn't require one to jump or jog.

At 1.00 p.m. sharp, you would rush to the mess for lunch. But reaching the mess did not mean you could start eating. You went into the dining hall and sat at the table and didn't move a muscle until the OD had taken his place at the head of the table. You picked up the napkin and placed it on your lap when the OD did so. Food, all beautifully and elegantly laid out was positioned at the centre of the long table across which the cadets sat facing each other. Of course, one was expected to use only a spoon, knife and fork and touch no morsel with the hand. Protocol required that you follow the OD closely. If the OD stopped eating the first course and jumped to the second, so did the cadets. This meant keeping pace with the OD or foregoing that portion of the meal. The OD kept an eye out for those who missed his cue, and they were flagged for the extra drill at the evening parade. This ensured you did not take too long with any one course.

Every meal started with soup of dubious coloration. And you soon learnt to move the soup spoon from the near to the far end of the bowl and to tilt the soup bowl not towards you, but away from you, with your left-hand forefinger on the far side of the bowl and the thumb towards you. The bulk of the meal was mutton, chicken or fish aplenty for the main dish, with a side portion of soggy rice and/or burnt shapeless rotis with the texture of a dog's ears. Vegetarians like me got a raw deal. Almost literally. For vegetarian fare, the main course would be an enormous portion of semi-boiled cabbage (smelling most disagreeable), eggplant (slightly less disagreeable, but with seeds), or okra (all slimy) on most days, with occasional portions of potatoes, all of which one was expected to sprinkle with some additional salt and pepper to taste and eat elegantly with the knife and fork.

The best part of the meal was—what in a parallel universe would have been the worst part of a meal—the mushy custard with mushy apples and bananas or dim-looking rice kheer or a piece of gelatinous cake. I nevertheless looked forward to this course greatly, having skipped my main portions since I did not particularly relish cabbage, eggplant or okra even when cooked by a mother—whether mine or anyone else's. No matter how hungry, I never could eat those half-boiled vegetables and the half-burnt chapatis, the smell of which entered through my nostrils into my brain and, from there, into my soul. The very sight of them was enough to want me to fast-forward to the dessert which was always served in a fixed portion. So, the OD's quick pace was never a real problem for me.

I wonder if I mentioned earlier that almost every cadet was a spy, and word of any long shelf-life goodies—from namkeens to laddus—that a cadet may have procured from an odd friend or relative in Cochin, or what one may have bought during the weekend liberties from town and stashed deep in the depths of the black trunks, would travel faster than the fake news that travels on WhatsApp today. And once the word was out, the marked trunks would be ransacked and the contents devoured in double quick time.

One poor worthy had brought a tin of ghee and was promptly nicknamed Tarzan. His can of calories was comprehensively devoured during a lunch or two by all the cadets and the OD, like good communists sharing common property. What belonged to one cadet, belonged to all, in a nuanced reinterpretation of one for all and all for one.

Lunch over, one fell into formation in a small clearing around the mess under a tree, for an informal session of sundry briefings with the OD. The OD, depending on our luck on a given day, could be smiling, scowling or sneering. They would all ask us encouragingly if we had anything to share with them. But any attempt to complain about any aspect of life at the base would invariably evoke a variant of the following response: 'Get comfortable being uncomfortable.'

It was during one such session of 'shooting the breeze', as the OD loved to call it, that he asked the entire assembly a general question: 'How many of you have an arts degree? Raise your hands.'

A few hands went up, including mine. I had a postgraduate diploma in statistics which was under the arts department of the university.

'Which ones of you have a science degree?'

A few more hands went up, including mine, for I had a B.Sc. in Physics, Chemistry and Maths.

'And which ones of you have a commerce degree?'

Another bunch of hands went up, including mine, for I had an MBA under the commerce department of the university.

The OD looked at me hard. He barked orders for me to fall out of formation. I did so crisply, as required.

'Are you looking for ten rounds around the parade ground?'

'No sir! Err ... not exactly sir ...'

'You son of a bachelor! What do you mean not exactly? You are raising your hand for every question I ask. You are clearly not listening to me, are you?'

'No sir ... er ... yes sirrr!' The problem was the cadets were not encouraged to say anything beyond 'yes sir' and 'no sir' when talking to a superior officer unless specifically asked to explain. Hence my apparent diffidence.

'Then explain yourself.'

'Sir, I have a graduation in science, a B.Sc.—so I have a science background; I have a postgraduate diploma in statistics, which was under the arts department of the university; and I have an MBA from the commerce department of the university.'

'WHAT? WHAT?? MBA? As in *master of business administration*?' (Remember, MBAs were still few and far between those days.)

I answered with a crisp, 'Yes Sirrr!'

'And a postgraduate diploma in statistics?'

'Sir.'

'Sir what?'

'Yes, Sir.'

'Then what the bloody hell are you doing here? Are you sure you aren't mad?' he asked involuntarily, making it very clear that he thought I was absurdly over-qualified for where I was just then.

'Er ... no Sir.'

'What's that supposed to mean? How old are you? You started attending school straight from your mother's womb or what?'

'Not quite Sir. I completed my undergrad by seventeen, started school at two,' I felt emboldened to respond.

'Close enough to the womb,' muttered the OD, and then there was some five seconds of silence after which it was time to break lines.

How I came to have a B.Sc., a postgraduate diploma in statistics and an MBA—all by the time I was twenty—is another little story, like a Panchatantra tale.

I wasn't a whizz-kid by a long shot in my school and college. It's just that by sheer chance I started kindergarten at two, just because I didn't want to be left at home by myself, with my two elder sisters going to school, and threw some mighty tantrums about it. From there, by a quirk of a practical joke played by providence, abetted by some abdication of parental responsibility by my father who admitted me to Class 3 when he should have entered me to Class 1 following a transfer from Ambala to Jammu, I found myself entering Class 10, back in Ambala after another transfer, by the time I was twelve, and therefore matriculated by the time I was barely thirteen. The matriculation curriculum of the Panjab University Board went so over my head that I would never ever top any class test, leave alone aim for anything higher. Ergo, my academic record was doomed to remain mediocre, no matter how hard I tried. I had therefore given up trying, hard or otherwise.

Turning thirteen, I huffed and puffed my way through matriculation with a first class by the skin of my teeth from Panjab

University Board in 1968. With that accomplishment, I was in no position to even sniff at an engineering college. I moved to the Pre-university class (called Prep those days) of the S.D. College of the same trust that ran my school. And by seventeen, I had acquired a B.Sc. from Panjab University, Chandigarh, in 1972, having missed my first-class by a narrow margin, notwithstanding some stupendous hard work put in towards the last year of my B.Sc. to make up for my atrocious performance in the previous years.

At seventeen, a job for second-class B.Sc. was pure fiction. So, I ended up enrolling for a course that was grandly called 'Postgraduate Diploma in Statistics' at the nearby and brand new Kurukshetra University—bifurcated from the Panjab University not long before—to kill a year as I figured what to do with myself. I took this up mainly because the diploma sounded close enough to mathematics, which I thought of as less of a challenge than either physics or chemistry. Even after the diploma in 1973, still too young to apply for most jobs—not that there were many going around. I would end up, at eighteen, applying for an MBA at Jodhpur University.

How I ended up doing an MBA could also be a tale within a tale, like the Panchatantra. A story of how life can change course on the whims of utter chance. We often underplay the role of randomness in our lives. But if you ask me, much of life owes itself to random chances at every turn. It is my belief that if you took all your major decisions in life at the throw of a coin instead of careful deliberation, your life may turn out not very different! The law of unintended consequences often puts paid to our carefully crafted decisions. But long story short, I landed up with an MBA thanks mainly to my decent prowess at chess, to which I had been introduced by my mother when I had been barely six or seven—another matter of chance.

I was visiting Jodhpur, representing Kurukshetra University, participating in the All-India Inter-Universities Chess Tournament that was being held at the Jaswant Campus of Jodhpur University, the vice chancellor of which at the time was the well-known educationist Prof. V.V. John. It was by sheer chance that, sauntering around between two games, I ran into an old classmate from my B.Sc. days.

'What on earth are you doing here?'

The guy looked unexpectedly superior all of a sudden, and said, 'Doing my MBA.'

'What on earth is that?' I asked.

Now, the knowledgeable is often one who is ahead of you on the knowledge curve by a whisker. Well, he had learnt about it equally accidentally (from his medical representative brother who had been posted in Jodhpur at the time) during the days I had been pursing my diploma in statistics. But he made sure I felt like an ignoramus as he explained what an MBA was. 'It is "master of business administration". You get good executive jobs (which to an average undergraduate meant something better than a clerk or a medical representative) even as you pass out. I suggest you apply as well. The admissions have just opened for the written test, and the forms are available in the department.'

It is interesting how advice, solicited or unsolicited, is more often given than taken. It is equally interesting to realise the potential that advice, when it is accepted, can have in our lives and, at times, change the very course of our lives. In the event, a casual piece of advice, by a casual friend, in a purely random meeting of a few minutes, perhaps changed my life significantly. I have often wondered what course my life may have taken but for this chance encounter. But let me not go on a tangent here.

I had only a few minutes to think about the advice. On second thoughts, there was really nothing much to deliberate. After all, what was the downside? Nothing. 'So go for it,' I told myself and in the next ten minutes I had collected the forms and by next morning, I had submitted them in the office of the commerce department.

Long story short, in the months following my application, I took a qualifying written test, followed by a group discussion and interview, and eventually made it to the final list of the small intake of fifteen out of some 900-odd applicants.

At the time, my actual knowledge of Jodhpur University or the Jodhpur Management Programme (JMP, or any MBA programme for that matter) could have been written behind a postage stamp. But soon after I had picked up the form and applied to JMP, I did a little more investigation, which basically meant procuring a copy of a recent issue of *The Illustrated Weekly of India*, which carried a lead article on Indian business schools. According to this article, there were two institutions fully dedicated to management education in the country, namely, Indian Institutes of Management (IIMs) in Ahmedabad and Calcutta (now Kolkata), which offered a postgraduate diploma in management, and some seven-odd universities that offered MBA degrees. Of these, Jodhpur was ranked fourth (and had Prof. V.V. John as vice chancellor), probably because their placements were good, which probably was because their intake of students was extremely low. But truth be told, even if JMP had been ranked last, I may have done nothing differently, especially because in my wisdom of the time, a degree was better than a diploma, of which I already had one in hand, and so why go after another at some IIM? Ergo, MBA from JMP it was!

So that's how at twenty, I had my B.Sc., postgraduate diploma and MBA.

Back to the main story. After the afternoon briefing, it was time to head for the practical seamanship sessions starting at 2.30 p.m. at the jetty.

At one level, this was the most exciting part of the day, when we were introduced to real seamanship skills under the tutelage of a coxswain—usually a leading seaman—in charge of the boat and our training. The leading seaman in charge would lecture us competently on the parts of the boat and corresponding parts on a ship. We would learn to tell a cruiser from a destroyer from a frigate from a corvette and their respective purposes. Or a canoe from a cutter from a dingy from a skiff from a dory and such. This was fun and we would all be somewhat relaxed, especially as a leading seaman would not be too hard on us.

An hour of lectures and we would be allowed to board the rowboat to learn applied seamanship. There would be thirteen to a boat, sitting facing the back of the boat with oars in hand. We would soon realise that holding the oar in a steady position even for ten seconds against the thrust of the waves was a chest-bursting exercise. Each 45-minute session in the sea seemed to drain us of enough sweat to raise the water level.

At 4.30 p.m., barely able to walk, we would jog half-heartedly to the mess for watery tea, samosas and nankhatais.

At 5.00 p.m., it was time for the gym. Boxing was compulsory for all. After some coaching by the petty officer, it would be time to box with the opposite number in the designated pair. If you tried to pussy-foot around each other in a tacit understanding of the 'you don't hurt me bad and I won't hurt you bad' kind, you could bet your backside you would be spotted by the petty officer, who would then box with you for real. That fate would be worse than fighting each other really hard.

Some days, this slot would be spent in the swimming pool. After some basic instructions:

'All you dumb fXs who don't know how to swim, fall aside.'

A large chunk of the dumb fXs fell aside. Some comfort, as I was among them.

'All right, now, line up one behind the other, aft of the steps to the diving board (25 feet high, we would learn later). Each of you will climb up and on the count of three, you will jump into the pool. Feet first (into the deep end). As the preceding one touches the water, the next will start his ascent on the steps. Understood?'

'YESSIRR!'

Most of us learnt to swim by the second session, even as a particularly bad case or two was dragged out of the pool from time to time like drowning rats by the two or three seaman lifeguards on duty posted precisely for this purpose. No one to our knowledge was ever injured, and no one came close to drowning.

But one cadet who found learning to swim particularly difficult was neatly dubbed dense as a brick, hydraulically speaking, by the OD during one of those post-lunch sessions.

By 6.30 p.m., it would be time to go to our rooms and dress up for dinner in dinner formals. We had half an hour free to ourselves. Dinner was at 7 p.m., which would follow the exact same procedure as the lunch with the OD.

Post-dinner, on most days, the OD would engage the cadets in the same patch outside the mess as the afternoon sessions.

'All cadets to fall in, double quick.'

'All right boys! You are in your dinner outfits now. I give you exactly 5 minutes. You will all go to your rooms and change into your physical training outfits and report back here and fall in exactly where you are now. Is that clear?'

'YESSIRR.'

Invariably there were some laggards, who earned a round about the parade ground the following morning.

'All right! Now you are in your trainers. Because you b***ds were lazy last time, I now give you 3 minutes. You will go back to your rooms and report back here in your sleeping gear.'

Three minutes later, most of the batch came back in pyjamas and kurtas or striped sleeping suits. A couple of worthies, standing in the fourth row trying to make themselves as invisible as possible, were caught wearing their white canvas shoes under their night pyjamas.

'You clown, you sleep in your shoes or what? Trying to cheat me here, are you? Two rounds of the grounds in the morning.'

'But sir, I am wearing my slippers and I don't sleep in them,' I muttered in reflex, a tad encouraged by the informal atmosphere. These were early days and clearly, one was still wet behind the ears.

'Hey you! Bloody MBA.' (I thought I saw him suppress a smile.) 'Fall out! Trying to give me lip are you? Four rounds before the parade.'

'Now all you jokers, go back and change into formals and report in 2 minutes and 30 seconds.'

Once again a few were caught out with their pyjamas showing from under their trouser cuffs, and more extra drills were handed out liberally all around.

Such sessions continued and would continue until each one learnt to change from one gear to another within 90 seconds flat.

Around 8.30 p.m. we would stagger into our rooms, tired to the bone and beyond, bruised and blistered from the day's toils, and had an hour and a half or thereabouts to revise the day's theory classes if one had the energy and will—for 10 p.m. was supposed to be lights out. This meant, if the lights in your rooms were found burning after 10 p.m. by the OD, who may choose to come on a spiteful round at any time at random past 10, and often at 10.02, you had a round or two added to your fate in the morning at the parade ground. Most lights would be out long before 10 p.m., though it was not unknown for someone desperately writing a long letter home or revising the trigonometry lesson or whatever, to be caught occasionally and signed up for those early morning extra drills.

The next morning, the algorithm would repeat itself. And the next morning. And the next.

And thus went our introduction to the naval life. Talks of wanting to quit and go home weren't entirely rare. But most often we would talk each other out of it. In any case, most cadets had a plain undergraduate degree to their names, and nobody saw their prospects outside the Navy being very promising, with jobs nearly impossible to come by. Often during our evening drills, the OD would introduce us to the traditions of the navy and such, and even tell us some inspiring stories. Incidentally, most of the time we had our OD who was known to be a fine but tough officer—the kind of tough who, when he asked you a question, you wanted to answer 'Yes Sirrr' first and figure out the question later—for guidance. But every now and then the OD would be replaced by a temporary stand-in officer. These could be any of the four or five other lieutenants posted at the base. These ODs would often be more relaxed and they were the ones who would tutor us to have some fun.

And then of course there were the joke sessions, sometimes even joined by one of the more lenient ODs during the post-dinner drills or during the odd Sunday afternoons in smaller groups, often with the constraint that the gags had to be related to the navy, and better still if the jokes involved certain actions which in nature usually result in a baby nine months later. And the navy being the navy, the bawdier the jokes, the better they were considered and the louder the hoots.

Once we even had a ribald jokes competition, and some of the bad ones went thus:

> *What's long, hard and full of seamen? A submarine of course!*
>
> *What's the vice of a vice admiral? The rear of the rear admiral of course!*
>
> *How do they separate the men from the boys in the navy? With a crowbar of course!*

But these one-liners were regarded tame, and another time we had a *real* bawdy jokes competition, best left out of polite conversation. And on and on we would go. The jokes may have been both bad and bawdy, but they provided us cadets much needed mirth in an otherwise tough regimen, especially in the early weeks.

We had been in the Academy only a few weeks. It was a Sunday. I was gasping and grunting around the airport on a 14-km run. The course I was jogging on was a narrow public road running around the airport (a travesty of phraseology, given that it was I who was doing the running and not the road). My legs were all but packing in, as if of a mind of their own.

A lumbering and rickety bus stopped just ahead of me, to pick up a passenger. I was looking at the bus longingly. We had heard stories of how it hadn't been unknown for a few daring cadets in the earlier batches to have taken a ride in the bus, part of the way. The idea was tempting and nearly within grasp. But I hesitated a shade too long. And just as well. For just as the bus was taking off again, I felt a sharp sting on my calf, followed by a bellow, 'MOVE!'

Alarmed at the unexpected smack, I turned and saw the face of a petty officer astride a bicycle. He had just smacked me, albeit lightly, but smacked nevertheless, with the leather strap of his whistle, as he exhorted me to *MOVE*!

I knew that it wasn't unknown for PT instructors to follow the joggers on bicycles precisely to discourage the kind of thoughts that I had just entertained. But for a petty officer to whip a cadet officer seemed excessive, even if he had read the turmoil in my head about the bus through the back of my skull. I looked at my calf and saw a light welt (to be fair, he hadn't hurt me seriously) and something in me gave. It was one thing for him to report me to the OD (But report what? That I was looking at a bus longingly?) or call me out for a prescription drill (though I had violated no rules and was aware of none that prohibited looking at a bus longingly), but quite something else to use the 'whip'. I knew that if I reported him, he would be in some trouble. But ratting on a mid-career man for his momentary foolishness—which was not really unlike my momentary temptation, except that he had given vent to his impulse while I had delayed it by a whisker—would not do. I did not report the matter, but the episode hurt my ego way worse than my calf.

I was still smarting under this dual assault on my calf and ego when a few days later, just as I returned from the post-dinner drill to my room, there was a crisp knock at my door. I opened the door and was not surprised to see the OD, who would inspect one's wardrobe at random to ensure that shirts, trousers and undergarments were all neatly stacked in their places.

'Evening, Sir.' I stiffened my arms in brief attention and waited.

The OD silently entered, pulled forward the only chair in the room and occupied it. I remained standing, facing him.

'At ease! So, you are an MBA right?' This was a week after the post-dinner incident I referred to earlier.

'Yes, Sir'.

'All right. Here is an assignment for you. The Royal Navy, UK, has called for essays from navies worldwide on "Management for Naval Communicators". The idiots in Delhi have asked INS Venduruthy to enter the essay on behalf of the Indian Navy. Now you say you are an MBA. So, you have three weeks to write the essay and turn it in. There is no time to lose. Better do a good job.'

I gulped some air like a fish pulled out of water. He added helpfully, 'The essay is to be 25,000 words.'

Incidentally, 25,000 words is about half the size of a decent-sized pocketbook. This chapter up to this point is about 7,500 words. You are talking two and a half times that size on a technical subject. And I was twenty-something and barely a few weeks old in the navy.

'Question, Sir.'

'Shoot.'

'Do I get access to a library, Sir?'

'The library is at the other end of the base and besides, ours is a rather technical library. Won't be any good to you. I am afraid you'll be on your own.'

'So how do I go about it, Sir?'

'You figure out. You are the bloody MBA.'

'Will I get some free time to do the writing, Sir? Three weeks seems too tight.'

'You son of a gun, are you here on a holiday or what? You have to manage the time yourself. No special concessions. You are doing nobody a favour. Your time belongs to the Indian Navy. Is that clear?'

There was nothing to it but say, 'SIRR!' and leave it at that.

'You will write out the essay by hand. You will be supplied requisite stationery.'

Thank God for small mercies!

I sat in a daze. Until lights out.

It took me a week to understand the broad issues surrounding the topic 'Management for Naval Communicators'. The communicators in the navy provide a staff function that is a supporting role to the hard-core naval personnel in the Executive Branch (EB). These officers in the Communications Branch are required to be electronics engineers, while those in the core hands-on arm of the EB, the line function, could be just graduates with maths and physics in their Class 12—as was our cohort. To join the navy even as a seaman in the Communications Branch, one had to be an electronics diploma holder, while to be a seaman in the regular EB, one just needed to pass Class 12. What is more, the core EB officers, and the non-commissioned officers, received a higher pay than their communications counterparts because of the sundry allowances they received when aboard a warship, submarine or aircraft, or when on sundry tactical exercises. That was not all either. If you were a core EB officer, you had the possibility of going all the way to the top, to becoming an admiral, while the officer from the communications branch would have to stop a rung lower at vice admiral. And to make matters worse, promotions for the core EB officers were much faster than for the communications officers.

So how on earth do you attract and retain talent in the Communications Branch? Easier asked than answered. Especially by an officer cadet.

Well, that's what the essay had to be all about. Or at least what I made of it all. I now had to don my thinking cap and put my meagre skills of report writing learnt in my not-so-rigourous MBA to work. Start with a problem definition; maybe toss in a section on literature survey (not possible, except for what I could recall of Abraham Maslow, Douglas McGregor, Henri Fayol, Peter F. Drucker and ... that about exhausted the names I could recall of management scientists—not that I had read any of them beyond my textbook references); bung in some leadership styles from autocratic to democratic to laissez-faire; supplement it all with a goodly dose of incentive systems; hold forth on pay and promotion corrections and stuff; round it all up with a conclusion—preferably with an executive summary up front—and most importantly, use three words where one would do, and I would have my essay; or rather the Indian Navy would have theirs. In short, I had to do what my half-baked and immature understanding and abilities permitted.

But the problem was time. I had two weeks to go; no free time and a soul-sapping schedule by day, with many of the technical sessions demanding undivided attention. I would seriously have to consider turning a believer if I had to turn in the essay in two weeks.

I did the only thing I could. A trick also used by some to read pornographic material which had appeared magically amidst the cohort and circulated stealthily.

I took to putting the blanket over the table lamp after lights-out to keep the light from showing through the cracks of the door or windows and working furiously for the next hour or two. For the next two weeks, I had to average nearly 2,000 words each night, which amounted to about ten pages of handwritten A4 sheets. In my MBA days, I had amply contributed to *Executive Reflection*—the house magazine that I had founded with a classmate, and the experience now came in handy, by virtue of which I could add titles, sub-titles, sub-sub-titles et al. to bulk up the body of the essay.

I had been lucky in not being caught out on lights violation thus far. I had another day or two's work ahead. It was a Saturday night. I was furiously writing the conclusion segment. It must have been 11.45 p.m. I had just removed the blanket covering the lamp and had gone to the loo. Expecting to be back within a minute, I had been careless. There was a knock on the door.

I opened the door to face the OD.

'What time is it?'

'11.45 Sir.'

'A.M. or P.M.?'

'P.M. Sir.'

'What time is lights out?'

'10 p.m. Sir.'

'Then why are your lights on? Report for extra drill tomorrow morning.'

And he turned to leave.

'Excuse me Sir ... but I was only ...'

'Speak only when you are spoken to,' barked the OD. 'I said report for extra drill. Now doubled for speaking out of turn.'

I couldn't help but recall what one of my brother-cadets had wryly remarked, 'In this f**king place, you can't fart of your own free will without having to run two rounds around the parade ground for it.' Well, he wasn't far off the mark.

I knew that one was not supposed to answer or explain anything out of turn. But I neither took that literally nor did I think, under the circumstances, I was wrong in pleading my case. But this was a bummer beyond all bummers. Here I was slogging my butt off to write an essay which was certainly not part of my course, and well beyond my pay grade; I was not given a library facility; I was not even given some spare time off from some of the other activities; and when I was doing my damnedest to do the job in my own time, I was being punished. I thought the entire establishment was heartless and mad.

Perhaps the excessive work over the last two weeks with little sleep told on my health. One morning, soon after the above episode, I woke up with a high fever—which I measured with my personal thermometer at 103^{0}F. I could feel the fever radiating heat through my face. I felt weak even standing up. I just washed my face, shaved, skipped the cold-water shower and got into PT gear. The walk to the parade ground nearly did me in. As soon as I reached the ground and was in formation, I reported sick to the OD.

'Extra drill! You know damn well you are not supposed to report sick before the drill. And don't forget the oath you signed about obedience until death.'

There was nothing to it but plod on as I was still breathing. By now, I had lost any capacity to think. I was on autopilot. But things were getting progressively worse. Post the drills, on the way back from the 7-km run, I collapsed nearly senseless on reaching the parade ground. I was moved to the Sanjivani Hospital.

I walked out of the hospital four days later, my physiology and psychology equally bruised. Something had snapped. To me, the training at the Academy seemed brutal beyond reason. I had barely four days left to turn in the essay. Given the recent developments, I wondered if I should ask for some extra time. But my personal pride forbade me from doing so. I had been given a task with a deadline and I was going to meet it, systemic unreasonableness notwithstanding.

Long story short, I managed to turn in the essay, beating the deadline with an hour to spare. Ah, at last I could sleep a couple of hours more!

It had been some five weeks since I had submitted the essay. One evening I heard another knock on my door. It was the OD again.

'Evening Sir.'

'Evening. At ease.' He had a smile on his face. 'Congratulations!' He extended his arm in my direction.

'Thank you, Sir,' I replied taking the proffered hand slowly, waiting for the reason for this congratulatory handshake.

'Your bloody essay got a consolation prize. We just got the word. I thought I should let you know. Good job. They are all very happy up there,' and with that he smiled, turned and left.

That news should have made me happy. Well, in a way it did. It helped me concretise a thought that had been sloshing around my head for a while. Had I made a monumental error in the choice of my career? Could any system, even the one of the defence forces, be so pointlessly callous, cruel and cold-hearted? Well, it could, considering I was in one such system; or at least that's what I thought of it at the time. I just had to do something about it. I had to leave the navy and take up a job in the industry, which I had foolishly bypassed not too long ago.

But should I really quit?

Quit?

Yes, quit. Wouldn't that make me a quitter?

This 'quitter' is a monster of a word. It can sap one's self-confidence. It can plunge one into depression. It can shame one into a spiritless sod. It conjures up visions of a weak-willed, weak-spined and weak-spirited loser, defeated by life. Seldom do we stop to consider the flip side of quitting.

After all, one would be stupid not to know when to quit an inane enterprise. If you walk into a dead end and cannot find your way ahead, is retracing your steps back and getting around the cul-de-sac, quitting? Is having the wisdom of cutting one's losses early, recognising the sunk cost and pursuing more profitable ventures, quitting? Is resigning from a job you don't enjoy and looking for another one quitting?

OK, so I had made a serious mistake in the choice of my career. What sense did it make to pay for it for the rest of my life? If that's quitting, so be it.

I knew that in my case quitting didn't come cost-free. The cost of training in defence academies is significant; in technical branches even more, because of the enormous resources committed on training. So, my quitting would mean my father having to pay for the cost of training incurred thus far, a log of which the navy would have. That meant putting my poor parents to another round of serious expenditure. Right at the outset, they had been against my bright idea of joining the Indian Navy. I had given big lip about *following one's passion* and what have you, putting them to significant expenditure to get myself in here. And now, before all my white shorts had been worn even once, here I was tucking my tail in and scurrying back to them asking for a bail out. Everything inside me cried out against it, even without counting the loss of face before the rest of the family and friends. But there was nothing to it but to grin and bear it, even if there wasn't much to grin about for my parents. But bear it, I supposed they would, parents being parents.

The decision was agonising and not to be taken in a hurry, having been guilty of haste already once—in joining the navy. But the longer I agonised the higher the metre of compensation was ticking. I couldn't afford the inertia of inaction for long.

———•———

With the news of my essay winning a prize, suddenly it was as if weeks of tension hissed out of me, even though I had scarcely given the essay a second thought after submitting it. But somehow, my dilemma on whether or not to call it quits in the navy was suddenly resolved. I had proven something about myself to the establishment. Against all odds. Even if I chose to quit the navy, I wouldn't be leaving as a loser. Why, I had just helped them win a prize in an international competition. I could now leave with my head held high. Yes, I would still be putting my parents to some additional expense, but there was nothing to be done about it.

The next morning, I spoke to the OD and stated my resolve to put in my papers.

'Are you serious? Why! You have just been recognised by the authorities in the stratosphere and you talk of putting in your papers? Are you out of your mind? Perhaps you are. After all, you joined the navy after two postgraduations, one of them being an MBA!' he said sardonically.

'No, Sir.'

'All right, you may cut the crap of 'Yes Sir' and 'No Sir' now and speak. What's bugging you?'

'Well Sir, I have been thinking about it all. I clearly made a mistake joining the navy. I want to correct the mistake while I can still afford it.'

'I won't disagree with you that you were a bloody fool in the first place to join here after an MBA. But now that you are here, why, it makes no sense to leave. I personally think with a start like this, you do have an excellent career ahead.'

'Excellent career being whipped around by a leading seaman ...' I wanted to say but didn't. As a matter of fact, I offered no reason for my decision.

At long last, he had no option but to forward my relieving petition to the commanding officer, Naval Academy (NAVAC), Commander Gupta, whom I had seen but once, when he had addressed the new cohort during the initial weeks. An elegant and no-nonsense officer of a serious demeanour, a Mahaveer Chakra awardee, the commander was respected very highly for running a tight ship at INS Venduruthy.

The commander listened to me, without offering me a seat. I stood at attention, with the lieutenant standing on the side at ease but without moving a muscle. He started with congratulating me on my essay and asked how I managed to do such a fine job. I had a hundred things to say about my experience on that particular aspect, but I put on a modest cap and said, not without irony: 'With cooperation from the establishment, Sir.'

The commander looked at the lieutenant and they both exchanged Mona Lisa-like smiles.

'Do you have any problem with the training here?' he asked.

'No, Sir.'

'Then what's your problem?'

'Nothing, Sir.'

'Then why do you want to leave?'

'I have changed my mind, Sir.'

We were going around in circles. On my part, deliberately. I had enough sense not to criticise any aspect of the training at INS Venduruthy. I had to hedge against the possibility of my release being refused.

So finally, I was informed that my resignation would be placed before the FOC-in-C, South (the Flag Officer Commanding in Chief of Southern Naval Area) with the commander's recommendation, and the final acceptance of my resignation would rest in his hands.

'Until we receive the final orders, you will continue with the training as if nothing has changed,' I was told.

Fortunately, within a couple of weeks, the OD informed me that the FOC-in-C would like to see me. He informed me also that this was the first time in his memory when the FOC-in-C would be personally meeting a cadet officer who wanted to leave. I was told that Commander Gupta would be the one accompanying me to meet with the rear admiral. I was advised to relax and not be nervous—an advice largely irrelevant, considering I didn't even know I was supposed to be nervous about meeting the admiral. To me the meeting was hopefully the last of the naval interactions before I was out of there.

So, that's how I found myself in front of FOC-in-C, Rear Admiral Ronald Lynsdale Pereira, AVSM. Admiral Pereira was as impressive a man as his name conjured up visions of. He was incredibly handsome and infinitely tall, made even more handsome by his spotless white uniform with impressive golden epaulets. His office was enormous and his table must once have doubled duty for billiards. Everything in the office and on the table, including half a dozen little flags, were absolutely in their place; spic and span. As we were ushered into the office by the admiral's adjutant, the admiral was in the process of signing some documents. The commander clicked his heels smartly and saluted, while I remained standing at attention. Almost immediately, the admiral put his pen down, got up and returned the commander's salute, and with a broad smile on his face, came around the table, shaking my hand affably, as a father would welcome a son returning from a vacation. He took me to a small round coffee table and had me seated. He took the seat opposite, while the commander remained standing.

'Ah, you so remind me of myself, when I got my commission ...'

For the life of me I couldn't imagine what the tall, fair and handsome admiral could possibly have had in common with me, when the admiral completed his sentence:

'... Yes, I too was twenty when I was commissioned, except that I didn't have an MBA.' he complimented me.

I didn't know what to say to that. In the next moment he added, 'Commander, you can wait outside. I have to convince this young cadet not to leave us. I need to be alone with him. Give me 15 minutes. I promise you, he'll stay in the navy.'

I cringed. I certainly didn't want to be talked into continuing in the navy by this charismatic man.

Fifteen minutes rolled by in no time. The good admiral instructed his adjutant on the intercom to inform the commander that this could take longer. As it turned out, it was 45 minutes (by the clock on the side wall) and the admiral was still working on me. By now I had learnt that his friends called him Ronnie. I also learnt that no sooner had he been commissioned in the Royal Navy at twenty, he had been put in command of a rag-tag wooden leaky fishing tub, aboard which, assisted by a crew as wet behind the ears as he was, he saw active service during World War II.

'Now where else will you ever be given such an opportunity to lead, my boy?'

I almost wanted to agree with him, so I could be off on the morrow leading a leaky dinghy full of seamen into some desperate battle. But to the best of my knowledge, there was no World War III brewing on the horizon.

The admiral pressed on, as if sensing his advantage over my momentary indecision, and went on to ask me about my experiences at the Academy thus far. To start with I held my reserve, as I had resolved to. But he wasn't an admiral for nothing. He was so affable and so smooth that before long he had me singing like a canary at the 'cruelty' and 'heartlessness' of the training and such. However, I never let out any specifics.

'Look here son, in times of war, it would hardly matter if you were terribly sick or running a high fever. There, not only your own life but the lives of all the men under your command would be at stake.

So, the force must prepare you for the worst. Your OD and his petty officers and seamen are doing nothing but what they are supposed to. Yes, a petty officer is not supposed to strike a cadet officer, but believe me, the same petty officer, who has given pretty much his life to the naval forces, would salute you the day you graduate and beg your pardon for any acts of excessive commission which were always committed in your best interest. Every time you even think of violating a disciplinary norm, you will recall that sting and hopefully it would help you make better decisions. The very idea of the armed forces is to rise above personal egos and all our training is aimed at that. Even the smallest details, for instance ... umm ... say, aren't you guys made to change your outfit in double quick time during your post-dinner drills? (I was surprised that he knew about it, for I had said nothing of it.) Well, even that exercise is meant to have you battle-ready in a matter of seconds. (I had thus far thought the OD was just harassing the heck out of us out of a sadistic streak.) Imagine you are sleeping after your watch, getting some shut-eye on a submarine and an enemy is spotted in the vicinity. You must be ready to take charge in seconds, don't you think?'

I fought against nodding my head affirmatively, because I feared that my nod would make my wiggling out of the navy that much more difficult.

'Yes, we squeeze every drop of your energy out of our would-be officers and then some more and then some more again because these situations which happen during times of war are not otherwise easily simulated. You thought you were nearly done for, but you are still on your own two feet now, aren't you? We inspire you to find your limits that you didn't know existed. That's what the Indian Navy expects of its officers and that's what we have been training you here for, and that's what you will expect of your subordinates tomorrow. Do you think that's wrong? Do you think we can do it the softer way?'

Oh God! The admiral was making me squirm. As a totally inexperienced young man, I hadn't ever thought of the training along those lines. But just then, my only objective was to seek my escape from a system where your vocabulary had to be limited to three words—Yes, No and Sir.

But the admiral carried on, 'I understand you are a vegetarian, my boy. I know that the vegetarian food in the Academy is unpalatable. Well, that's because we deliberately discourage a vegetarian diet in the navy. It is so much easier for us to run a single kitchen in the confined spaces of the ship, which aren't restaurants by a far shot to cater to different palates. Vegetables rot fast, even in the freezer, in the humid sea air, when out on a two or three-month exercise on the high seas. In the limited confines of ships, there is only so much storage space. Storing or even catching fish in the sea and feeding the seamen is so much easier. All in all, we want the vegetarians to convert. Of course, this is not an official policy, but that's the truth. Is that terribly unreasonable?'

The admiral had all but demolished my resolve to leave the navy. But his last remark sunk in, hitting home with the law of unintended consequences. The navy may have a million reasons to ensure that everybody ate a uniform diet of animal flesh, but vegetarianism was deeply ingrained in me. And if what the admiral said was true, and it was indeed, apart from anything else, my gastronomic future in the navy was bound to remain impossible. Food is a big part of one's life, like it or not. You must engage with it three times a day, seven days a week, fifty-two weeks a year. Both the options, that is, converting into a non-vegetarian, or reconciling myself to boiled cabbage and eggplant, would be an enormous cost to pay for any career. Or so my logic went.

Yes, I had to remain steadfast in my resolve. I was almost thankful to the admiral for having unwittingly given me a good reason not to waver from my initial resolve.

Interpreting my silences as his nearing checkmate, the admiral continued, 'Look here son, the navy is an extremely complex organisation. Why, even a large ship is practically an enormous enterprise. A war itself is nothing but a complex web of logistics. An MBA would indeed be a most useful qualification to have whether you are dealing with men, material or maritime movements. I'll tell you what. Why don't you let me know what would make you happiest? Submarines? Aviation? Gunnery? Navigation? You name it and I have the power to give it to you. Is that fair? We need leaders in the navy. You will make a fine leader.'

I remained silent and felt like a creep before the magnanimous admiral. But fear lent me wings and I mumbled weakly, 'Sir, I only want out of the navy. I have thought through it all. I made a mistake enlisting. I want out.'

'All right. Tell me young man, what do you intend to do if you leave navy?'

'Sir, I'll take up a job as an executive in the corporate sector.'

'Look here young man. Take it from me. While I am sure you will get a job somewhere someday, it's not going to be easy. You are still too young. And jobs aren't easy to get, even for an MBA, once out of business school. Besides, the navy offers you a fine career. I had wanted to be a doctor or a dentist, but I somehow joined the navy. And I have been a happy man. Never regretted it. Look at me ...' he stood up, towering over me, gesturing towards his epaulets and the array of ribbons on his chest. 'I am an admiral. An admiral in the Indian Navy. I get to shake hands with presidents and prime ministers. Now you can't do that as an executive in a company, can you?'

The affable admiral was treating me as the young rookie that I undoubtedly was, helping me see the glamorous side of the job. Nor did I know enough to know that I couldn't backchat an admiral. But Admiral Pereira was so affable, so easy-going, so friendly and so father-like that I forgot who he was, and in a moment of inspiration, answered: 'Sir, if I continue in the Indian Navy, my best bet would be to shake the hands of presidents or prime ministers. But if I leave the navy, who knows, I may be a president or a prime minister myself someday, Sir.'

The admiral looked at me for a few seconds. Absolutely silent. Most admirals may have kicked my butt out of the office then and there.

But not Admiral Pereira. He just looked at me for a moment before bursting into a loud guffaw that fairly shook the room and declared, 'Well, well, well son! There is no way I am going to be able to stop you. This time, I have lost the argument good and proper. You did well with that essay too. I know we could have got a better essay with a little more handholding, but we had our constraints and we also wanted to see how far you could stretch over and above the routine. And boy, you sure did pull that one off! However, don't you think it was a remarkable run of luck that you weren't caught with your lights on until the last night? Or that you were never given extra drill during those three weeks, until that last morning? Of course, you outdid yourself. But before you go, do you have any suggestions for our training?'

The enormity of what the admiral had said would sink in only much, much later. But just then, I reflected for a moment and replied, 'With respect Sir, I have but one observation. The defence forces or the Indian Navy places enormous emphasis on the leadership potential of the cadets they select. But the opportunity to exercise one's leadership qualities and judgement probably comes only towards the fag end of one's career, when one makes an admiral maybe. But until then, an average officer only carries out orders for most of his career. So, I think, apart from leadership potential, the navy should also be trying to spot the potential propensity for unquestioned obedience—the very opposite of leadership—among its potential officers.' In other words, the selection should balance the potential for leadership with the potential for obedience.

The admiral gave another hearty and indulgent laugh, like he knew I was wrong, but he let it pass, saying, 'I won't stop you now. I will give you the earliest release and write off a good part of the training cost, because the full training cost will be prohibitive. I know you will in any case go a long way in life. I wish you all the very best.'

My discharge letters came a week later, and I had to pay a very reasonable (though hard on my parents) compensation to get out. I had found something else obliquely in common with the admiral. He had never regretted his joining the navy. I did not ever regret quitting it.

And yet, I knew that I had met a very remarkable admiral. I did suffer from a tinge of regret for not abiding by the great man's advice.*

---

* When Admiral R.L. Pereira superannuated from the Indian Navy, he simply retired into a home he called 'At Last', in Bangalore. When he passed away at seventy in 1993, of cancer, apparently there was not a single dry eye among the present sailors who had come from far and wide—including those who had never served under his command—to pay homage.

CHAPTER TWO

The Price of a Piss—The Value of an Extra Operator?

Authenticity and the courage to express oneself honestly and fearlessly are virtues worth striving for...

1976–78

The mammoth boom of the machine swayed rhythmically, back and forth, back and forth, in a hypnotic rhythm of a metronome that held my gaze transfixed. ... I suddenly realised that the boom had come to a halt. My reverie broke, and I found myself waiting, and waiting, and waiting, for the machine to resume its work. But no, it remained still ...

... the dragline had been idle for a good 25 minutes. One heck of a long time. I could not even see the operator in the cabin through the window. I had read that in developed countries, when such a piece of equipment goes idle for anything more than say 5 minutes, automatic hooters on the machine go off and the general manager of the shift is at

the site post-haste to check out the reason. I waited another 20 minutes. And then I decided to find out what was happening.

I walked down the long incline to the dragline and caught up with the shift supervisor, who appeared entirely unconcerned.

'What happened?' I asked.

'Nothing,' he said, looking perplexed at my question.

'Then why is the dragline silent?'

'Oh that,' said the supervisor, 'Tanki khali karne gaya hoga.' (He must have gone to empty his tank) ...

Out of the Indian Navy after that long chinwag with Rear Admiral Pereira in late 1975, I spent a good six months like the classic unemployed youth of the 1970s that I was, with the full-time job of looking for employment. I parked myself in Bombay (now Mumbai), at my elder sister's apartment on Pedder Road, and started working on the enterprise systematically.

Finding a job in those days was like looking for a black cat in a coal cellar, MBA or not, and landing a job through a newspaper advert only slightly more probable than winning a lottery.

And yet, I had to try every trick in the book, starting with picking up the hefty Bombay telephone directory, forever nestling on the lower shelf of the coffee table at my sister's, and from a mental list of such companies as the names of which I could readily recall, mustering a catalogue of addresses and phone numbers.

Next, I got to work 'botoxing' my curriculum vitae (CV), adding a few creative embellishments here and there. And because this was the pre-digital age, I had to physically type out copies of my CV and mail them to all the addresses I had compiled, each addressed to a 'Dear Sir'. Ah, the joys of snail mail and waiting weeks for a response.

Looking back, I realise that my approach was pretty outdated—gender sensitivity was still far off. But hey, as a twenty-year-old I was doing what I could to get noticed and land a job. And who knows, maybe my 'voluptuous' CV would catch someone's eye and lead to a job offer. There is no downside to dreaming, right? Go for it!

To further seal chances of my success, I also decided to spruce up my covering note to really sell myself to potential employers. I wrote something along the lines of, 'If you doubt my claims in the CV, all you have to do is call me for a face-to-face interview.'

Nor did I stop there. I started calling each one of the companies, one by one, and trying to pitch myself as the perfect candidate for the job, to whoever I could find on the other end! Looking back, I realise that I was basically doing telemarketing before it was even a thing. Talk about being ahead of the curve! Of course, I cringe a little at my youthful immaturity and chutzpah now. But then, I was doing whatever I could to stand out and land a job.

My job search wasn't exactly off to a roaring start. The only response I got to my letters was from a company that appreciated my boldness, but also gave me a verbal spanking for coming across as a tad too entitled. They took issue with my use of the term 'claims', saying the phrase 'if you doubt my claims ...' implied I was asserting a right to a job with them! I was left scratching my head for weeks, wondering if it was their English or mine that needed a little work, but the word 'claims' didn't roll off my tongue with the same confidence for a while.

Undaunted by my lack of success, I decided to start making cold calls. Armed with my briefcase borrowed from my brother-in-law, and a slim CV, I marched into various office buildings with a spring in my step and the broad tie of the times around my neck, asking to meet with the HR manager. Alas, I never made it past the front desk anytime, as the receptionists were quick to point me to the exit. It was like they could smell the likes of me from a mile away. Ah, those were the good old days!

Unattained grapes are always sour. With much time on hand despite my 24x7 job of looking for jobs, I took to delving into the works of existential and left-leaning authors like Albert Camus, Franz Kafka, Simone de Beauvoir, Jean-Paul Sartre and Søren Kierkegaard—in between my sporadic interview calls for salesmen, advertised in the classified columns of *The Times of India*! Slowly but steadily, I was coming to the view that the private sector was not my calling, and that I should set my sights on the public sector. However, this also meant that I had to take the hard and lengthy road, as the public sector recruitment process could take months, even upwards of a year. And so far, lady luck wasn't smiling at me. If I didn't start soon, I might start sprouting grey hairs on the temples.

To cut a long story short, I scoured the newspapers for public sector job advertisements and shortlisted three organisations—Coal India Ltd (based in Calcutta), Bank of India (Madras) and Hindustan Aeronautics Ltd (Bangalore). I took their written tests on different dates and locations, and a few months later, I was called for interviews by the first two. Eventually, I received a thick cardboard-like appointment letter, signed by Lt General K.S. Grewal, Chairman of Coal India Ltd, inviting me to join as a management trainee with a monthly stipend of ₹800. I was asked to join before 31 May 1976, and I happily accepted the offer.

Ironically, soon after I had accepted the Coal India offer, I also received the Bank of India offer. The bank's offer was appealing in many ways, but the idealism of youth can often be too real. Would it be ethical to renege on a commitment I had already made? Should I not keep my word given to a general no less? Plus, the appointment order from General Grewal, the very chairman of the company, printed on an electric typewriter, was way more charming, gracious and personalised—complete with my name handwritten by the general—

than the Bank of India offer, which simply addressed me as 'Dear Sir', typed on a clunky manual Remington.

Looking back, it was this dash of idealism that influenced such a significant decision in my life. It only reaffirmed my belief that most of life's major decisions could easily be made by a toss of a coin, given the countless variables that can interfere with our choices.

I made my way to Calcutta with barely any money in my pocket, counting on Coal India to provide accommodation in their executive hostel for management trainees, as indicated in their offer letter attachments. Their headquarters were located at 10, Netaji Subhas Chandra Bose Road, and that's where I was headed.

I landed in Calcutta on a rainy Sunday afternoon, 9 May 1976, to be precise. I made my way to Naktala, where I had decided to anchor overnight with my close friend, Jayanto Bhaduri. Jayanto and I had become very close friends during our time at the Jodhpur Management Programme. He had since been working as a consultant with a good consulting firm in Calcutta and was living with his parents. I thought I would stay with him overnight and report at Coal India the next morning. From there, I would be taken care of by Coal India.

So, on Monday morning, another rainy day, I took a minibus from Naktala to Dalhousie Square (also BBD Bagh). A good one hour later, during which we passed through the beautiful Victoria Memorial and the enormous expanse of open grounds, the bus entered the terminal stop of Dalhousie Square, facing an enormous red building. This I would learn was the Writers' Building—housing the state's secretariat.

After a few minutes of deploying the customary Indian modus operandi of finding one's geo location—stopping folks at random and asking for directions—I set off towards the dusty street of 10 Netaji Subhas Road, which was not more than a ten-minute walk. It was about 11.45 a.m. when I arrived at a handsome three-storey colonial building. Upon reaching the reception area, I presented my letter of appointment and informed them of my purpose to report. The receptionist, sporting a puzzled expression, furrowed her brow, dialled a few numbers, and eventually instructed me to proceed to the HR department on the second floor for further information. It was evident that my arrival had taken them by surprise.

As I ascended four flights of steep stairs to the second floor, a sense of shock washed over me. The floor sprawled out before me was an immense hall—I thought the size of the very Howrah station where I had alighted the day before for the first time—with row upon row of tables at the centre, and cabins ring-fencing the perimeter. Seeking guidance to locate the HR department, I was directed to a specific door adorned with the title, 'Assistant Controller (HR)'.

I knocked.

'Come in,' came a gruff voice.

There were three gentlemen sitting in various states of relaxation on three chairs around a table, with some tea and small samosas (I would learn that what looked like small samosas of the north were in fact the standard shingaras of Calcutta).

'Yes, what do you want?'

'Sir, I am V. Raghunathan ...'

'Yes, so?'

'Sir, I am here to report as per my appointment order as management trainee?'

'What order? What management trainee?'

'I have my appointment order with me, Sir.'

'What are you doing here today? You are supposed to report on 31 May.'

'Sorry Sir, that's not what my appointment order says.' Saying so, I took out my appointment order and showed him, adding, 'it says any day *on or before 31 May 1976.* Today is 10 May.'

He did not look at the letter I had pushed in his direction.

'Didn't you hear me? You are supposed to join on 31 May!'

Clearly, he knew what the letter contained, but didn't want to acknowledge it. I continued: 'But Sir, that's not what the letter says. If the date for joining was changed, I received no intimation. I have travelled all the way. Now that I am here, why don't you please let me join?'

'What's your problem? Didn't you hear me?' he said impatiently. And then he immediately assumed a patient tone and said, 'What's your problem? Why don't you understand that we cannot have different fellows joining on different dates? Come back on 31 May.'

Well, I did have a problem. Where was I to hang around for the next three weeks? I could hardly stretch my friend's hospitality for so long. I had too little cash on me to go back home and return in two weeks, leave alone stay in a hotel or a lodge for two weeks. I was desperate.

Clearly somebody had goofed up somewhere and I was being made to carry the can. So I said, 'Perhaps you meant us to join on 31 May. But the chairman's letter clearly gives us a twenty-day window. So perhaps his office made the mistake and that's why I am here to report today. Why don't we get a special approval from the chairman for me to join today? I am sure I will not be the only one. If a similar letter has gone to others, I am sure others will have the same problem too, don't you think?' I said, genuinely thinking I was helping solve a knotty problem.

I wasn't therefore prepared even to understand his train of thought just then, as the man exploded, saying, 'Ah, so you have already started behaving like a union leader, have you? And you haven't even joined! You want to complain to the chairman, do you Mr V. Raghunathan? Do you know, my friend, I can find a dozen different reasons to cancel your appointment if you don't just go back and report on 31 May.'

Only much later would I learn that this precise man had goofed up in drafting that letter sent out by the chairman and he knew that if the matter went to the chairman, he could be in a spot of trouble. So he had been covering his backside by bullying me. But just then, young, inexperienced and desperate as I was, I thought retreat the better part of valour and left to ruminate my future course of action—future as in the next three weeks.

I walked out of the building and started wandering around. I remembered the beautiful wide expanse of the Maidan and I recalled that it was close by. So I walked towards it, though the walk was a good sight longer way to walk than I had imagined.

I was nearly in tears. How could I just impose on my friend, who himself lived with his parents and siblings? Staying outside, anywhere, was hardly a real option, since I didn't have the money and I didn't have the stomach to borrow from my friend. Calling home for help was an option, but unpalatable, as I didn't want to burden my parents any more than I already had. Besides, a money order from home would take at least a week to reach me. What was I to do until then?

There's only so much one can do when one has loads of time and very little money in the pocket, anywhere in the streets. And I had done my bit: eaten puffed rice snack twice over (which I would learn was the famous moori) and watched traffic flow past in the distant—what I would learn later—Chowringhee Road, and finally it was time to head home to my friend's.

One look at my face and my friend knew something was seriously amiss. There was nothing to it but confess the quandary I was in. He asked me to wait for ten minutes, after which he came and said he had discussed with his parents and that I could cheer up, for there was nothing to it! They had a disused room on the terrace. They would clean it up and I could stay there as long as it took me to get my hostel. After some persuasion, I got my friend to agree on my being a paying guest, with the rent to be paid only at the end of the next month, my first payday! He and his family never even made me feel that they had done me a favour, the burden of which I shall never ever be able to undo.

Coal India was an ocean and we, the management trainees, were the bottom-feeders. As we were the first batch, or maybe it was their default setting, the HR department was clueless as to what to do with us, and we were shuffled around from colliery to colliery like a pack of footloose and fancy-free vagabonds. From underground mines to open-cast mines, and from East India to Central India to West India and back again, we travelled like a lost tribe, with no schedule or training detail to speak of. It was like an endless expedition through coal mines.

But the travels were not without their little perks at that stage in our lives. For one, we got to travel in the first class on Indian Railways—none of that cattle-class anymore. And wherever we went, executive guesthouses awaited our arrival, along with a trusty, and rusty Jeep to whisk us away to our next destination.

I couldn't help but feel the weight of my own potential in a modest way. Who knows? Maybe someday, I too would be sitting in a plush office, surrounded by teak furniture and sipping on a cup of tea while making big decisions that would shape the future of bottom-feeding management trainees like myself, meaning, evolving into a slightly larger fish in a layer above the bottom-feeders as I progressed through life. But hey, just then, I got to travel in style.

Even as we roamed the many collieries without specific tasks or responsibilities like so many castrated bulls on our streets, there was plenty to learn in the new world of mining that had just opened before us, if only we were so inclined, and mostly, in the vim of our youth, we were so inclined.

It was 1977. My two-year training was cut short after six months and I was posted to Western Coalfields (WCL) as the finance officer, Budgets Wing. Happy at the development, I hauled my meagre belongings to Nagpur by train.

The finance function was headed by a venerable general manager (GM). The chain of command under him ran thus: controller of accounts, additional controller of accounts, joint controller of accounts, deputy controller of accounts, assistant controller of accounts, and finally the humble finance/accounts officer (and even an assistant accounts officer to accommodate those who had come up through the clerical cadre)—just so you know where to flag me on the totem pole.

As a crew of bottom-combers in the Budgets Wing of WCL, our job was to keep a watchful eye on the budget figures of each of the 130-odd mines. The numbers were rounded off to two decimal places of rupees in crores, which made me feel like a financial aristocrat. The GM, who preferred to work directly with us, would give us broad guidelines and we would prepare the initial budget. Our *de jure* boss, the deputy controller, was, in our perception, a relic of the past, who seemed to have lost all interest in his job after nationalisation, or maybe even before.

Preparation of the revenue budget was simple. The previous year's production and costs were the benchmark. The variable costs, adjusted for inflation, would increase in proportion with the increase in the volume of production in each mine, from year to year. The fixed costs would increase by a flat inflationary per centage, assumed usually at about 9 or 10 per cent. The aggregation of all the revenue and cost data of all the mines was the total revenue budget.

The capital budget was predicated on the new equipment required, estimated based on the replacement of old equipment going out of commission, and such additional equipment as may be required to cope with the increased production requirement of a mine, or discovery of a new coal face in a mine and so forth.

During these meetings, some area GMs would often voice their concerns and suggestions on various cost parameters, capital expenditures, productivity targets and production figures. Sometimes, they would even dispute the prescribed numbers, citing the technical realities of their respective mines. For instance, a mine with more water ingress would require additional electric pumps, resulting in higher electricity consumption. Similarly, a mine with a hard coal seam would require more workers to extract the same tonnage as a mine with a softer seam. These factors could lead to adjustments in the previously agreed-upon budgetary provisions for each mine.

Our GM would convey these changes to us, which we would then incorporate against individual mines, either based on some specific reasons, or pro-rated across all mines of an area, because the budget for the area as a whole had been cropped, say for labour, power, explosives or whatever.

As if we hadn't dealt with enough changes already, the budget had to go to Coal India headquarters in Calcutta where the chief managing directors (CMDs) of all five subsidiaries would defend their budgets. It was like a big, fancy game of budget Jenga, with the CMDs carefully removing and replacing blocks of numbers until they were satisfied. And of course, these changes would then trickle down from the CMDs to us poor little slopsuckers, and we had to painstakingly recalculate every cost item for each mine. And let me tell you, doing all of that without computers was a real Facit-ache on our wrists.

And just when you thought the budgeting process was over, there was more! Two budget seasons, budgeted estimates and revised estimates. The first before the new financial year began and the latter halfway into the year. And to add to the muddle, Coal India had to send its estimates to the Committee on Public Sector Undertakings (COPU) in New Delhi for approval. This committee, made up of the respective ministry and finance ministry, had the power to make cuts to the budget in the broader context of the national annual budget. The higher up you go, the fonder of budget cuts they are, it seemed to us! And if that wasn't enough, uppermost on the totem pole, the finance minister could make further apportionments across all the public sector organisations, which could mean even more cuts (seldom increases) for the budget of the CMD of Coal India. All this without the aid of computers, just good old-fashioned manual calculators. That was our good life.

No light at the end of the budgetary tunnel yet. This is when the entire budgetary juggernaut would start rolling all over again, but backwards. The CMD, Coal India, would pass on the cut down in whatever proportions to the CMDs of his subsidiaries, who would further apportion the cuts to this or that area in consultations with the executive directors (EDs) and GMs of the area in this or that proportion, and which would finally drip down, via our GM, on to us minions to work out the mine-wise cost figures. And of course, at each level there could be errors, which would again and again come back to us to rework.

It wasn't unusual for the GM (Finance)—our ultimate boss—a venerable chartered accountant in the twilight of his career, to summon one of us to accompany him to the meetings for budget finalisation with the chairman and managing director of the company. Our task was to assist him with any essential numbers if needed unexpectedly. But such was his elephantine memory that I or my colleague were usually silent spectators, seated in a back row in the boardroom.

Mr Balram, the CMD of our company, was a force to be reckoned with. He was a mining engineer with a reputation for being tough as nails and taking no nonsense. He had a knack for chewing up GMs and EDs for breakfast and swallowing them whole. If you made the mistake of presenting incorrect numbers during his meetings, you could consider yourself cooked in slow fire. And to make matters worse, he had a memory for numbers that could put a computer to shame. Luckily, our GM also had an impressive memory for numbers, which spared him from the frequent tongue-lashings that other GMs were subjected to.

One day, my GM summoned me to grab all the budget documents and join him for a high-level meeting. As usual, the bigwigs—the EDs, the GMs, the controllers and the like—occupied the large boardroom table that could accommodate thirty people. These meetings were typically male-dominated affairs, with no female representation. As mere sidekicks accompanying our bosses, we sat in chairs lined up against the walls, behind our respective bosses. If my GM needed a number, he would turn to me and whisper what he was looking for, and my task was to provide the figure in a similarly hushed tone. The only challenge during these whispered communications was that my GM had a slight hearing problem, so I had to be extra careful.

This morning, during the meeting with the formidable CMD, our GM nonchalantly supplied some budgetary figures, which I, the faithful sidekick, recognised to be dated, not reflecting certain revisions. I attempted to whisper a warning to my boss. Unfortunately, my words fell on a deaf ear (I don't know if the pun is intended or not). As the discussion heated up, it seemed that the GM's numbers were causing more confusion than a chicken at a rodeo.

In a panic that our GM was in danger of falling flat on his face, I leapt up and took a stooping stride forward, and spoke a bit louder, practically breathing into his ear. When he finally turned to face me, I inched my file closer and gave him the lowdown in a jiffy.

'Young man! Will you shut up and take your seat,' I heard a booming command.

For a moment I didn't realise that the CMD had just lashed out at me. And when I did, I looked at him, and found him gazing at me as if to ascertain from which crevice I had emerged. And then he thundered in a voice that could carry a mile in a moderate wind: 'Don't disturb the meeting! Go back to your chair!'

In theory, I should have slunk back into whatever fissure I had emerged out of. But something inside me snapped, like a short-circuited electrical wire. I could feel my blood rushing to my head. If my skin had been lighter, you would have seen my face turn red as a tomato. But no matter.

I stood to my full modest height, and responded in firm words, 'Sir, I beg your pardon, but I am not disturbing the meeting. I am merely assisting my GM, who brought me here for a purpose. I believe I just served that purpose. If my actions are deemed inappropriate, my GM may certainly let me know, and I will leave the room immediately.' With that, I sat back in my chair, feeling a small sense of triumph for having stood up for myself.

The atmosphere in the room turned taut as a guitar string, each person holding their breath, waiting for the inevitable snap that would come with a single strum. And no one wanted to be the one supplying that strum. I sat there, feeling small and vulnerable, wondering if the atmosphere created was due to Mr Balram's intimidating presence or my foolishness. In the end, the GM quickly corrected his numbers and the meeting resumed its course, the tension dissipating like a balloon slowly losing air. I breathed a sigh of relief, grateful that the moment had passed.

During a brief break, while the CMD was out of the room, one of the production GMs approached me and said, 'Kid, you may be small in size, but certainly not your b**ls.' My own GM was uncertain about how to react to what had happened.

But it was after a couple of weeks that the GM called me to his cabin and said, 'The CMD is setting up a special committee to study costing of opencast mines. He specifically asked me to include you.' He said he wanted someone who was fearless. Within a week a cyclostyled circular went around naming the members of the committee, where I stood out incongruously amidst some very senior officials.

As a member of the committee, I had to travel across opencast mines extensively. Opencast mines or open-pit mines are typically mines where the coal deposits are easily accessible, relatively close to the surface. All that is required to get to the coal is to remove the overlying soil and rock, called overburden, exposing the coal seams which can then be hauled away.

In contrast, underground mines are located where the coal deposits lie deep beneath the earth's surface, necessitating the construction of steeply inclined or vertical tunnels to reach the strata and then horizontal tunnels to extract the coal seams.

Now, the removal of overburden can be done two ways depending on various parameters.

Some mines prefer using rippers or explosives to loosen things up, and then use the good old shovel-dumper combo. Once the overburden has been loosened and the shovels work in tandem to get it hauled away, a convoy of trucks with tiltable payload, also known as dumpers or tipper trucks, takes charge. And when it's time to remove the coal, well, you guessed it—the same procedure applies.

The dumpers were not just big; they were humongous, with capacities that could range from 20 to 100 tonnes and even more. Back in 1976–77, a single giant dumper—often imported from Russia—could cost anywhere between ₹1 and 2 crores. In today's value, that would be equivalent to a whopping ₹40–75 crores! It's safe to say that these dumpers were not your average pickup trucks.

The other method for removing the overburden and coal, depending on the topography of the land, is the use of a walking dragline. The walking dragline is the ultimate dinosaur (in terms of size) of mining equipment. It's not just humongous, it's titanic—the kind of thing that would make Godzilla jealous. Its boom, which can stretch up to 100 or 150 metres long, is attached to a bucket the size of a large house. And the walking part? Well, let's just say that it does not win any races. This thing moves slower than a snail on a hot afternoon. But when it's in action, it's a marvel to behold. The entire contraption, the size of a four-storey building, lifts up on two short fat legs and then swings forward before the two legs are retracted and the machine is pushed forward. In the meanwhile, the dragline continues to lift the overburden or coal 100 or 150 feet away with ease and then gracefully swings it away 180 degrees, thus depositing the overburden some 200–300 metres away. All the while, it's slowly walking along on its two hydraulic fat feet like a giant, robotic sloth. And the cost? A tidy ₹50–75 crores in the 1970s (or around ₹2,000–2,500 crore in today's money), depending on how much tonnage it could handle.

At 11.30 a.m. one day, I found myself standing on the precipice of an opencast mine, entranced at the spectacle of a dragline in full swing. The mammoth boom of the machine swayed rhythmically, back and forth, back and forth, in a hypnotic rhythm of a metronome that held my gaze transfixed.

As I gazed at the minuscule figure inside the cabin of the dragline, deftly manoeuvring the mammoth machinery single-handedly, I couldn't help but marvel at the skill and precision required for the job. These operators were the cream of the crop, earning a pretty penny for their expertise. In fact, they made more moolah than airline pilots and top-notch bureaucrats combined! And why not? While we struggle to judge the distance of the far-corner of our car's hood 6 feet away, these guys need to accurately assess objects 100–150 metres away, manipulate a 150-metre boom, collect the overburden in one go, turn 180 degrees and deposit it 125–150 metres away at a specific location—all without breaking a sweat! It's no wonder that dragline operators aren't mass-produced in colleges—they're born with the gift of spatial dexterity and then spend years polishing their craft.

I suddenly realised that the boom had come to a halt. My reverie broke, and I found myself waiting, and waiting, and waiting, for the machine to resume its work. But no, it remained still.

I glanced down at my trusty HMT watch and realised that the dragline had been idle for a good 25 minutes. Quite a long time for a piece of equipment worth more than a mid-sized firm. I strained my eyes to catch a glimpse of the operator in the cabin, but to no avail. I recalled reading that in developed countries, when such pricey machines remain idle for more than a few minutes, automatic alarms blare, and the general manager appears on the site post-haste. Another 20 minutes crawled by, and my curiosity finally got the better of me—I decided to investigate.

I walked the long incline to the dragline and caught up with the shift supervisor, who appeared entirely unfazed.

'What happened?' I asked.

'Nothing,' he replied.

'Then why is the dragline idle?'

'Oh that ... 'said the supervisor casually, '*Tanki khali karne gaya hoga*.' (He must have gone to empty his tank.)

'Forty-five minutes for that?' I exclaimed.

The supervisor looked at me as if I was a joke and gestured to the other side of the pit.

'*Voh dekho, shift office. Vahan jaana padta hai. Bees minute jaaneke, aur bees minute aaneke. Lo voh aa gaya operator.*' (Look there. That's where the shift office is. That's where the job has to be done. Twenty minutes to go and 20 minutes to come back. Anyway, there's the operator coming now.)

As I walked away, I couldn't help but chuckle at the absurdity of the situation. The cost of a 45-minute bathroom break for an operator of such an expensive machine was surely something worth investigating.

And to add to the irony, it wasn't unusual for dumper operators to drive their 50- or 100-ton dumpers home (the colliery quarters) for an hour-long lunch break! Now this was transportation more expensive than being driven home and back in a Rolls Royce Silver Cloud.

As the committee's costing study drew to a close and the draft report was being finalised, I noticed that my fellow senior members were hesitant to include a particular section that I had written. The section contained some comments and recommendations that I believed were crucial to the report's completeness. Despite their reluctance, I stood my ground and insisted that the section be included in the final report. Eventually, the section was included, and the report was complete.

The heading of the section I introduced was: '₹10,000 Piss & ₹500 Lunch'.

My explanations were simple. An equipment worth ₹50 crore in 1976, when idle for 45 minutes, cost the company about ₹10,000 (about ₹3,70,000 in present day terms) given an economic life of five years (20 per cent straight-line depreciation) and annual interest of 12 per cent on the cost of the equipment. And this is what every piss of the operator cost the company. I suggested a mobile toilet placed right next to the dragline.

Alternatively, I suggested having an additional operator attached to a dragline. Even at ₹10,000 per month, the monthly cost of the additional operator would be recovered in a single trip to the pee-pot. Two operators could ensure that a dragline was never down, except for breakdowns.

Similarly, a ₹2 crore dumper at an annual depreciation rate of 20 per cent and 12 per cent cost of borrowing, put the cost at ₹500 (about ₹18,500 in present day terms) per hour, or for every hour that it was missing in action during lunchtime, not counting the diesel cost of travel back and forth. Now a dumper driver earned about ₹2,000 every month including overtime etc. So having a standby driver at that rate would pay for him in a matter of four lunches!

Incidentally, when you travel abroad, you seldom see heavy earth-moving equipment like dozers, shovels, road rollers or construction cranes standing idle. You would typically notice eight times out of ten, the machine would be at work. In India, it is the reverse (based on my actual observations and research articles). Eight times out of ten, you see a heavy machine idle. Check this out for yourself next time you travel by our roads.

I had recommended that most large earth-moving equipment should have two operators instead of one to ensure that no machine time is lost. However, the recommendation was rejected with the argument that it would set a wrong precedent for workers. Oh, for crying out loud!

I couldn't help but wonder if any commercial company could afford such wastefulness. It wasn't even a principal–agent conflict because there was effectively no ownership, and so no principal. The government's job was done with nationalisation, and the agent, the managers, didn't seem to care. It was obvious that cost consciousness was lacking in our public sector undertakings and government.

Ultimately, the senior committee members discouraged me from emphasising the dragline issue, and watered it down significantly in the report, as it didn't reflect well on the germane coalfield's GM!

I was growing increasingly disenchanted with the public sector and was eager to move on. Apart from the lack of concern for efficiency and the desire to do a job well, the excessive bureaucracy and innovation-stifling hierarchy, I had witnessed sales officers getting rich quick, purchase officers turning into millionaires and general managers and contractors becoming billionaires. I was convinced that the public sector was not for me. The romance of the public sector was behind me—I had seen it all—the warts, moles, pimples, pustules, boils and furuncles.

I knew I had to make a change. By the third year at Coal India, my itch had grown into a veritable rash. At long last, in 1979, I decided to take a shot at one of the IIMs for a PhD to shift my career prospects up a gear. I was determined to redeem myself after a mediocre MBA and a less-than-satisfactory work experience. It was time for a fresh start, and I was ready for it.

CHAPTER THREE

IIM Calcutta—Cutting My Academic Teeth

In moments of despair, it is important to remember that nothing remains the same forever. Lows are frequently followed by highs ...

1979–81

Doctoral students are a species unto themselves, living in a time-warp all their own. Because the end is not a fixed point, they don't seem to feel any pressure to get up and get to work every morning. They start with all the time in the world, but before they know it, deadlines are flying past them like the Mumbai local ...

I landed at the Joka campus of IIM Calcutta (IIMC) in July 1979. I was on a mission to turn my mediocre career prospects at Coal India into something more promising, and so I had taken the famous Common

Admission Test (CAT), and entered the doctoral programme, called the Fellow programme at the time, at IIMC. I figured since I was already in the finance function at Coal India, why not just stick with what I knew, however modestly, and join the finance stream at IIMC? Once I heard that they had the best finance faculty at the time, making the decision was a no-brainer.

The doctoral programme was to be no picnic. It involved two long years of coursework, coterminous with the postgraduate diploma (de facto MBA) students, and at least two more years thereafter for the doctoral dissertation, and often much more, with no bright light at the end of the tunnel to tell you that you would get there. Dropouts weren't unknown. To make matters scarier, one learnt that the median time for the completion of the programme was a staggering six to seven years, and those taking seven, eight or even ten years to complete their PhDs weren't entirely unknown either, which was almost longer than it took to finish school! These delays reached such a pass that at some stage, the institute, like some strict parents, cut off the scholarship after the first six years, so thereafter you either flew or fell flat—meaning you had to fend for yourself.

For me, a key attraction in choosing IIMC over IIM Ahmedabad (IIMA) was that IIMC permitted those who had an MBA from any institution (like me), to skip the first-year coursework and jump straight into the second year, while IIMA provided no such waiver. Only later, when I started teaching at IIMA, would I realise that skipping the first-year coursework at an IIM was like building a skyscraper without ensuring a solid foundation—one would have to work much harder later in life to make up for the omission. But then wisdom invariably kicks in with hindsight, doesn't it?

IIMC was India's first IIM, established in 1961 in some sort of loose collaboration with the MIT Sloan School of Management. The institute had moved to the new campus in Joka on Diamond Harbour Road only in 1975, so that at the time of my joining the campus in 1979, the buildings were still fairly in plastic wraps.

Let me paint a picture of the IIMC campus for you—when I first saw it, I was blown away. The lush green surroundings were like a scene out of a nature documentary, complete with man-made lakes so full of water that you were tempted to go row-boating right away. It was a slice of heaven on earth ... until you came to the buildings, that is. Whoever designed them—and it was the Public Works Department you could bet safely—clearly suffered from an aesthetic deficit. Awkward and unattractive summed it up. Even as the campus has grown and improved over the decades, even today the buildings remain ugly as sin; a few of the newer buildings may not be bad in themselves, but a coherent whole they do not form.

But back in 1979, where I came from, the campus could not have been more alluring. In terms of student composition, nearly 95 per cent of the cohort (which included eight doctoral students and about 120 postgraduate students) were engineers. It could well have been an engineering convention. Everyone was here for a business degree, mostly to shed their engineering backgrounds and sell soap for Hindustan Lever or lend big bucks for banks.

As I had joined the second year directly, most of my electives were in the field of finance and control systems, and I hit the road running. The received wisdom was that having been built on the foundation of their collaboration with MIT, the curriculum at IIMC was highly quantitative. Well, if so, either my modest mathematical abilities were better than I thought or my received wisdom needed a serious reality check. Because even though I barely broke a sweat, I managed to comfortably stay in the top ten per centile of the class every trimester. All in all, the coursework phase at IIMC wasn't terribly demanding.

IIMC was a fun place, with a brilliant cohort, among the finest brains any academic institution could boast of. The institute would go on to produce many internationally distinguished alumni and no less distinguished a faculty. It was a bonus that I made several lifelong friends. Some of us in small groups would often make forays to the city and back by the only bus, namely 12 C, which would halt at every stop with the conductor exhorting the driver to take it easy with the shout of '*Ahiste* ladies' every time a female passenger boarded or disembarked.

And then there were those night-time boating expeditions in the tiny old tub moored at the little jetty opposite the hostels. While the hostel food was nothing to write home about, we had compensations at Mihir's Dhaba situated opposite the main gate of the institute. Plates of scrambled egg and bread, shingaras (samosas) accompanied by extra sweet tea in little mud pots and fluffy rosogollas kept us alive and thriving discussing esoteric authors and their abstruse books. This was the high life.

The classes were conducted by excellent teachers, even if the dominant pedagogy centred around straightforward lectures. It was simply that on occasion, in Calcutta's oppressive heat and humidity without air conditioning, the afternoon classes conducted in a non-interactive mode—especially in economics or some of the other social sciences—could make it a challenge to keep one's eyes open! The happy-go-lucky cohort, though brilliant, did not necessarily prepare for each class with any prior reading, especially as it was not a stipulated requirement. There were surprisingly few surprise quizzes to keep us on our toes. In short, the system treated students like adults, with the underlying philosophy that they were offering the best of education from the best of scholars, and it was up to us to make the most of it. Or not.

Many would compensate for the lackadaisical classroom habits with last-minute crash courses in finance, accounting, statistics, probability, operations research and such from one of the more earnest classmates and clear the exams splendidly. Mid-trimester and the end-trimester exams were the key exams that mattered.

Time flew as an arrow and soon it was March 1980. For the doctoral students, the next six to eight months were supposed to be devoted to preparing for a comprehensive examination which would qualify us to move to our dissertation phase. However, I chose to be a Hermione Granger of sorts, working extra-hard preparing for the comprehensive examination during the third semester, and managed to have the department arrange for my comprehensive exam practically back-to-back with the end of the third trimester in March 1980. This released a good six extra months for my dissertation work.

Life on the campus certainly wasn't all work. There were enough trivialities to keep one tirelessly occupied. There was this informal competition to name one of the cats that made it its business to make rounds of the hostel blocks with the regularity of Skimbleshanks, the Railway Cat. But of course, neither Skimbleshanks, nor Rumpelteazer, Deuteronomy or Mistoffelees were considered seriously, as much because that would violate the intellectual property of one late Mr T.S. Eliot, as because our cat was a feline of the fairer sex. Suffice to say, the winning name, though not one from *Old Possum's Book of Practical Cats*, would have done Eliot proud: it was B. Uma Vijaylakshmi, a name complete with initials, which could well have been in the attendance sheets in one of the classrooms.

And there was this inter-hostel gaali (cuss words) competition, held the day after semester-end exams. The competition involved teams standing on their balconies trading gaalis with each other across buildings. The winners were to be decided on the colourfulness, imaginativeness and originality of the 'gaalis', without being offensive or vulgar. Now I was born and brought up in Punjab, Haryana and Jammu. With my fluent Punjabi, I knew that much of the offensiveness about Punjabi lay in the intonation of how a sentence was articulated, and that you could sound quite offensive, even if the words themselves were not offensive at all. For that matter, even when the words were actually innocuous, you could make it sound like a gaali. Here is one example. '*Teri maa nu ... maasi akhan ...*' merely means your 'I call your mom my aunt'. No harm there. All innocence. But if said in a certain Punjabi way, it can sound like cussing of the worst sort! While I chose not to actually shout out the gaalis, I stayed as a consultant to my hostel mates. No awards for guessing whose hostel won.

Not all the non-academic time spent was trivial. The doctoral students faced myriad problems of their own, ranging from delayed receipt of their monthly fellowship money, the quantum of the fellowship amount itself, the number of books they could borrow from the library, approval of research expenditure, some of the processes involving the doctoral programme and such. The Fellow (doctoral) programme was run by a Fellow Programme Committee, comprising several faculty members, and chaired by a senior member of the faculty. This committee also included a student representative—a responsibility which the doctoral students had asked me to shoulder, as I was the most vocal voice asking for whatever reforms the system required. And this claimed a goodly bite of my time.

One of the major battles I fought with the institute management was of systemic significance. It came to our notice, and was also supported by data from prior years, that after spending three or four years in the programme, some doctoral students had still not been able to clear their coursework requirements in more quantitative areas such as production, statistics, finance and the like. These students were being asked to leave the programme without receiving so much as a master's degree or diploma (which would be granted in comparable circumstances in US universities). These cases were predominantly from one of the social sciences disciplines, while they were rare in certain other disciplines. I soon developed the hypothesis that this particular social science area was admitting students with much lower CAT scores in quantitative sections than the other departments. This automatically meant that such students were weak in their quantitative skills from the outset and were predisposed to failing such subjects because their non-quantitative background did not prepare them to clear such courses. It was then not so much the fault of the students, but rather that of the concerned department or the institute for admitting them in the first place and then requiring them to clear courses for which they did not have the background. To ask them to leave after three or even four years was patently unfair.

To test my hypothesis, I asked for the CAT scores over several years of all the doctoral students, department-wise, to compare them against the CAT scores of the postgraduate students, etc. Only then would we know whether some of the departments were admitting their doctoral students much below the minimum cut-off score of the master's students.

To my surprise, the institute refused to part with the data. This lack of transparency infuriated me, and I hardened my stand and made myself more and more vociferous, accusing the institute of patent unfairness and opacity. The fact was, in those days, no IIMs, unlike today, shared the CAT scores with students. And yet, my issue was a little different. Because it involved compromised scores at least vis-à-vis some doctoral students, I wanted the full data to test my hypothesis.

Long story short, the institute with much reluctance finally shared the CAT scores with me, to be viewed only by me in a closed room and not carried away. Based on the data, I was able to suggest significant improvements in the admission process of doctoral students, which the institute, to be fair to them, agreed to abide by. This was a significant victory for the doctoral students.

Now doctoral students are a species unto themselves, living in a time-warp all their own. Because the end is not a fixed point, they don't seem to feel any pressure to get up and get to work every morning. They start with all the time in the world, but before they know it, deadlines are flying past them like an oncoming Mumbai local on the opposite track.

It's as if they are in a maze of confusion, unsure which way to turn, or how much time to devote to any one task, like comprehensive evaluation, thesis proposal, literature survey, data collection or thesis writing. They spend way too much time in profound discussions and sterile reflections, which frequently take them into wildly unrelated areas, leaving them twiddling their thumbs so that that they end up with a pile of missed deadlines and a dissertation which is still a twinkle in their eyes, long after when they should have been nearing completion.

No doubt, a PhD is the time of life for intellectual exploration, for discussion and debate, for going wide and deep into a subject. But if this is done without the end goal constantly in sight, even if at a distance, it becomes a self-indulgent exercise that doesn't necessarily lead anywhere.

I had had a window into this life during my postgraduate diploma in statistics, when we were lodged in the hostel meant for doctoral students, who were also my chess buddies. I had seen many of them going that route, little realising that doctoral work was after all merely a stepping stone towards more significant research pursuits in the future. To make Einstein envious, there was the rest of life.

I had resolved when entering IIMC to be very hard-headed and practical, and complete a dissertation of decent quality well within the stipulated time and move on. After all, how hard could it be to come up with a half-decent idea with due literature survey, develop a clear hypothesis and methodology, collect relevant data and write up the thesis on the results? That was the reason I had tried to expedite matters by finishing my comprehensive examination well ahead of schedule.

With the comprehensive examination behind me, my immediate concern was to identify a problem for my dissertation. It wasn't before I submitted my idea of modelling the pricing mechanism of consulting assignments in the industry to my thesis advisor, the venerable Prof. S.K. Chakraborty, that I realised that it was about as clear as mud.

It took me four months to realise that I was attempting the impossible. But fortunately, at this point I realised that the time had come to let go of this topic and identify a new one. And when a new idea did flash in my head, I had to find a new thesis advisor, as the topic was in an entirely different field of finance, and it took all my meagre store of tact and diplomacy to do that. But it's a miracle, and the generosity of the two thesis advisors, that the changeover did not cost me a year, or even half a year.

Fortunately for me, after just a few weeks of brainstorming, I had identified a problem in the field of cost of capital for my dissertation. Once the idea began to take shape, I lost little time in putting it in the form of a proposal. Fortunately, I had been reading up on this topic for quite some time, so that I didn't have to spend several months on surveying the relevant literature. And luckily for me, the proposal idea appealed to Prof. N.K. Rao, who kindly agreed to be my new thesis advisor.

Well, you could say I was like a guided missile when it came to focus and the speed with which I worked. I girded up my loins and took to working fourteen-hour days, and made rapid progress with my dissertation.

This may be the right time to say something about my dissertation, which was in the broad area of corporate finance.

In corporate finance, capital structure and dividend decisions are crucial. Capital structure decisions involve finding the right balance between debt and equity to maximise a firm's market value and minimise its cost of capital. Debt is seen as risky due to fixed repayment obligations, making capital structure management essential to avoid bankruptcy.

Similarly, dividend decisions are about what proportion of profits should be paid out as dividends—again something that firms agonise a great deal over.

My dissertation was concerned with the first of the above.

Franco Modigliani and Merton Miller, the presiding deities of corporate finance since the early 1960s, introduced the Capital Structure Irrelevance theorem in 1958, later refining it in 1963.

They argued that, aside from tax and bankruptcy considerations, the amount of debt a company carries is irrelevant to its market value. This perspective challenged the common concern over capital structure decisions. While their ideas faced considerable academic scrutiny over their overly simplistic assumptions, their theories found adherents, even if not universally.

According to M&M, debt may be favoured over equity primarily due to the tax benefits of interest payments, assuming bankruptcy costs to be negligible. However, empirical evidence suggests that firms do not maximise their debt levels in their capital structures as their theorem would predict. As debt increases, initially the firm's market value rises due to the injection of cheaper capital, but eventually, the risk of bankruptcy leads to a decline in market value, resulting in a saucer-shaped curve for the value of the firm or inverted saucer-shaped curve for the firm's cost of capital. This indicates the pervasiveness of an optimal cost of capital where market value peaks.

Throughout the 1970s, critiques of M&M's theory focused on its idealised assumptions about perfect markets, which often didn't align with real-world conditions. Empirical evidence suggested that even in near-perfect markets, the cognitive behaviours of stakeholders (shareholders, lenders, management, etc.) would prevent debt from being entirely irrelevant, even in a tax-free environment. Debt carries negative connotations both psychologically and sociologically, unlike equity. Terms like 'debt-laden', 'indebted' and 'loan-sharks' or even basic terms like liability, debt recovery or debt burden etc. evoke negative associations, impacting perceptions and valuations in the market. Therefore, it's not surprising that even in a tax-free world, firms with high debt levels may be valued lower than those with lower or no debt in their capital structures.

My dissertation aimed to explore the disagreement between Modigliani and Miller's views and the traditionalists who favoured the saucer-shaped curve. I sought to show that equilibrium would result in firm values reflecting investor perceptions appropriately for their respective debt levels, rather than being necessarily equal. I began with a thought experiment and then provided experimental evidence to support my hypothesis.

In the thought experiment, envision two identical debt-free firms in a tax-free environment, initially valued equally. We introduce debt to one firm while injecting an equal amount of equity into the other. M&M argued that in a perfect market, any resulting inequality in firm values would be corrected through investor portfolio adjustments and arbitrage (buying the undervalued-firm and selling the over-valued firm) until both firms are valued equally.

I questioned the above argument, asking why, if market rationality dictates equal firm values, they become unequal in the first place. One explanation could be that there is an overreaction to the introduction of debt at first. However, if investors are perfectly rational, why do they 'consistently' overreact and later correct their overreaction through arbitrage? This inconsistency challenged their assumed rationality. Investors are not seeing debt injected into a firm for the first time, so why the overreaction? I sought answers elsewhere.

What if the initial reaction wasn't an overreaction but stemmed from the underlying reasons? Why is the term 'debt' so negatively charged? Why do we speak of 'debt burden' or quote phrases like 'the borrower is the servant of the lender'? Why do figures like Benjamin Franklin advocate 'going to bed supperless than rise in debt'? There are numerous reasons that could steer a firm away from the risks and perceptions associated with debt.

Of course, there are many reasons to borrow, including obtaining cheaper capital, generating higher returns for shareholders, embracing risk, and addressing liquidity issues. In many cases, bankruptcy may seldom materialise, as is the case in the Indian context. Firms that avoid borrowing entirely may be deemed irresponsible, as equity is typically more expensive. Ultimately, how investors perceive debt is subjective and influenced by behavioural heuristics. Even if there was some initial overreaction, fundamental differences in values of leveraged and unleveraged firms may persist, albeit at a slightly reduced level, after the arbitrage process proposed by M&M.

In light of this, my fieldwork included a survey of stockbrokers in Dalal Street, Bombay, aimed at understanding their perspective on investor attitudes and perceptions towards debt and valuation. The survey focused on why M&M's arbitrage argument might not eliminate differences in the values of two similarly structured but unequally leveraged firms.

By December 1980, I had more or less completed my fieldwork in Dalal Street. With the distance of time, I make it all sound easy, all sunshine and rainbows. Well, it wasn't. I did have my share of gloom and doom and that feeling that usually comes with banging your head against a brick wall, cured only with gallons of black coffee all night followed by feeling like a zombie the next morning.

By March 1981, I had wrapped up my conclusions and was all set to commence the writing of my dissertation work. I had estimated three to four months for this phase and was well on track to submit my dissertation by July 1981.

But fate had a somewhat different plan for me—a curveball, as they say. My father, who was 58 and working as an executive engineer in Ambala Cantonment, was hospitalised with diabetic complications. I had to drop work on my dissertation and rush to his bedside, where my mother and two younger siblings were taking care of him at the hospital.

After ten days of hospitalisation, my worst fears became a reality. My beloved father breathed his last in early April 1981. It was a bolt from the blue. At twenty-six, as the eldest son, the responsibility of my family fell squarely on my shoulders. My two elder sisters were married. Now, with two younger siblings and mother to look after, I had to urgently look for a job that would allow me to support them.

I had to find that job super-quick. Fortunately for me, the IIMC system allowed for a doctoral student to take up employment if the fieldwork had already been completed. And I found a position as a consultant with the Administrative Staff College of India (ASCI), Hyderabad, towards the end of May 1981, which just about gave us enough time to wind up the Ambala house. It was rough, especially for my mother, to wind up the establishment of several years in Ambala and move to a new and unknown city.

Of course the process of resettlement and the new job did throw a wrench in my dissertation work, but working extra hard, and using the portable Remington typewriter which was a gift from my mother, I nevertheless managed to type up and submit my thesis by November 1981—a delay of five months from my original plans—but still by far (I think even till date) the fastest completion of a doctoral dissertation at IIMC (I think I can be pardoned some bragging given the circumstances).

It has always been my firm belief that events in life are usually random. If lady luck scowls at you one moment, you never know that she would be smiling at you the next. It's merely a question of hanging in there and not letting adversity weigh you down for too long. One has to learn to roll with the punches and adapt to the curveballs that life chucks at one without surcease. That's what makes life an adventure!

I had been deputed to the Indian Bureau of Mines, Nagpur, on a several-months-long assignment by ASCI. I had only just submitted my short eighty-four-page doctoral dissertation. It was when I was visiting Delhi on some consulting-related errand that someone drew my attention to an advertisement for faculty positions at IIMA. Unfortunately, the last date for the advert was already over.

But where was the downside to applying for the position anyway? If I didn't get called for an interview owing to the late application, it was no different from my not applying at all. I hurriedly borrowed some paper, wrote out my CV, had it typed at a kiosk and sent it to that exalted institution, with little hope of hearing back. This was another of the momentous decisions in my life.

But luck decided to switch on one of its random smiles. IIMA promptly called me for a faculty seminar, as part of their recruitment process for the position of assistant professor in the finance and accounting area.

My mind was in a bit of dilemma. I was doing well as a consultant at ASCI. The ASCI pay scale was significantly better than that of IIMA, quite apart from a generous travel allowance as a consultant. Principles of economics clearly suggested the move from ASCI to IIMA to be a losing proposition, at least in the short term, given that my brother was still in his undergraduation in a hostel in Ambala and my sister had just completed her masters in English literature and was at a crossroads as to what to do next. And yet the possibility of a faculty position at IIMA was way too alluring to let pass. I was convinced, and I convinced myself further, that in the long run, IIMA would prove a far superior alternative and it would be foolish not to respond when opportunity had come knocking. And my conviction would prove me right.

So of course, I would attend the faculty seminar towards the end of 1981. But before giving the seminar, I would also be meeting various members of the finance and accounting faculty, the dean of the institute, and the director.

The seminar was typically meant for the faculty body (usually comprising all the primary and secondary members of the concerned area—finance and accounting area in this case—and anybody else, including doctoral students, who may be interested). The success or failure of one's performance in the seminar played a significant part in deciding the fate of the candidate.

While the topic for the seminar was usually left for the candidate to decide, for a rooky candidate like me, it was only expected that the topic would be nothing other than the subject of my doctoral dissertation that went by the stilted title, 'Unifying the Basic Cost of Capital Theories'. I was to give my seminar on this subject before a room full of academics and doctoral students.

Well, even if my topic turned out to be a snooze-fest, the audience would not fall asleep as they could be assured of seeing me fried during the presentation. But my one consolation, or so I imagined, was that I probably knew more about the subject than anyone in the audience would. After all I had logged in many more hours on the narrow subject of my dissertation than most others had reason to.

It was this dissertation that I was presenting at IIM Ahmedabad, with the confidence only a neophyte can display (I was yet to defend my thesis in public, which would be scheduled by IIMC only a few months later).

In retrospect, my dissertation was a rudimentary behavioural explanation for why, notwithstanding M&M's arbitrage, the differences in valuation of high debt and low debt firms may persist. I had not actually used words like 'behavioural heuristics' in my dissertation. As a matter of fact, there wasn't a single reference in my dissertation to the works of any behavioural economists of the times—not that there were many then. Nor was my dissertation written in the 'language' of behavioural economics.

It was after all the dawn of behavioural economics and at least in our part of the world, in 1979 and 1980, when I was working on my dissertation, Kahneman or Tversky or Thaler were not the names they are today. Simon and Becker belonged more to departments of economics than finance. And our familiarity with international research trends was near-zero. Besides, I was an average bloke and hardly either a genius or a cutting-edge researcher. Even my good and gentle thesis advisor, Prof. N.K. Rao, was unaware that a discipline called behavioural economics was already beginning to raise its head.

Looking back, it may be said that if behavioural economics today is equated to a Boeing, I had made a crude 'Wright Flyer' of my own, pretty much unaided and untutored.

After all, it wasn't the Google era. Access to research literature, especially in India, even in a leading IIM, was highly limited. Researchers like me, and even our professors, were not in the 'publish or perish' culture. We had zero exposure to the high academia of the US. Our papers on the efficiency or otherwise of Indian stock markets were routinely rejected by the US journals with the comment that the journal readers were not interested in the Indian capital market; or that our English was bad (meaning un-American in style); or that the papers were typed on poor quality paper (our bond papers weren't as white as they are today) on manual typewriters, and not electric. One look at the appearance and our manuscripts would elicit a terse reject note post haste. Framing bias?

In such an ecosystem, I can hardly complain if editors of journals had missed to spot the potential contribution the dissertation may have made to behavioural economics! Alas, my dissertation remained unpublished!

I had met the entire finance faculty, about six or seven of them, and a few secondary members, in the morning. It was now 2.30 p.m. My seminar had begun. My understanding was that usually the attendance in such seminars was about fifteen to twenty. But I saw the seminar room full, with at least thirty-five individuals. Apparently, there were quite a few secondary area members and members of the economics faculty too, and quite a few doctoral students. And then there were a few miscellaneous folks who had to be somebody or the other!

I had begun well. I was crisp, clear and confident. At least, most folks were listening to me intently, nodding their heads. They say well begun is half done. Well, I thought I was more than halfway through with my seminar, and it was still going good. So, I must be well more than half done. I was coming to an inflexion point in my presentation when I spotted two among the faculty members I had met in the morning, who kept shaking their heads. It soon came to a point where they wanted to stop me and ask me a question, which would disrupt my flow. I deployed the standard gambit of reserving all questions and answers to the end of my presentation and soldiered on. And after some 45 minutes, and much to the impatience of my two head-shaking members of the audience, it was question-answer time. And that's when the two gentlemen systematically started taking me and my seminar apart for the next 45 minutes that the session lasted. The gentlemen were S.K. Barua and G. Srinivasan.* Samir Barua, a primary member of the production and quantitative methods area, with secondary membership in finance area, and Srinivasan, a faculty in the finance and accounting area, I would learn, were among the brightest young faculty of the time, and were for now staunchly arrayed against me. (They would both become my very good friends later.)

But on that day, they were anything but friendly! And the truth was by the time they were done with me, the confidence I had in my dissertation disintegrated against the onslaught of the formidable Samir and Srinivasan, who criticised the entirely unheard-of methodology like an opinion survey in the context of critiquing M&M, no less. Barua and Srinivasan's aggression, combined with my not being mathematically proficient enough to capture the behavioural side of the argument more robustly, led to my well-structured seminar

* S.K. Barua retired as the director of IIMA and now lives in Ahmedabad and Goa. G. Srinivasan left IIMA within two years of my joining to teach at the University of New Brunswick, Fredericton, Canada, from where he is now retired.

crumbling like the proverbial cookies, and I was convinced my prospects at the institute were entirely bleak.

For the longest time thereafter, I would be hesitant even speaking about my dissertation with any degree of self-assurance. But a semblance of consolation did ensue when, post my thesis examination, a distinguished academic from Indian Institute of Technology Madras, one Prof. L.V.L.N. Sarma, commended it as a notably 'original' piece of work.

I left the seminar, feeling crestfallen deep inside but trying my best not to show my emotion externally and keeping the air of confidence alive with sheer will. The process ended with meetings with the dean, Dr Mohan Kaul, and the director, Dr V.S. Vyas. Both of them were senior figures who were very polite, pleasant and almost affectionate in their demeanour towards me. They told me that they had sauntered by through my seminar briefly. But because I did not know them by face and because I was nervously engaged in my losing duel with Samir and Srinivasan for much of the second half of the time, I could not recall their entry and exit!

I returned to Nagpur the same evening, where I was deputed on my IBM (Indian Bureau of Mines, to remind you) assignment.

And then one day when I returned to Hyderabad over a weekend, I found a letter from IIMA on the dining table. The letter had come just the previous day. My mother urged me to open the envelope and read the contents. I postponed opening it until the next day, as I was convinced that it would be a polite rebuff. And who loves rebuffs? But of course, I had to open it sooner or later. And when I did, I was in for a pleasant surprise. I had been made an offer, albeit as a visiting assistant professor—not a permanent position—as I was yet to defend my thesis at IIMC. So, either I had held my own against Samir and Srinivasan better than I thought I had, or the other parts of the process had gone well enough to outweigh the seminar.

The offer put me on a back foot, at least temporarily. The temporary position made the offer worse than what I had originally envisaged.

After all I was in a secure and permanent position at ASCI, which was a respectable institution, even if not quite in the same league as IIMA. Also, the pay scale I was offered was significantly worse than what I was drawing at ASCI, not to speak of the hefty daily allowance that I earned on my out-of-town consulting assignments, which was nearly twenty-five days in a month!

I agonised briefly on whether to accept the offer, knowing all the time that I was going to accept it! And I did. I joined IIMA in May 1982 and would go on to spend my next twenty years at the excellent institute with Samir Barua, who had nearly cost me my appointment at IIMA, becoming a lifelong friend and collaborator in many a project.

CHAPTER FOUR

IIM Ahmedabad—Living the Academic Life

Opportunities abound, but it is crucial to discern and select the ones that align with our goals and values ...

1982 ...

'Sir, I have come to you once again, with the same request. Please take another look at my paper. It's only a matter of one extra mark. Sir, puhlease ... it would mean so much to me.'

'But did we not go through all this only a couple of weeks ago? Didn't I show you the model answer sheet, and how there was no scope for me to grant an extra mark?'

'Yes sir, you did. But sir, this is extremely important to me. It is a matter of a whole year for me.'

'How so? What has changed between then and now, that I should review your paper all over again?' I asked.

'Sir you see, I have one F and six Ds this year (equivalent of eight Ds). The PGP Office has asked me to repeat the first year. If I get just one extra mark in your course, that will make it one F and five Ds, and I would be promoted conditionally to the second year. Sir, please sir ... after all I am just on the borderline. A single mark from you can put me on the right side of the line ...'

I moved lock stock and barrel from Hyderabad to Ahmedabad in May 1982, with my mother, sister and brother, in a second-class unreserved compartment. I had rented a house just behind the institute in the suburb of Azad Society, which was within walking distance, but cost me about 50 per cent of my post-tax salary. The line for campus housing ran four years of waiting!

The early years were an enormous challenge. But for my mother pitching in with her meagre savings, it would have been difficult to make the ends meet in our household of four. As a rookie twenty-seven-year-old, consulting income would kick in only after I had established some credibility among my new peers. The take-home salary of an entry-level academic even in a hallowed institution like an IIM was lower than the belly button of a worm, and our monthly budget would go into a spiral if I so much as bought four sets of Jockey briefs, not counting the vests. My thesis defence at IIMC was still pending (it usually took a year for it to be organised, as the thesis examination committee involved two external examiners). My sister had decided to pursue her M. Phil at the Gujarat University next door, while my brother planned to pursue his Master's.

I was pressed into teaching almost immediately, which meant nearly ten hours of preparation time for every one hour of teaching. Fortunately for me, the daily grind of preparing for classes left me with little time to dwell on my overall bleak situation. And as they say, if you hang on long enough, life has a way of simplifying complications as readily as it piles them on in the first place.

Soon the clouds of doom cleared and luckily for me, my arch-nemesis, Samir Barua, who had nearly cost me my opportunity at the institute, became my very good friend, guiding light and mentor of sorts (and remains my best friend to date). He guided me all the way, showing me the ropes, both in terms of academic preparation and navigating the administrative maze. He even let me sit through his classes and co-instructed my first course.

By the end of 1982, I had successfully defended my thesis at IIMC, and IIMA promptly regularised my appointment as an assistant professor retrospectively. Talk about lemons turning into lemonade! Things started looking up in my family life too. In 1983, my sister completed her M. Phil and married a genteel academic from the famed Jawaharlal Nehru University (JNU), and in 1985, my brother landed a job as a probationary officer with a public sector bank.

My next twenty years would be spent at this splendid institution, the iconic IIMA, represented by the 600-year-old Siddi Saiyyed Jali. I can safely say I enjoyed every single minute of my time at this wonderful institution. These were among my most productive years.

I learnt very early that in the IIMA environment, a member of the faculty was expected to perform well on four dimensions—the mix of which could vary with the seniority of a faculty. The four dimensions were: dissemination of knowledge, namely, teaching; creation of knowledge, namely research and publications (though not in the publish or perish sense); application of knowledge, namely consulting; and institutional development, namely participation in the administration of various activities such as admissions, placement, postgraduate programme, doctoral programme, library, hostels and such, which were all managed through committees comprising mostly faculty members and occasionally some co-opted student members as well. These committees were also chaired by one of the members of the faculty.

I started to systematically work on each of these dimensions, except for consulting, which was still a couple of years away. Always given to complementing my average abilities with extra hard work, my productivity, in terms of teaching, research, publications and administrative work rose to the top ten per centile of the faculty, and as did the rankings of my courses. What added to the pleasure was the good fortune of teaching some of the best brains of the country especially in the postgraduate programme.

In my early years at IIMA, I found myself barely three or four years older than the students I taught, and probably even younger than some who arrived with significant work experience. Leading a class of exceptionally bright students nearly one's own age was not unlike a ringmaster amidst a pack of lions. If one didn't take charge of the class decisively, it could go south in minutes. I had to think and plan hard about managing my classes effectively.

I was teaching Management Accounting – I (MANAC – I) or Financial Accounting for the first time. The first thing to do was to prepare well, which of course I did. As providence would have it, my first ever class of MANAC – I fell on the first day of the first trimester. I entered the classroom with a bunch of quiz papers. The class was in an uproar! 'But how can you have a quiz on day1 when nothing has been taught yet! Besides this is our first day in the institute!' was the general refrain. This allegation was easily defended.

I pointed out that their welcome kit had clearly described the ethos of the institute. The kit containing the timetable for each course in each trimester, the session schedules for each course, and all the related teaching material was provided to the students before the commencement of the term. I asked them if they had all collected their material. They had. I asked them if they had read the instructions about class preparation. They said they had. And here was the crux. The institute expected, nay *demanded* of our students, and made it clear up front, that they needed to go over the prescribed reading for a given session before coming to the class. Surprising? The IIMA philosophy was that a class was supposed to be based on discussions, not just a lecture. And if the students had not read the teaching material as required, they could not meaningfully contribute to the discussions. 'So that's what this quiz on Day 1 is all about—to assess if you have at least perused through the prescribed reading even casually; nothing more.' The class could not object to this reasoning. I had to lay down my expectations and the ground rules from the start and that's what I did. I would do this again and again in the coming years in many of the courses that I taught.

Short quizzes like this one ensured in due course that students came reasonably prepared to the class, given that both surprise quizzes (about six in a trimester) as well as class participation each carried 15–20 per cent weight.

But in the process, I also gained early notoriety as a tough b***d. And the infamy only strengthened with time, given that I was also in the habit of closing the doors of my 8.30 a.m. classes as the classroom clock struck the hour sharp. It was my stated case that the onus of being a minute ahead of me rather than a minute behind was on my students if we were to respect the integrity of the classes. Every classroom had a large wall clock and all of us were supposed to synchronise our watches to that clock. While there was a bit of demur at this initially, soon my infamy preceded me, and it saved precious minutes of teaching time. And more important, it instilled a respect for non-negotiable deadlines in the students!

But it was still only 1984. I would be turning thirty later in the year, and my mother was keen, as mothers usually are, that I too get married, now that both the younger siblings were 'settled'. Fortunately, my elder sister, married to a banker, lived in Jodhpur, and happened to know my future parents-in-law. My sister had taken a shine to their daughter, Meenalochani, or Meena, recommending her very highly as a potential partner for me!

Thanks to my sister's matchmaking skills, Meena and I were introduced in late 1983, leading to six months of intense correspondence. After all, choosing a life partner may well be one of the most important decisions one makes in life and the cost of a wrong choice can be monumental. Fortunately for me, in retrospect, my decision to marry her turned out to be my best decision ever. Bless all elder sisters!

We were married in 1984. My only condition for the wedding was that I wanted no part of any religious rites and would just like to sign marital papers in the local matrimonial court, and that Meena would join me in Ahmedabad with just her personal belongings. A moment of mirth ensued when we visited the Jodhpur Marriage Registrar for giving notice of our forthcoming wedding, and the Registrar earnestly wanted to know if we were eloping or belonged to different castes or communities!

She being the only daughter (plus a brother), her parents were a tad disappointed at this stipulation. Besides, Meena's father, who headed a defence R&D establishment in Jodhpur, had a vast array of well-wishers whom he wanted invited to the wedding. But my being a PhD from IIMC and a faculty at IIMA trumped all other considerations in her scholarly father's eyes. On my side, I yielded somewhat and went along with her parents' wishes to hold a large reception at their residence, while I held none in Ahmedabad, choosing instead to donate to a cause.

As I stated earlier, one of the joys of teaching at IIMA is the sheer brilliance of the students, who were also deeply ambitious and serious about their work. Most of them would have been toppers in their respective schools and colleges. It was highly challenging to teach them—if they could trip up a faculty, they were heroes among their peers. It was almost like a spy vs spy game—anticipating their questions and preparing answers, along with gentle snubs to keep some of them in their places or from pre-empting or hijacking a class.

I recall a period around 1986–87. There was this student, an IITian, who sat on the last row and almost never opened his mouth during the raucous classroom discussions. He would sit quietly with a seemingly bored expression through every class. In a bid to draw him in, anytime I asked him a question, of any complexity, he would invariably provide a brilliant and ready answer. I was always impressed by this quiet tall young man. I also noticed that his grades in my courses were always high. If I recall right, he passed IIMA with a gold medal too. He went on to become the governor of RBI.

And then there was this quiet and petite young lady—a Stephanian—very earnest, almost shy, bright, and very diligent. She would often ask questions outside the classroom and invariably did very well in all my courses. Three and a half decades down the road, she would be the chairperson of Securities and Exchange Board of India (SEBI).

I could go on with the list of students who would all make it big as CEOs of large banks, corporates, big-time start-up entrepreneurs, renowned academics and more, quite apart from equally distinguished colleagues in the faculty.

But let's make no mistake about it. There's only so much credit one can take for having taught students of such calibre. These students would have been RBI governors, SEBI chiefs, corporate honchos or whatever else regardless of who taught them!

Ah, wait, there was something else to IIMA's organisational prowess. We even had seating charts available to us for each class, complete with the pictures of the students, so that faculty could readily identify and get to know each student personally.

I wanted to make the most of these. I would take the seating charts to the postgraduate programme office to get the first name of each student. To me, getting to know my students by their first names was a top priority. Many times, I surprised them by calling out to them by first name like a long-lost friend, which always earned me some brownie points! (The class nameplates and the seating charts only carried their initials and the surnames.)

But that was only a part of it. I also made it my business to find out their educational backgrounds, so I could tailor my approach to each student's unique strengths and weaknesses. With a quick glance at my seating chart, I could immediately tell, for example, who had an engineering background, who was a chartered or cost accountant and who had a commerce or arts background. Asking an engineering student an advanced question on accounting made little sense. Similarly, if you wanted to discourage a CA topper from hijacking the accounting class, you asked him or her a particularly advanced question in accounting that they couldn't answer, and that would dampen their enthusiasm just enough to go with the pace of the class, which was geared to carry everyone along. This gave each student an even chance at learning.

If teaching the postgraduate programme ensured that we were absolutely thorough in the fundamentals of theory, teaching in the executive programmes was enriching in a different way. One met and interacted with CEOs and CXOs, senior bureaucrats, family business owners, senior and mid-level executives, et al. Each had their own rich experience and insights, which were of immense value as many of us had come into teaching with little or only junior level corporate experience. It was no less challenging—why should a person who had spent twenty years running his or her company or department listen to person half their age just because the youngster had a PhD tagged to their name? The beauty of it was that by the end of these programmes, immense mutual respect developed. On the part of the faculty, for the real-life problems that the executives faced and overcame, and on the part of the executives when they understood how to place their experiences and challenges in a theoretical framework and how it facilitated their finding solutions to some of their vexing problems.

In 1986, I was coordinating an executive development programme in capital markets, which was attended by many professionals from stock exchanges. I was always a stickler for punctuality.

A quiet star among the participants in the cohort of the Management Development Programme I was coordinating was M.R. Mayya, the then executive director of the Bombay Stock Exchange. So impressed was he with my punctuality and earnestness (and hopefully my lectures), that he invited me to join the Ahmedabad Stock Exchange as a public representative, a role I played for the next seven years. This was my first board position. Every time I enter any boardroom even today, I always think of Mr Mayya!

By the early 1990s, we had formed a nice quartet: Samir Barua, Jayanth Rama Varma, N. Venkiteswaran and I. Together we were a very productive group which wrote numerous papers, articles and books, and undertook several consulting assignments together.

Over time, without meaning to be immodest, I found the IIMA experience propelling me to several corporate and stock exchange boards. These included the Derivatives Board of Bombay Stock Exchange, the Primary Market Board of SEBI, boards of well-known educational institutions, banks, financial institutions, and several national level advisory committees of the Ministry of Finance, National Stock Exchange, Institute of Chartered Accountants of India, among others.

But through it all, teaching remained the biggest and the most rewarding love, especially because the feedback from teaching was so immediate, even if the formal feedback would come with a lag. So exciting was teaching that the weekends often weighed heavy, and I couldn't wait for Monday mornings.

It didn't take me long to figure out why IIMA consistently ranked among the very best worldwide (including IIMC and IIM Bangalore) despite their similar student populations. The difference? IIMA followed a dynamic, discussion-based pedagogy, complete with riveting case studies that often sparked lively and energetic debates and discussions, which kept everyone active and on their toes. One could feel the electric buzz in the air as spontaneous and brilliant questions from students required extensive preparation on the part of the faculty members to field. As far as rigour in teaching went, there was no beating IIMA, and certainly not in the case-based pedagogy. Alas, much of this would be truer of the first year than the second year of the programme, by which time the students would learn to 'play the system'!

A never-to-be-forgotten case was Smoky Valley Café—always taken up on the first day, first case and first class of Management Accounting – I (or financial accounting course). The case was complete with a business, protagonist, an extramarital affair and an elopement, which left the business with incomplete accounting details. Using the meagre information, the class had to string together a whole balance sheet. This Harvard Business School case, taught for decades at IIMA, went on to become a mini-celebrity case, spawning more stories in the form of epilogues to the original and such. (The case would later find mention in one of my own novels, *Return to Jammu*.)

In academic affairs, faculty had near-complete freedom in designing courses, prescribing reading material, grading systems for their courses, and grades awarded to students and such, subject only to peer consultations of the concerned functional or sectoral area members of the faculty. I do not recall that such powers were ever misused by the faculty.

Faculty meetings were often as disputatious as parliament and could be emotionally charged as well. Every aspect concerning the institution was deliberated upon without reservation. This approach, grounded in the conviction that each member could contribute to the institution's betterment through a candid sharing of ideas, fostered a robust and cohesive community.

From time to time, faculty meetings were also held to discuss specific instances of students who had not met their institutional academic requirements of keeping one's grades above stipulated limits.

The three semesters of the first year comprised about eighteen courses, and the second year had about fifteen or sixteen courses. The institute norms permitted up to four Ds, or one F and two Ds in a year for a student to be promoted from first year to the second or to graduate at the end of second year. The implicit logic for this was that even though one may be weak in a handful of courses, it need not come in the way of one being an all-round manager, provided they had good grades in the rest of the courses.

It was not uncommon for students to struggle and receive multiple Ds and Fs, exceeding the permitted limit of four Ds or one F and two Ds, particularly in the first year of the postgraduate programme. In principle, those failing to clear this hurdle could be asked to repeat the year or could be promoted conditionally.

One April afternoon, when the summer break had commenced and I was busy in my office preparing for the new term which would commence by the end of June, there was a knock on my door. I hollered a perfunctory 'Come in!'

As the door opened, I recognised the student who had recently approached me about re-evaluating her Corporate Finance answer paper. She sought a small mark increase to elevate her grade from D+ to C-. Annoyingly, only the previous fortnight, she had involved her father, a senior IPS officer, in this pursuit.

The end-term examination had consisted of objective type questions, leaving little room for subjective judgement in grading. The evaluations were conducted by a research associate, albeit an experienced one, who had scrupulously followed the model evaluation sheet I provided. Upon re-examining the paper, I diligently explained to the father and daughter duo why there was no possibility of altering the marks I had assigned. Consequently, I maintained that her grade could not be altered and would remain a D+. I addressed all their doubts and queries methodically, ensuring they understood that no additional marks could be awarded.

Now, at my door once again, she said she wanted 'five minutes' of my time. I asked her to come in.

'Sir, I have come to you once again, with the same request. Please take another look at my paper. It's only a matter of one extra mark. Sir, puhlease ... it would mean so much to me.'

'But did we not go through all this only a couple of weeks ago? Didn't I show you the model answer sheet, and how there was no scope for me to grant an extra mark?'

'Yes sir, you did. But sir, this is extremely important to me. It is a matter of a whole year for me.'

'How so? What has changed between then and now, that I should review your paper all over again?' I asked.

Incidentally, the faculty body had already met and deliberated several times towards the end of the trimester and decided that notwithstanding the standard four-Ds stipulation, students who had got up to seven Ds may be promoted to the second year conditionally, meaning the students would have to retake their courses of the first year to remove the excess of three Ds from their first-year coursework, alongside their coursework of the second year. However, those above eight Ds, but less than ten Ds would have to repeat the year. And those upwards of ten Ds would be asked to withdraw from the programme.

The student continued, 'Sir, you see, I have one F and six Ds this year (equivalent of eight Ds). The PGP Office has asked me to repeat the first year. If I get just one extra mark in your course, that will make it one F and five Ds, and I would be promoted conditionally to the second year. Sir, please sir ... after all I am just on the borderline. A single mark from you can put me on the right side of the line.'

'Look here young lady. You are not actually on the "borderline". Borderline would have been four Ds, or one F and two Ds. You are at one F and five Ds! The border has been expanded enormously already. So you have crossed the borderline by a huge margin and now holding me responsible for preventing you from crossing it. The onus of remaining within the borders is the students', not the faculty's. What grades you have obtained in other courses cannot be a consideration for you to get an extra mark in my course.

'But you are being inconsiderate!' she wailed hysterically, and went on to appeal to my sympathy, empathy, humanity and more.

Truth be told, giving her an extra mark to bump her grade a notch up was within my discretion. It's not as if I was being heartless. The fact was, the student's case didn't align with the spirit of the requirements. Moreover, I had discovered after her visit to my office with her father last time, that she had narrowly avoided F or D grades in three other courses by just one mark. This implied she had unsatisfactory grades in nearly ten courses, not just seven. She was gaming the system. I stood firm and declined to grant her the grace mark.

The fact is, such requests were always morally and emotionally troublesome. In my heart and conscience, I knew that I was doing my duty as an academic and in upholding the standards of the institution. But such decisions are never easy on the human front. And moreover, led to the reinforcement of my image as a tough son of a b***.

In that era, IIMA was primarily a faculty-governed institution. Important decisions required faculty consultations, seen not as a director's weakness but as a bolstering factor. These collective decisions gained support from the board or government entities. Fascinatingly, faculty members operated without a hierarchical structure. Everyone, including the director, had equal-sized offices and furniture. House allocations were independent of faculty ranks, determined solely by the date of joining the institute. Area chairmanships rotated, allowing an assistant professor to hold the position, not solely senior professors.

The same spirit of equality that governed the faculty also percolated down to faculty-student interactions, characterised by fairness and equity. Students, competitive as they were, would often argue, debate, negotiate and even fight for every single mark after each quiz, mid-term or end-term examination. There was no room for arbitrariness or negligence in the grading process. Even crafting a question paper was a delicate task, for any question that could be interpreted equivocally had the potential to cause chaos. Giving in to the arguments of one student could result in a flood of requests for grade adjustments from other students, which could ultimately undermine the credibility of the process, the instructor or the examiner.

Living in a country rife with corruption at every level, I was constantly impressed by the unblemished reputation of esteemed institutions like the IIMs or the IITs. It was unheard of for any candidate to gain admission through unfair, unethical or irregular methods. It is not as if attempts were not made by powerful politicians, bureaucrats or corporate bigwigs to secure seats for their children. It was not uncommon for high-ranking officials to make phone calls in an attempt to exert influence.

So how did these institutions insulate themselves from giving in to influence-peddling, and remain untouched by corruption? After all these institutions employed people from the same population as the rest of the country. So what was different?

Firstly, these institutions ring-fenced themselves with strong systems and processes which were highly transparent and had in-built mechanisms to thwart any hanky-panky with those processes. Secondly, unlike the typical Indian society which suffers from high power–distance index, these institutions of excellence made an exception of themselves. The collegial, scholarly and committed faculty wasn't easily impressed by influence peddlers.

Let me give an example or two. Take a bank. The power–distance index in it is typically such that few would dare challenge the decision or directive of a chairman-managing director (CMD). Leave alone a directive, the gentlest suggestion or request of the CMD would be taken as a command. That's how obliging credit committees frequently clear bad loans—because they are highly pliable in the face of subtle, or even not very subtle, signals that a corrupt CMD, or a CMD pressured by the powers that be 'from above', may send their way.

On the other hand, even assuming an IIM director is highly corrupt or weak-kneed when it comes to a phone call from a mighty power-peddler, there is nothing the director can do to oblige those calling for the favours. The director can influence neither the written test not the interview process in the slightest. So the one and only response of the director to those pressuring them has to be, 'Sorry, but it is simply not within the director's powers.' And that would be the truth, unlike in the case of a bank CMD. It further helps that the power–distance index in these institutions is such that even the gentlest of such suggestions would be laughed out by the faculty concerned, and would seriously erode the credibility of the director making such a suggestion. Few faculty members are cowed down by a director.

But that's not all. The selection process at IIMs is typically multi-layered. It starts with the preparation of the CAT paper, progresses through the printing and administration of the CAT, determination of CAT cut-off scores, subsequent interviews and group discussions, and culminates in the creation of the waiting list, among other steps. The comprehensive and complex process engages several faculty members from different IIMs, none of whom wield significant authority over any specific facet of the procedure.

The carefully developed process of complex checks and balances has contributed significantly to the test's resilience against corruption. In the history of CAT spanning decades, the process was compromised only once, and that was when a government press oversaw the printing of the question paper.

Broadly the process worked like this: while the system may have changed somewhat today, in those days the admissions committee of each IIM comprised nearly ten faculty members, with a tenure of two years or more. The Inter-IIM Admissions Committee, which had representatives from each IIM, changed its membership annually. This committee formed a subcommittee, called the CAT committee, involving about a dozen odd members in those days—who were sequestered for three days while preparing the CAT questions. During this process no telephones were allowed, and nor could anyone leave the premises where the questions were being worked on.

Each member could contribute only for a small segment of the CAT, and all papers were surrendered by the members before leaving the premises on the final day. Furthermore, the questions submitted by one member could be tweaked by another, and the original contributing member would not know what the tweak was. The final selection of questions was done by a yet smaller group.

This complex process of checks and balances helped to ensure the integrity of the CAT and prevent any manipulation or favouritism. While the system may have changed somewhat today, the basic principles of transparency and confidentiality are still maintained to ensure that the CAT remains a fair, robust and transparent filter for all candidates.

The system of generating the question papers itself ensured that even if there was a bad apple, such an apple could do very little damage to the integrity of the system.

The pride that the members took in their role and the deep sense of responsibility for the system also played a significant part in maintaining its integrity. The faculty members involved in the CAT preparation saw it as a matter of personal and institutional reputation to maintain the highest standards of transparency and fairness in the exam, which made it unlikely that any member would be able to compromise the system, even if someone wanted to.

That was not all. Even the process of interviews was elaborately designed to minimise the chances of corruption. Each IIM would constitute a bank of interview committees, each consisting of three faculty members from different disciplines, an industry expert and an alumnus. Which candidate would face which panel would be unknown to both the candidates and the members of the interview committee. These committees would be assigned to one or more interview centres in accordance with their availability and the interviews would be conducted within a span of about three days.

The blind date format of the interviews aimed to minimise any bias towards a particular candidate. Even if, by the slimmest chance, an interviewer encountered an acquaintance in a panel, their influence on the candidate's evaluation would be absurdly miniscule. This is because the individual subjectivity in candidate evaluation during the interview accounted for only 15–20 per cent of the total interview score.

In short, the IIMs' admission processes were like a fortress with several layers of defences. Little wonder that they have managed to protect their integrity all these decades and their admission system has remained one of the most credible in the world, assuring a purely merit-based system.*

---

* With more than twenty-odd IIMs today, I do not know if all of them follow the same tight and secure practices. Living up to brand IIM is a tough call and one can only hope the integrity of the brand will prevail.

In other words, the systems at IIMs and other similar institutions of excellence, like the IITs, showed that it was possible to design fool-proof systems against corruption if only there was the will to do so. The reason why we do not have more extensive prevalence of such systems to curb corruption can only be chalked to the lack of will among our political 'masters' (since they are certainly not political servants anymore) to curb corruption. Perhaps NEET (National Eligibility cum Entrance Test) administrators today have something to learn here.

The near twenty years at IIMA would pass as if in no time at all. Not once did I ever suffer from Monday blues. As a matter of fact, weekends were a bump in the enjoyment of living as a teacher at IIMA! Fortunately, there were always students—especially non-commerce graduates wanting special tutorials in accounting or finance—keen to have an extra class or two even at 9 p.m. over the weekends. So my weekends were not always without a connect with the students.

I would grow with the institute, and grow as a teacher, as a management professional, and grow as a columnist and more, as scores of challenging opportunities came my way, most of which I guess I grabbed. These opportunities would have been unthinkable outside of IIMA. Perhaps that's one reason why IIMA strikes a deep chord among the ex-faculty and students alike. No, I would not retire from IIMA. In fact, I would leave the great institution midway through my career, when the midlife bug bit me, exhorting me 'not to die teaching'. The field of management was nothing if not practised. Being a consultant or on the boards of companies was never quite the same as 'managing' real-life challenges. This I would proceed to do in 2001; but I didn't know it just then.

CHAPTER FIVE

The Lion Is a Gentleman—Manners of the Jungle

Developing the ability to heed expert advice is a valuable skill to cultivate ...

1987

We had just turned around a large ber bush, when we came face to face with this enormous lion with his humongous golden mane just sitting there on his haunches, as if waiting for us, as if knowing we were coming, and watching us intently as if contemplating what to make of our insolence. He was barely 15 feet away. We stood frozen mid-step. You have my word that the free-ranging lion looks three times as big as it does in a zoo.

Ravi murmured softly to me, 'Don't be scared. Don't turn your back. And no matter what, don't run. Trust me. I repeat, no matter what, don't turn your back and don't run ...'

I was set in the groove of academic life and was still a relatively young thirty-one-year-old associate professor of finance and accounting, complete with my share of papers, articles, case studies and teaching notes, and even a board position to boast of.

So, what was I, a hardcore academic, doing in a stand-off against a full-grown magnificent specimen of an Asiatic lion in the Gir, you may ask. Well, that's what this adventure is all about.

I had just returned from a weekly spin in my 1937 Austin 7, which I had acquired from Jaipur, for no good reason, except that I could just about afford it. By now, accustomed to some of my quirks for things ancient and decrepit, my good wife had just smiled, tacitly 'permitting' me my indulgence. It was a tiny, boxy little two-door green contraption with four black mudguards, a luggage rack at the back and a windshield that could be lifted 90 degrees from its hinges at the top.

I was just recovering from the heat, sweat and exhaustion of a laborious Sunday, because the spin had been preceded by a good half an hour of tinkering with the simple engine until the motor ultimately showed some signs of life, sputtering, then spluttering, and finally roaring to life. Besides, it was 43 degrees in the shade. It hadn't helped that the spin just concluded had been with a full load of boisterous kids—my 'campus friends'.

A man needed to catch his breath. It was then that my good wife, Meena, knowing my fringe love for adventures, mentioned casually that an acquaintance of hers, Ravi Chellam, was passing through the city in the coming week, en route to the forests of Gir, and asked whether I would like to accompany him for a 'spot of adventure', watching lions up-close. Ravi was a young man—maybe a tad younger than myself. He was completing his PhD, studying the Asiatic lion in its only and last habitat, the Gir forest.

If Meena and I hadn't been on the best of terms, Agatha Christie could have been pardoned for putting her centre-stage in one of her novels, plotting a convoluted and ingenious idea of murder masquerading as a lion kill, by planting the idea of the trip into my head.

But suggest it she did, and I fell for the suggestion like a stone chucked skywards. After all it was summer break time, the month of May, free from classes. So, I was in; jaws, claws and paws, as it were.

My first impression of Ravi was that he was wild, like the very *Panthera leo persica* he had embarked on studying. I recall him, nearly three and a half decades later, as the strong-silent kind, more floating in the air than walking, communicating more in gestures than talking, attired in olive-greens from his military Fidel Castro-style cadet patrol cap, down to his rubber-soled canvas boots.

He scarcely spoke unless spoken to; scarcely smiled unless the jokes were really good; and scarcely ate except when he had to for biological reasons. My world of cash, finance and economics, and his of big cats, forests and ecology had little in common.

The following weekend, before 7 a.m. on Saturday, after an early breakfast, we set off for Junagadh—a 320-km journey—a good nine-hour drive those days, in his beaten-up ancient grey Mahindra Jeep, with plenty of faded khaki canvas covering the seats and the top, with a jerrycan of water (largely for effect, I presumed).

This was the month of May perhaps the hottest of the year anywhere in the country, but in Gujarat it seemed only a touch colder than the core of the sun. Within an hour of leaving the city of Ahmedabad on the narrow highway, the air that blasted us from the sides of the Jeep stung us like solar flares. But Ravi was unflappable, even as by about 11 a.m., the road ahead rose in a haze and inverted reflections of the oncoming vehicles confused the mind, and the iced water we had filled up in the bottles heated up halfway to being steam. But, by 12.30, even the stoic lion-man needed a break.

We stopped at a dhaba in the middle of nowhere, ate the meagre Saurashtra spread on offer for lunch, recharged the boiling water bottles—even the Jeep's radiator needed a generous fill of water from the jerrycan (which wasn't for effect after all)—and resumed the mind-numbing ride.

To help Ravi (and myself) keep awake, I tried some conversation. I vaguely recalled a story about him that I had heard second-hand from a common friend not too long ago. I wanted to know if the account was true. He confirmed the story in minimal words. Apparently, he had once fallen asleep exhausted, in his sleeping bag, his back against a tree, at about 2 a.m. in the Gir, when he had been watching a pride of lions on a sambar-kill, barely twenty-five feet away. He had woken up feeling the weight and movement of a cub jumping over his legs sheathed inside the sleeping bag. It had taken much tact and nerve and gentle wiggling of his toes to get the cub off him, and walk out of the situation, for the slightest alarm on account of any unexpected movement from him could alarm the cub and get the mother lioness to make short work of him. Unlike African guides and researchers, researchers in India do not enter the forest with a gun. The lion-man had confessed matter-of-factly during the drive, that it was the one time he had been *really scared*. He also showed me a freshly developed picture which he took out from the open glove compartment, of a rare frontal shot of a lion (with a camera) taken from a low angle, without tele-lens. I learnt that most shots of lions tend to be taken from top-below, because often the shutterbug is perched on higher and safer ground, like a tree or a vehicle. A low angle shot on the other hand is taken from a level below that of the lion, which leaves the photographer at the mercy of the beast. The picture was a jaw shot of a lioness sleeping with her mouth open.

We were passing through the Saurashtra countryside, a first for me, but I had little eye for the landscape; the sights registered feebly in my mind in the heat-induced trance.

We hit the outskirts of Junagadh by about 6.30 p.m. at dusk, but we had to drive an hour or so further west, to reach the Forest

Department rest-house. To be fair, Ravi had referred to the rest-house but once, but somehow, I had visions of a sprawling jungle bungalow rich in wood, complete with khansama and such, to end the hard day of a rough and hot ride.

No such luck. The rest-house was a two-bedroom apartment on the ground floor of a dilapidated (not old) cream-coloured, three-storeyed building, housing two apartments on each floor. Except for one apartment directly above the rest house, the rest showed no lights.

Apparently, the apartment with lights was occupied by four functionaries of the Forest Department—a cook for the rest-house, a driver and a couple of forest guards. The cook in a dishevelled pyjama and kurta—a far cry from the khansama of my fancy—soon got busy rustling us up a very basic dinner of dal, roti and rice. In the meanwhile, some glucose biscuits served us for starters.

We entered the rest-house. It was furnished for a Zen monk. No curtains on the windows or doors. No blinds. The apartment, letting in all the heat of the day through the shut glass panes, was worse than a furnace—a live demonstration of the greenhouse effect. The surrounding scrub jungle did little to bring down the heat. There was no question of an air-conditioner. The fan blew such hot air that any cinder in there would have caught fire. I could also sense quite a few mosquitoes all but crashing against my forearms and neck. I was beginning to get worried as to how we were supposed to sleep in the mosquito-infested oven of a room. I was hungry and had already demolished five of the biscuits.

As for Ravi, he seemed indifferent, or rather incapable of caring whether it was hot or scalding, whether one slept or not, whether one ate a dinner or did without. He hadn't touched one of the biscuits yet, and he had driven all day.

Dinner over, I suggested that we drag the camp cots out on the verandah to sleep in the fresh air which, even if not much cooler than inside, offered a less claustrophobic surrounding. The cook cheerfully informed us that only three days ago, a lion focused on a chinkara had come rushing by right next to the verandah of the rest-house where he (the cook) was sipping a cup of tea at sundown, and had skidded to a stop opposite an equally bewildered cook and slowly retreated into the jungle, as the quick-witted chinkara ambled off in the opposite direction (much later in life, National Geographic would educate me that prey animals are known to seek human company when chased by predators). But he assured us that there was no activity of any lions observed in the vicinity that day. His encouraging conclusion notwithstanding, my enthusiasm to sleep on the verandah waned as quickly as it had surfaced.

We thanked the cook, who left for his apartment upstairs, and promptly hit the camp-beds placed in each room, switched off the lights, and went to sleep. I needn't have worried. Having been tossed around all day like popcorn in a pan, I couldn't have slept better had this been Queen Elizabeth's retreat at the Balmoral.

I woke up in alarm, thanks to a bunch of quarrelsome babblers screaming as if from the next room, and I could see the grey rectangle of dawn through the curtain-less window. It turned out to be the alarm clock—probably one of the few fancy indulgences of Ravi's travel kit, befitting the jungle theme. My watch confirmed it to be 5.00 a.m. I found myself drenched in sweat and mosquito bites and promptly went to the only bathroom in the rest-house for brushing and shaving, followed hopefully by a nice cold shower for some relief from the unrelenting and suffocating heat.

I had left home without a bar of soap in the belief that government rest-house bathrooms were bound to provide standard-issue Hamam—miniature green rectangular bars of soap. But to my surprise, there was none. At least no fresh one, even though there was a razor-thin remnant left on one half of an old yellow plastic soap-holder with slatted bottom. I knew better than to use this apology of a soap for my bathing, anticipating it might have to serve more dire needs, if you know what I mean.

As I emerged some ten minutes later after a painstaking 'bucket bath', the bath towel wrapped around me, Ravi had boiled some tea on the gas in an aluminium saucepan. He poured the brew into two ribbed glasses on the only table in the living area. Being more than somewhat sensitive to personal body odour, I seldom travelled without some eau-de-toilette and a small bottle of Old Spice was forever to be found in my kit. I took out the 100 ml bottle to dab some on my face, when Ravi gently stopped me, telling me it would be best not to use any. As if anticipating my question, he said we were going to be in the forest, probably in close proximity to lions and it would be best not to wear any strong scent upon oneself. In fact, he underscored that when on the field, he favoured the local datun over the strongly flavoured toothpaste.

Well, wild-lifers have their quirks, I thought, and went into my room to dress myself in a dull brown trouser and a matching sweatshirt, feeling pretty smug in what I fancied to be jungle-friendly attire. Only much later would I learn that when treading into a jungle, it is best not to wear freshly laundered clothes with their strong laundry smell. I grabbed a few biscuits and some dry bread lying on the table as an apology for breakfast. Ravi took another ten minutes to get ready in the same olive greens of the day before and by 5.30 a.m. we were standing around the Jeep. Two assistants, or helpers, who were apparently going to accompany us, were loading the Jeep with sundry bundles of things, such as a couple of small cartons, a few bamboo sticks, a black box (which I would learn shortly was a receiver) and what appeared to be a standard zig-zag television antenna made of aluminium tubing, attached to a short handle, with a long plastic wire ending in two naked copper terminals hanging from it. Soon the stuff was loaded, and we were on our way, the two helpers on the two lateral canvas-covered benches at the back, me on the front passenger seat, with Ravi at the wheel. One of them informed Ravi that some activity had been observed about 5–6 km away, at the edge of the national park.

Apparently, Ravi had radio-collared a male lion which we were now on our way to track. The antenna was to catch the signals transmitted from the radio-collar of the cat. We were presumably headed towards where the helpers had received information of some lion activity during the night—surely the direction of the jungle, I thought. We travelled some half an hour on a narrow belt of a road lined with a variety of evergreen trees. Beyond, as far as the eye could see, the dominant spread on the scenery was that of the bush-like babool (acacia) tree, dotted with larger trees of jamun, banyan, teak, dhak, flame of the forest, and plenty of dry bushes including those of ber, et al. The landscape was not very dense, with fair visibility far and wide, though a trifle dimmed with the morning mist. I wasn't expecting to see lions amidst such landscape and thought we must soon enter more dense foliage, forgetting this was supposed to be a dry deciduous forest. But I saw a fair sprinkling of the other famous residents of the Gir—the moustachioed maldhari tribesmen in their distinctive white headgear, white dhotis and short frock-like white kurtas with penny-sized golden studs on each ear, carrying long bamboo staffs, ambling along lazily, herding some cattle. I understood they may well have left those cattle in the vicinity to graze under their overnight collective watch, and were now collecting them, shepherding them back to their villages.

Soon the road ended, and we turned into a narrow and rutted mud track. Within a short distance, Ravi braked hard and jumped out of the vehicle. As did the two assistants and I. Ravi went about ten feet in front of the nose of the Jeep, bent down over the dust looking keenly at something, and craning his neck left-to-right-to-left again. For the life of me, I could not fathom what could have caught his fancy on the plain dusty track. As I went closer, he pointed out a row of faint lion pug marks crossing the trail into the bushes, from right to left. 'Could be twelve to twenty-four hours old,' he announced quietly and returned to the Jeep to resume our journey calmly. This was my first-ever gander at lion's pug marks in the wild; the zoo's cemented cages never show pug marks in any case.

The trail was bumpy, and we were tossed around the vehicle in every direction, like corn in a popping pan. Within ten minutes, even this meagre track petered out. Ravi parked the vehicle under a small bamboo thicket and all four of us dismounted. The cartons were left in the back of the Jeep under cover of a faded khaki tarpaulin, as we began our silent march with one of the helpers carrying the receiver on a sling and Ravi holding the antenna by the handle. Each helper carried a bamboo stick in his armpit. It wasn't 6.30 a.m. yet and the air around us was still somewhat cool, though the nip in the air was rapidly disappearing, as the sun struggled to rise above the horizon.

The surroundings were silent, except for sundry bird noises. The landscape was hardly jungle-like, and the visibility extended a good 50 metres. I asked Ravi softly (the surrounding silence somehow forced you to be keep your voice low) when we would hit the jungle. He just said this was it and that we were headed towards the area that bordered the national park territory.

We commenced our march towards a small hillock. As we reached its base, Ravi and the helper with the receiver ascended the mound some twenty feet high, while the other helper and I stayed at the base. Soon I saw Ravi brandishing the antenna held perpendicular to himself, in an arc of 270 degrees. I knew enough to figure out that he was scanning the environment for the beep on the receiver to gauge the direction in which the radio-collared animal was likely to be. Within five minutes, we descended the hillock, and recommenced our march in a particular direction. Ravi informed me that the lion should be well within a kilometre from where we were, and I felt the excitement travel up my veins.

We resumed our slow and silent march for 15 more minutes, until we spotted another hill. A jungle fowl, slightly larger and longer than the standard rooster, landed clumsily ahead of us and then took off equally clumsily. The suddenness of it gave me a near heart attack.

We continued to walk, and the exercise of ascending the mound and waving the radio antenna about was repeated, except that this time, there were three of us atop the mound, as I joined the other two. I distinctly heard a faint beep as the antenna swung around a particular direction. 'Less than 300 metres ... must be on the boundary of the national park,' murmured Ravi. And then, as if he had just remembered something, addressed me, 'I am expecting the lion we have set out to track to be outside the national park. But in case it turns out to be inside the park, you will have to return to the Jeep with one of the assistants. You will accompany me only if we are certain of making the contact outside the national park.' My heartbeat accelerated a tad more, and I fervently prayed for the lion to be outside the national park boundary.

We had been walking for over a half an hour now and so far, there had not been the slightest trace of any of the fancied wildlife (unless you count the fowl). It was as if the jungle, if you could call it one, had been systematically cleared of any animal, small or big. And then suddenly, the helper whose hands were free, except for the bamboo stick, stopped us with a hand signal, and pointed towards a slump of bushes about 90 degrees to the direction we were walking. I could see nothing. Then the friendly helper pulled me a little closer to himself and pointed once again in the same direction, asking me to look harder. And then one of the animals twitched, clearly alarmed by our presence and then I saw it and then its companions. It was a herd of cheetal.

Barely 30 feet away. I could spot a mature stag munching on the upper reaches of a bush, as the rest fed on the many leaves and berries fallen on the ground. There must have been between a dozen to fifteen deer in all. What was amazing is that even after it was pointed out, it took me a great deal of effort to see the entire bunch of them. And then we saw a few black-faced langurs.

We commenced our silent march, even slower this time, with Ravi constantly keeping the antenna pointed in the direction of our march. I kept hearing slightly louder, but low-intensity beeps at constant intervals. My heart was pounding like an iron-smith's hammer, as Ravi continued to mutter periodically, as if to himself, 'Not over 200 metres' ... 'Less than 100 metres' ... 'Ah, almost there' ... as we walked.

And this time when the helper pointed towards a termite-mound, I managed to spot a porcupine just disappearing behind it. I had been able to spot it more quickly as the animal was on the trot. Ah, so the 'jungle' did hold some wildlife after all.

Ravi kept shushing me to not make such a ruckus with my steps which confused me, as I thought I was walking as on eggshells. But clearly the eggshells were crunching, as I simply couldn't help stepping on twigs that carpeted the ground. But by now, I was hardly concentrating on my walk. I had just noticed as I turned my neck that the two helpers were nowhere in sight. They had stayed back. I would learn later that once the lion's presence had been localised, their job was over. I suddenly felt half-naked and shuddered with a deep fear the like of which I had never known.

A deer barked, followed by a couple of monkeys vertically above our heads. Ravi stopped short, and held me by the arm, as he looked around to see which way the monkeys were facing when they barked. He was apparently satisfied as he released his hold on me.

The jungle had been silent all along, except for the occasional bird calls and the periodic stridulation of the crickets. But the silence that ensued shortly was of a very different quality. It is like the difference between dark and pitch-dark. The jungle was pitch-silent now. It was as if the birds had stopped chirping. Even the crickets seemed to have fallen silent. It was as if even the smallest animal knew better than to let their presence be betrayed through any movement or noise.

It could mean only one thing. And then it came to me—my meagre knowledge of lions. Softly but very firmly I asked Ravi, 'Ravi, you say you have radio-collared one lion towards which we are headed. But don't lions live in a pride? What if one of this radio-collared lion's cousins is lurking nearer than you think, like around that next bush?'

Ravi shushed me with a firm squeeze on my left arm and with his forefinger on his lips, bade me be silent. And then proceeded very gently and very slowly further, with me sticking by his right side.

We had just rounded the bush ahead and emerged on the other side, when we saw a male lion, framed in an enormous golden mane, sitting on his haunches a bare 15 feet ahead of us. The expression on the face of the lion was serene, as if he had heard us from far afar and had been expecting us all along.

This was obviously my first sight ever of a lion outside of a zoo or a circus, in the natural setting, with no barricade or vehicle's window separating me from the lord of the jungle. The lion, at some 15 feet away, looked three times larger than lions behind a barricade at the same distance. My feet froze almost as if of their own volition. Fortunately, Ravi stopped too, for I would not have wanted him separated from me. On his haunches, the lion's eyes were at my eye level (granted I am not a tall fellow).

But none of these were the predominant sentiment of the moment. The dominant sensation of the moment was fear, absolute fear, and nothing but pure, unadulterated and supreme fear. Everything inside me wanted to turn and run; run as fast as possible; as far as possible; as soon as possible. My bowels wanted to rebel, loud and clear. I was suddenly sweating, and not from all the walking.

And then I heard some gentle words, repeated twice, thrice, reaching my ears. It took me a few seconds or perhaps an hour to realise Ravi was talking to me in a loud whisper, 'Raghu, no matter what, I repeat no matter what, please do not turn your back and please do not run. Trust me. I repeat: do not turn your back and do not run.' I realised that I was receiving my first-ever whispered but firm lesson into my ears, a la Gayathri Mantra, from 'Professor' Ravi Chellam—the man of few words—about what to do, or rather what not to do, when you find yourself staring eyeball to eyeball, standing on your feet, 15 feet from a wild lion in a forest.

The problem was I was thinking of doing nothing of the sort. Actually, I was thinking of nothing at all, except how to control my bowels and get a grip on my abject fear. My legs seemed to have developed a mind of their own and were screaming to turn and run and I was at the verge of agreeing with them. At the same time, something told me I should listen to every word and every letter of the man next to me. That, and that alone, could save me from the situation I was in, which as a simple professor of finance and accounting, I had no business being in, in the first place.

The lion on his part just sat there watching us both keenly, as if contemplating what to do with us, or more likely wanting us to make the first move. Ravi was frozen in his place and I stood right by his side, my bowels still waging a war of their own to gain an upper hand.

The lion was clearly bored with the waiting game. He slowly got off his haunches, and just as he did so, Ravi took two slow steps backwards, gently pushing me rearward too, with his extended right hand pressing against my stomach, at the same time gently muttering in a soothing but emphatic tone, 'Relax buddy; relax ... relax'. It took me a moment or two to realise that he wasn't addressing me (even though my nerves needed much addressing), but rather, the lion.

The enormous lion was standing tall, facing us. He slowly stood up, his tail twitching just a little, and yawned, his enormous jaws opening and opening, till I could see the ribbed insides of his gaping mouth. As he stopped yawning, he charged—the charge being three rapid steps in our direction, stopping short about 6 feet from us, and snarling. It was hardly a full-throttled roar, but it was enough to curdle my blood, fry my brains and melt my gizzards. Shitting and peeing would have been the most natural things to do; and I didn't know who I was braving myself against more: the lion, or my viscera which were screaming for an exit.

The lion had narrowed the gap between us to about 10 feet, since he had taken three rapid steps in our direction. 'Mock charge; don't panic ... mock charge; don't panic,' again the gentle and firm instruction rang in my ears, as Ravi took two more steps backwards, gently pushing me back at the same time.

Fortunately, my terror gripped me, else I would have had a nice throaty laugh: 'Ah, so only a mock charge, thank God! For a moment I was afraid.' I nearly bolted. Ravi and the lion could settle their business as they wished, but all I wanted was to be out of there. I nearly put my plan to action, except that the back of Ravi's right hand was still in contact with my stomach gently pushing me backwards, and that contact felt like my only lifeline.

Whatever Ravi's assurances to me, I was convinced that this was the last day of my life. I mean how often can you be within 10 feet of a charging lion, mock or not, and survive to tell the tale? Several lines of thought crowded my imagination.

One line of thought was that Ravi was the expert of the moment, for whatever it was worth. If I was going to be dead anyway, where was the downside in strictly abiding by his counsel? So ideally, I should just desist from doing what Ravi didn't tell me to do.

And then there was another line of thought working in parallel. If I broke contact with that lifeline, I was sure to be the beast's snack. After all, Ravi was supposed to be an Asiatic lion expert, while I was a layman. But dang it! The lion doesn't know who the expert is. If I bolted, at least I would be putting some distance between the beast and myself, and Ravi could use his expertise to deal with the animal. The idea was persuasive and tempting, even comforting. But then again, if I stuck right by the man next to me, there was a 50 per cent chance the lion would go for Ravi instead of me. Again comforting. Under the circumstances.

(*Please note that these and some of the other sage and smart thoughts are all after-thoughts; at the time these events were unfurling, I was only concentrating on controlling my bowels, and nothing but the bowels.*)

We took a few slow steps backwards, while the lion, his 'mock-charge' executed, stood gazing at us expressionless; I thought maybe even a bit contemptuously. His eyes were yellow, like two golden coins. Standing petrified, I noticed some injury marks on the lion's elbow. I could even see some dry leaves and a small twig entangled in his golden-brown mane.

In the meanwhile, Ravi had pulled out a soiled little notebook from his hip pocket and a ball-point pen from his shirt pocket, the antenna looped in his left hand. And now, instead of continuing to walk backwards putting a little more distance between the lion and us, I was terrified to observe that he was circling leftwards around the lion, which I would learn later was to confirm if this was indeed the radio collared animal, as through the dense mane, the collar wasn't easily visible. I was left with no option but to move too, my leaden and lifeless legs notwithstanding, for I knew that without the calm presence of Ravi by my side, I was bound to panic and do something stupid.

The lion slowly moved his head in tandem as we moved around its front until we were somewhat on his side. And now Ravi started jotting down some notes rapidly ... Oh my God ... his eyes were off the lion. What if the lion chose precisely this moment to attack us? I thought the man was insane, for nothing else could explain his actions and the calm.

Presently, the lion turned once again, facing us directly, wrinkled his face into a snarl, rushed at us another three rapid steps and came to a dead stop a mere 6 feet from us, as once again Ravi spread his hands and chanted:

'Easy boy, easy ... easy does it (to the lion) ... and more softly, 'Relax, relax, mock charge, don't panic ... don't turn your back ... do. not. turn. your back ... do. not. run. Whatever happens (to me),' even as he took a few more steps backwards, with me in tandem. I must have made a very funny sight to the lion, but the lion didn't show any signs of mirth.

Just when I thought nothing in life could be worse than being 10 feet away from a charging lion, mock or not, something truly out of a nightmare happened. Two lionesses, their curiosity apparently aroused by the commotion, came on the trot from a distance of about 30 feet from behind a bush to investigate the scene of the fuss: one on each side of the lion. They both came to a halt, about five paces behind the lion but about 60 degrees to each side, about 15 feet from us. So now there were three lions in front of us in a wide arc. I don't recall if I felt comforted by the fact that the lionesses did not show any agitation and seemed calm, if curious.

I figured that my chances of fleeing had just diminished. Steeply. Three lions and two men. If I tried bolting, one or the other, lion or lionesses, hardly mattered which, was bound to swat me down. That's when I decided to throw in my lot with Ravi and decided to pay heed to his advice verbatim. No turning back? I shall take it frontally should the lion decide to charge. No running? Rooted to the spot in attention it shall be. In for a penny, in for a pound. I was going to die anyway. At least listening to the expert would give me that sliver of a chance at life.

And now, even as Ravi took down quick notes every now and then, we braved a couple more of the mock charges, with Ravi imploring the lion to relax ... and take it easy. The lionesses held their peace though, as if they were leaving it to the men folk to sort it out. That's when I chanced a look backward, on my right side, and emboldened a wee bit out of sheer helplessness—call it the bravado of the doomed as it were—murmured to Ravi that in any case, even if we wanted to turn back and run, we couldn't, as there was yet another lioness at our back, approaching in our direction at an angle, on my right side.

But thankfully, this lady too stood at about 15 feet from us, making an arc of four lions around us in an arc of nearly 270 degrees. Believe me, that's a lot of lions and I fairly gave up. So far starting from our sighting the first lion, it had been barely 10 minutes, which of course felt like an eternity. I was sweating copiously. That's when I heard the first welcome words from Ravi, spoken firmly but softly:

'OK Raghu, you are doing great. Hang on ... just hang on ... we are slowly backing out now. Just stick by my side ... make no abrupt moves. Don't run whatever happens ... just spread your arms and holler loud if they come too close but don't run ....'

'*Yeah right,*' was my feeling, but I had no real option in any case.

It took us a good 15 more minutes to gradually manoeuvre and wriggle our way slowly so that all four beasts were to our front, and then back out slowly, as Ravi carried on his reassuring and calming chat with the lion, with his arms slightly raised every time the male showed his canines and made mock charges.

At last, we managed to put nearly 40 or 45 feet between us and the lions, who stood watching us passively, after which we slowly turned and walked away.

Looking back, abiding by the expert's advice, doing nothing silly and getting a grip on my raw panic was what had kept me alive when death had danced naked right in front of me. I had come as close to religion as I ever would in my life.

It took us another 15 minutes to find the assistants and another half an hour to reach our Jeep. Ravi seemed nonchalant. But I was still weak in the knees, and trying to put up a brave front. And when the assistants asked 'How did it go?', Ravi's answer was one word, 'Fine', or more literally, '*Achha gaya.*'

The assistants put out a kettle of water on a small gas stove, and brought out some sandwiches, bananas and biscuits for breakfast. 'Ah, so our upstairs chef hadn't entirely forgotten us.' I felt thankful, though I wasn't sure whether I had any appetite, after so nearly having been breakfast material myself to the lions.

As we munched on our breakfast, Ravi asked me, 'So how was the experience?' He obviously knew that I was a nervous wreck, and his eyes were mischievous. Partially cross that he had prepared me so little on what to expect and partly jealous that he seemed to treat it all as just another day in the office (which it probably was; *for him*), I deliberately controlled my excitement as if nothing out of the ordinary had happened, shrugging my shoulders, and said, 'Scary, but fun!'

'Yes, the trick is never to panic and never to turn your back or run. You did well,' he said.

The rest of the morning was spent moving around the forest in the vehicle for which he had official permission. Every now and then, the assistants would ask Ravi to stop and then point at something, which for the life of me, I could barely spot, until it moved. One of them was a porcupine, which revealed itself only when it scurried away from near a termite-mound. Then there were a couple of wild pigs, which I could not spot from 10 feet, until they decided to run for it. We spotted a lone jackal and a pair of chinkaras. But black-faced langurs and peafowl were plentiful.

Before long the sun was at its apogee, and I was thirsty. The hot water in the water bottle did little to quench the thirst. We saw the occasional Maldhari enjoying a siesta carelessly under the shade of a tree, with his turban under the head for a pillow, and his staff and his hard-leather pointy slip-on footwear by his side. Our noisy passage did nothing to disturb his slumber.

The sun had moved well past the zenith into the 2 p.m. locus in the sky, and hot and exhausted—I more than the others—we halted under a big banyan tree by a mostly dry riverbed to have more of the same fare as breakfast, for lunch, downing it all with nearly warm water from the bottles. We could hardly relax under the shade of tall grass as the place was fairly buzzing with large flies and assorted insects. So, we reluctantly got up, while I went a little distance to pee. On my return I found Ravi had apparently sauntered off to the riverbed, may be for the same purpose as myself, but now he was beckoning us from there. One could read nothing from his wooden expression. But he made some signals for us to keep calm and not make noise.

The sandy riverbed where Ravi stood had some small puddles of water. Ravi pointed at what even to my untrained eye was a clear pug mark of a lion or lioness (I couldn't tell) into which water was just seeping. Ravi put his forefinger to his lips and pointed at another tiny pug mark or two, softly declaring that this was a lioness with two cubs. 'Maybe three cubs?' suggested one of the assistants. 'No. Two,' declared Ravi firmly but softly, pointing at a few other tiny pug marks with a twig in a pattern, which apparently established to the assistants that the boss-man was right. 'The lioness is about three minutes ahead of us in that direction,' he pointed downstream.

The import of this demonstration was clear to us all; even me! The lioness must have been relaxing, guarding her cubs by the bushes near the banyan tree. Lions usually always sleep or relax by the hot day and move only between dusk and dawn. And this one had been no exception, until we probably disturbed it. The lioness had merely made herself and her babies invisible by the tall grass, hopefully waiting for us to finish our business and leave. But just when Ravi had unwittingly walked down into the riverbed, the lioness had moved, to keep her cubs invisible from the prying eyes of humans.

'I simply have to check out the cubs, because I wasn't aware there was a lioness here with two-month-old cubs. The assistants are leaving for now, while one of them will be back with the Jeep later and wait here. If you are too tired, you can leave with them. Alternatively, you can wait here. I should be back soon,' Ravi suggested, matter-of-factly!

Like hell I would wait there! Not in this wilderness with the pug marks of a lioness with cubs right there under my feet! Nor was I ready to go back, with an experience of a lifetime ahead of me! Worn out as I was, wild lions wouldn't make me stay alone—pardon the bad pun. So, I feigned great keenness to see the cubs in the wild myself!

And thus, our march downstream by the bank of the river began, with little realisation that after the adventure of the a.m., I was in for the adventure of the p.m.

We painstakingly followed the clues of the trail being left by the lioness. Feeble pug marks on the dry sand; clear ones on the wet sand, movement of some grass a hundred metres away in the still air of the afternoon; plain guesswork by Ravi. We walked, and walked, and walked. Not once did we manage to sight the lioness, leave alone the cubs. We had walked some two hours in the hot sun, but still no luck. The river had entirely dried out and pug marks were no longer to be found, as the lioness seemed to have climbed the embankment. So, all the clues Ravi now had were 'circumstantial'. By the chatter of some monkeys. The hysterical screeching of a peacock. The swaying of grass, which looked more imagined to my untrained eyes than to Ravi's.

It had been nearly three hours of fruitless tracking and still the lioness chose not to show herself. I must have perspired a bucketful of sweat and my only ambition just then was to give my aching legs some respite under a shaded tree. But there was nothing to it but follow Ravi, who showed no sign of fatigue.

And then, a pug mark again! But the pug mark showed the lioness had decided to move inland from the embankment. It was nearly 5.30 now and the setting sun was getting closer to the horizon. We could see a belt of hills at some distance, perhaps half a kilometre away. Ravi was now treading each step purely by guesswork. It was as if he would guess the next big bush behind which the lioness and the cubs may be and head in that direction. As we managed to reach that bush, the lioness would be behind a new cover and so on. But no sight of the animal. It seemed impossible that a large animal with two little ones could remain invisible for so long.

The vegetation here was still sparse except for the usual deciduous bushes and babool trees and a sprinkling of other greens. And we were nearing the hill; perhaps some 50 metres from the foot of a long chain of hills, almost a small mountain.

At this point Ravi stopped and without a word, pointed towards some point in the hill. The light was not as good as it had been earlier. I looked hard and then I saw them! Two tiny cubs, dotted with black spots, tottering clumsily up the hill. But the lioness was nowhere to be seen.

Ravi whispered into my ears, 'Careful. The lioness may attack; but let's hope not. Let's turn back, when ...' Before he could complete the sentence, we saw the lioness galloping in our direction, from near the foot of the hill.

'Raghu, run!' screamed Ravi, ensuring I grasped the urgency, which I did. The command aligned perfectly with my instincts, reflexes, disposition, craving and yen, and I obeyed. He kept looking back, probably to keep an eye on me, and of course, I was sprinting like an Olympian. Actually, running for my life, like few in real life ever have to. I ran like I didn't know I could. My one and only objective just then—I am ashamed to say—was to overtake Ravi. Each one for himself and lion take the hindmost and all that. No kidding either. I must have set a personal record of sorts, as I overtook him in two shakes of a lamb's tail, till I realised looking back that he was nowhere behind me! Heart pounding, I stopped too and stole a look behind. Ravi was bent guffawing (a strange sight) for all he was worth about 30 feet behind me and the lioness a good 100 metres away, hurrying back towards the hill range, coughing and grunting, butt swaying.

Evidently, he had slowed down and then stopped. I decided not to walk towards him, which would lessen the distance between me and the lioness, even with its back turned on us, and waited for him to catch up with me. Suddenly, a distance of a hundred-odd metres from a lion's posterior seemed a safe place. But I was panting like a German Shepherd in the Gujarat summer, though Ravi had recovered very quickly and his breathing was nearly normal, as he approached me. He wasn't laughing any more. It was a few minutes before I felt strong enough to commence our walk in the reverse direction, when I asked the question screaming inside my head.

'Come on! Only this morning you made such a big deal of not turning our back and running away! What happened to your own advice just now? You ran faster than ... faster than ... Carl Lewis ...'*

Ravi laughed again and said, 'I know, I know. I am glad you didn't wait to ask me the excellent question at the absolutely wrong time when I urged you to run! But you see there is a big difference between the situation this morning and what happened just now. In the morning, we were barely 15 feet away from the lion or lions. Had we tried to run, the lion could have been all over us in a single bound. We stood zero chance in case of flight. The only option was to brave them. Confuse them. Buy time. I knew that the lions were all well fed. Didn't you notice their bulging stomachs? (I'll be damned if I did.) They did not consider us as food. But the lion was most certainly trying to let us know that we had come too close into their space and, with his mock charges, was making sure we backed out. He didn't regard us so much as a threat as a nuisance. That's why I kept backing away every time he charged. I also let him know with our calm demeanour—and I am glad

* The then reigning Olympic gold medallist in 100 metres sprint (1984).

you didn't panic—that we weren't all that scared of him, which kept him in check. Had he really wanted to charge us, there was nothing stopping him. It was our calm retreat that did the trick. You are alive, aren't you? Proof of the pudding, buddy!'

'But shouldn't the same wisdom have held true now? What if the lioness had caught up with us?'

'Oh, isn't that obvious? Look, the charging lioness was at least 50 metres away from us when she came charging. I knew she would chase us for only 50 or 60 metres and by the time she gained that much ground, we could gain another 20 or 30 metres.'

'And what if the lioness had kept coming?' Another 30 seconds and we could have been dinner.'

'Hardly. The lioness would not put a great deal of distance between herself and the cubs. After all, for four hours she had kept herself and her cubs out of sight. If she showed herself now, it was because she had chosen to do so.'

'So why did she decide to show herself now?'

'You see, she decided, going by our persistent tailing through the afternoon that we could be potential threats to the cubs. As a matter of fact, she was all along perfectly aware of our tailing her. That's why she kept herself and her cubs out of sight. She wanted to put as much distance between us and them as she could. So she kept going. She was not interested in us per se. She charged to put a greater distance between us and the cubs. And when doing so, she wouldn't risk widening her own gap from her cubs very far. That's how I knew she would not continue her chase. That's why I slowed down and stopped after a while, confident that she would be on her way back.'

'But how did you know the lioness would charge just when she did? In fact, she charged just when you were saying that she may charge any time!'

Ravi laughed softly. 'Well, you see we had caught the lioness and the cubs between the hill range and ourselves, leaving her no choice but for her and her cubs to move up the hill. As soon as the cubs tottered up the hill, the lioness knew that their cover, protected so assiduously through the afternoon, was blown and that they had been spotted. Also, a lion is a large animal and doesn't like climbing hills against her will. So I was almost certain the time had come for us to turn back, when she charged. Our only chance then was to run and put some distance from the cubs.'

'But isn't much of that guesswork?'

'You are alive my friend ... proof of the pudding ... '

Looking back, abiding by the expert's advice, doing nothing silly and getting a grip on my raw panic was what had kept me alive when death had danced naked right in front of me; not once, but twice that day. I had come as close to religion, and lion food, as I ever would in my life.

CHAPTER SIX

A Journey to Nowhere—A Fifteen-day Odyssey

Immersing oneself deeply and hands-on into any subject is the only way to gain expertise and the confidence that accompanies it ...

1989–90

'Hey, how old is this bus?' I asked the driver of the long-distance bus, distressed at the pathetic condition of this and many other buses that I had been travelling by in the last few days.

The driver pondered over my question gravely, like I had asked him a question about the meaning of life. After what seemed like an eternity, he replied, 'Sir, that's difficult to say.'

'I don't get you. I mean, I am asking a simple question. Which year was this bus commissioned? How many years ago?' I even spoke slowly, as if slowed speech would somehow make my question more intelligible.

The driver once again went into some contemplation and replied, 'Sir as I mentioned, that's a very difficult question. May be seven, ten, fourteen ... who knows.' And I could see that he genuinely wanted to answer me but was not able to.

'But why?' I was beside myself ...

The foregoing exchange between me and the bus driver transpired on a narrow highway, if you can call it one, somewhere on the west coast of the country, with about 5,000 km of my journey already behind me, and another 1,500 km or so to go. The bus was overcrowded. The passengers comprised an assortment of commuters, with such varied luggage as agricultural equipment, bicycles, poultry, even a buffalo calf, and any number of baskets of marine life, for we were on a bus driving along the west coast from Honnavar to Mangalore, in Karnataka. The bus had crossed Udupi only half an hour—or was it 45 minutes?—ago. Thanks to some road widening activity, which in the India of the 1980s as much as in the India of the 2020s, was a perennial pastime.

Thus the bus had been obliged to take a detour—essentially a dirt track—and before long, it rolled to a grinding halt, with an unnaturally loud clatter, with the gear-box being the suspect. After all, we are a thrifty nation, and then as today, we never believed in providing motorable bypasses even for highway traffic, even if the construction or repair on the main route was to take several months, if not years. The bus had looked suspiciously rickety even at Honnavar and I had wondered about its ability to negotiate the potholes on the patchy bypass, which in fairness, were only slightly worse than what they had been on the highway itself.

But our drivers and conductors are nothing if not masters of jugaad and an hour later, with some temporary fix made, the bus had staggered and swayed on its way, at a speed only slightly above that of a speeding bullock cart, to reach Mangalore some three hours late, well past midnight.

I hit the bed at the first hotel we found near the Mangalore bus stand. In the morning, we had some time before our next bus was due for Kasargod, where we were headed. We had some time to look for the driver of the same bus which had brought us into Mangalore, as usually it would be the same bus that would go back to Honnavar on a return trip. But understandably that particular bus had been sent to the depot for repairs, and in its stead was a replacement, another one which looked in an even more precarious condition. It was evident that the replaced bus itself had outrun its life aeons ago.

As the depot workshop was right next to the bus stand, we walked into it and seeing some of the depot officials, went up to them and asked casually, 'How old is this bus?'

A fair, straightforward question, one would think. But I soon discovered that this was not so. It was not a question easily answered. It took a while to figure out why.

It turns out that a typical bus comprises two key parts, namely the chassis and the body. The chassis is the underframe for the body-on-frame, while the body is the coachwork for the body on frame. In 1988, integrated bodies like the Volvo or the Mercedes Benz buses that we see on the roads today were scarcer than vegetation on the moon.

A chassis comprises a structural underframe, engine and radiator, gearbox and transmission, wheels, axles, suspension, dashboard, steering wheel and driver's seat. We often see the skeletal frame of the chassis being driven from manufacturers to automobile bodybuilders through the highways. And the body is built upon the chassis by the bodybuilders to the specifications of the client—in this case the road transport corporations.

Now the two being entirely different in their characteristics, being made of different material and subject to different stresses, wear and tear and so forth, have different economic lives. Intuitively one can understand why the chassis and the body do not necessarily give way at the same time. So when the body gives way, a new body may be built upon an old chassis, and at times, vice versa. Even parts of the chassis and bodies may be rebuilt or replaced from time to time; they may even be cannibalised from old vehicles. In short, after a time, significant portions of the original bus may have been replaced, and while on paper the registration documents may indicate a bus to be fifteen years old, both the chassis and the body may be relatively new, so that effectively, the bus goes without being superannuated for an indeterminate time.

The situation is not dissimilar to what is well known as the Theseus Dilemma, a Greek legend attributed to Plutarch. Theseus—the King of Athens—and a number of Athenian youths returned from Crete after the war in 490 BCE in a ship with thirty oars. The Athenians had preserved the ship right up to the time of Demeritus of Phalereus—that is some 200 years! This was achieved by replacing old planks with new planks whenever the old ones decayed. This raised the question among Plutarch and other philosophers of the time, whether the ship was still the same ship as the one originally used by Theseus! If the ship was still to be considered the original, what happens if we now built another ship made up of the old parts? Which of the two will be the original one? That was the Theseus Dilemma or Theseus Paradox.

Well, we understood why the conductor and the depot officials weren't able to answer our question on the age of the buses!

As we continued our travel, we would find several buses that would be so rickety, dilapidated, decrepit or damaged that we would frequently wonder if the buses had any 'retirement age'. Did the road companies follow a cogent policy to phase out a bus from the road in a certain time frame? No! At least not in those days. They remained on the road indefinitely as it were, simply because technically, they had no age! This came as a revelation to us.

I (though I was not alone) was on an approximately 6,500 km, fifteen-day journey, on road transport corporation buses, mostly public sector corporations. The journey was to be in two tranches with a short break interspersing the two legs of the journeys.

But who in his right mind would want to undertake back-breaking travel of more than 6,000 km over fifteen days by road transport buses on the Indian roads of the 1980s, you may well wonder. Surely either one was addled in one's head or one was a big-time bus-travel buff. Well, the truth is in this case, I was neither.

What was the objective of the travel?

Travelling 6,500 km over two weeks! The idea seemed daunting in the extreme; but that was the only downside. Of the upside, such a trip held much! In any case, to mitigate the downside, we ended up planning the trip in two tranches with a short break splitting the two legs of the journeys.

The destination would be largely irrelevant. Nor was the route of our journey of any import. While willy-nilly we would end up seeing a lot of India, Bharat Darshan was not on our plate. We weren't pilgrims traversing the four dhams either. In fact, we would neither be visiting places of tourist interest, nor meeting any specific people. We weren't researchers, sociological, anthropological or any other kind. We would also not be on a mission involving a wager like that of a twentieth century Phileas Fogg.

More than anything else, we wanted to keep moving. But why? I promise you will get the answer before the chapter is done.

The limiting constraint of our journey was that much of our travel would have to be by State Road Transport Corporation (SRTC) buses, with occasional rides on private transport companies not entirely precluded. And yes, we would be travelling light; just a good-sized backpack each.

Our purpose was singular. To travel that distance—nearly 6,500 km—in two weeks, by SRTC buses as much as possible.

The itinerary and destination did not matter, as long as the travel took us to the length and breadth of India. It could have been any city, say, in Orissa (now Odisha), West Bengal or Assam. We could well have flown to Bihar, Orissa, West Bengal or Assam and bussed it in the reverse direction.

And it was in execution of this project that we were caught, in the second phase of our travel, between Honnavar and Mangalore, learning about the life of buses.

After our planning had been completed, we figured that that it would be too onerous to do the entire journey in a single tranche. The map below provides a quick view of our overall routing. Our final plan ended up covering nearly 6,400 km—almost the exact length of the original Silk Road.*

Our first leg of the itinerary was to last about eight days and cover 3,500 km. This itinerary looked as under:

* In our original log we mentioned the distance in the first and second segment as 2,763 km and 2,960 km respectively. However, these were pre-Google-Maps days. The actual distances as checked on Google Maps are 3,450 and 2,900 km respectively.

I am more inclined to believe the current figures since sources to find out accurate distances between bus stands in those days were far less reliable. Some of the related numbers have thus been accordingly changed from the original logs.

<table>
<tr><th>Day</th><th>From–To</th><th>Distance in km</th><th>Nature of Transport</th></tr>
<tr><td>1</td><td>Ahmedabad–Indore</td><td>400</td><td>MP State Road Transport Corporation (MP SRTC)</td></tr>
<tr><td>2</td><td>Indore–Badvaha–Indore
Indore–Bhilwara
Bhilwara–Ajmer</td><td>120
550
140</td><td>MPSRTC
MPSRTC RTC
Rajasthan RTC</td></tr>
<tr><td>3</td><td>Ajmer–Jaipur
Jaipur–Delhi</td><td>135
270</td><td>Rajasthan SRTC
Delhi RTC</td></tr>
<tr><td>4</td><td>Delhi–Panipat–Delhi
Delhi–Aligarh</td><td>100
120</td><td>Haryana SRTC
UP SRTC</td></tr>
<tr><td>5</td><td>Aligarh–Etah
Etah–Shikohabad
Shikohabad–Bah–Shikohabad
Shikohabad–Kanpur</td><td>70
50
80
210</td><td>UP SRTC
Private RTC
Private RTC
UP SRTC</td></tr>
<tr><td>6</td><td>Kanpur–Ghatampur
Ghatampur–Sadh
Sadh–Kanpur</td><td>40
200
210</td><td>UP SRTC
Tempo (Intermediate Transport)
UP SRTC</td></tr>
<tr><td>7</td><td>Kanpur–Gorakhpur
Gorakhpur–Kasia
Kasia–UP-Bihar Border
UP-Bihar Border–Gopalgunj
Gopalgunj–Raxaul</td><td>360
75
30
37
96</td><td>UP SRTC
UP SRTC
Mahindra Jeep (Intermediate Transport)
Hindustan Trekker
Private Road Transport</td></tr>
<tr><td colspan="4">Here we forayed by cycle-rickshaw some 7–8 km into Birgunj, Nepal, for dinner, and back the same evening.</td></tr>
</table>

Day	From–To	Distance in km	Nature of Transport
8	Raxaul–Muzzafarpur Muzzafarpur–Patna	135 67	Bihar SRTC Mini Private Bus
From Patna, we flew back to Ahmedabad.			
	Total	**3,495**	

The second leg of the journey was to last six days, covering about 2,900 km, as under:

Day	From - To	Distance in km	Nature of Transport
1	Ahmedabad–Bombay	525	Punjab Travels (Private RTC)
2	Bombay–Chiplun Chiplun–Ratnagiri	258 90	Maharashtra SRTC Maharashtra SRTC
3	Ratnagiri–Savantwadi Savantwad–Goa Goa–Honnavar	176 74 174	Maharashtra SRTC Kadamba RTC Karnataka SRTC
4	Honnavar–Mangalore Mangalore–Kasargod Kasargod–Cannananore (now Kannur) Cannananore–Calicut (now Kozhikode)	179 52 91 91	Karnataka SRTC Karnataka SRTC Kerala SRTC Kerala RTC
5	Calicut–Ernakulum Ernakulum–Trivandrum Trivandrum–Nagarkoil Nagarkoil–Kanyakumari	171 199 70 20	Kerala SRTC Private SRTC Nesamony RTC Nesamony SRTC

Day	From - To	Distance in km	Nature of Transport
6	Kanyakumari–Madras (now Chennai)	707	Thiruvalluvar RTC
From Madras, we flew back to Ahmedabad.			
	Total	**2,877**	

Source: V. Raghunathan, G. Raghuram and C. Gopalakrishnan, 'Passenger Transport in India - A Customers' Perspective, *Journal of Transport Management*, September 1991.

Thus, in the two tranches, we covered, to be precise, 6,372 km over fourteen days.

Phew! By the end of the trip, we had reasonably accurate data of the proportion of travel by SRTC (about 75 per cent); the proportion of travel by ordinary, express, semi-luxury or luxury buses; proportion travelled by private transport and intermediate transport in regions not adequately covered by regular transport companies et al. We knew the average speed of travel and tariff structures state by state, the road conditions, the condition of the buses, the behaviour of the drivers, the conductors, the extent of honking, the state of bus stands, the facilities available in and around them and so on and on. We could compare the services in the state-operated corporations versus the private ones. We could point out the regions in various states not covered by the SRTC, and therefore opportunities for growth, etc.

Most buses were in poor condition, and bus stands and related facilities filthy. But travel costs were relatively easy on one's pockets. We figured out such trivia that the ordinary SRTC travel cost was a bare 12 paise per kilometre. But if you tried an express service or a semi-luxury service, the cost could inch up to 14–15 paise per kilometre. Well, India or Bharat may not have been travelling fast or in any modicum of comfort, but they certainly travelled cheap. Even the semi-luxury came at a mere 2 paise per kilometre incremental cost—some luxury, that.

The long travel threw up some other unexpected nuggets of knowledge as well. For instance, the tendency of the drivers to honk their shrill horns, even within dense towns, all day, all night, with scarcely a thought for the distress it could cause to the sleeping citizens, was on full display across all states. More charitably, the country had bigger battles to fight; bigger challenges to overcome; and nobody cared about a petty matter like honking, especially when signage at the back of every truck earnestly begged you to *Horn Please*. Not much has changed in this respect even today.

During such honk-fests one could not but wonder if the driver would not be better off sitting right atop a horn-button nesting under his seat for all the constant honking that he had to engage in. It may be way more ergonomic than using his hands every time. To our amazement, it turned out that some drivers had indeed precisely done that! They had a device rigged under their seats and every time they wanted to honk, which was often, rather than move their hands and press on the centre of the steering wheel hard, they just had to slant their butts, and hey presto—the piercing banshee shriek went off! With this jugaad-assisted honking, one was that much less hopeful that India would limit its propensity for sound pollution anytime soon. It hardly gladdens us that our pessimism has been proven right over these thirty years.

Another thought one could not escape concerned the pitch and frequency of honking. Even a short burst of the toot was so offensive to one's ears that one wondered why the drivers did not find the blast equally offensive—which should cause them to honk less often. Could one hypothesise, that over a period, the shrill horns had damaged the ears of the drivers so badly that they had perhaps become more acceptable, if not immune to the offensiveness of the horns?

(Incidentally, in 2010, I saw a paper titled 'Noise induced hearing loss risk assessment in truck drivers', which conclusively proved the hypothesis formed way back in 1987–88 and published in 1991.)*

The journey held other curious revelations as well. Among them was the propensity of various transport companies to fix the fares for various distances down to paisas. Typical fares, for short or long distances, would be something like ₹15.37, ₹67.63 and so forth. One constantly wondered why the fares could not be rounding off the nearest 50 paise if not a rupee (considering these were days when a rupee still held some value), as the change was frequently pocketed

* Karimi A., Nasiri S., Kazerooni F.K., Oliaei M., 'Noise induced hearing loss risk assessment in truck drivers', *Noise Health 2010*; 12:49-55. Also V. Raghunathan, G. Raghuram and C. Gopalakrishnan, 'Passenger Transport in India - A Customers' Perspective, *Journal of Transport Management*, September 1991.

by the conductors overtly or covertly, at the cost of the customers. Wouldn't such a policy, apart from minimising corruption at the conductor's level, also improve customer service, as it could reduce ticketing time and rationalise the ticket denomination to be carried by the conductor? Surely consumers would welcome that too? Besides, we wondered why tickets were rarely issued at terminals which could ease some workload for the conductor, especially in the overcrowded buses.

We also found that not all the SRTCs printed their timetables. Even where printed timetables were available, they were not marketed or made available visibly enough. For instance, very few passengers were even aware that printed timetablets were available at all in a SRTC.

And why weren't the SRTCs providing for greater differentiation among their services to cater to a wider range of clientele? For example, given the extreme pressure on the railways and high fares in airlines, wouldn't the RTCs be able to capture a larger share of up-market clientele, by offering better buses, more luxury services, including air-conditioning, in-bus catering, in-bus toilets etc? They could easily get one section of the market to subsidise another section and at the same time provide much desired services at least on some strategic routes.

And it didn't take us long to figure out, especially in the rural segments of our travels, that the RTCs could easily achieve a better trade-off between load factor and service frequency using smaller vehicles.

Where intermediate public transport (IPT) was active, it was obvious that they had become popular due to the flexibility of their operations in terms of frequency and operational economy. The low load factor of the SRTCs on many of the village routes pointed towards the relevance and preference of IPTs to suit the specific needs of the rural areas. One wondered why the RTCs were not seizing on the opportunity to offer more IPT-like services in the rural areas, which could be better organised and less overcrowded than the current IPTs in operation.

Thank you for staying with my narration this far. I am aware that I still haven't told you what this travelathon was all about. Well, there were three of us—my colleague G. Raghuram (then an assistant professor of public policy), Gopalakrishnan (a research assistant working with us) and I (an associate professor of finance and accounting)—all of us from IIMA. While the two Raghus did both the legs, Gopal could make it to only one of the legs.

Alright, so what on earth were we up to? Well, like it or not, the answer to that must be a little round about. Ready? It's like this.

Life as a professor at IIMA has never been known to be a comfy one. You have to be forever on your toes, especially if you are into heavy-duty teaching, if for no other reason than the fact that you typically teach some of the brightest students in the country. Take me for instance. When I started teaching at IIMA in 1982, if I had to be a few jumps ahead of my students in a financial accounting class which included some chartered accountancy toppers in the country, I had to work something like ten hours for every one hour of teaching. Equally, unless one was careful, one could be tripped on a point of finance, mathematics, statistics or probability.

Teaching the MBA students at some level was a little more predictable than was teaching executives in the management or executive development programmes (MDPs or EDPs), where one faced experienced executives. And if you were a faculty who had never worked in industry, your goose was already half-cooked. No matter how well armed with theory, a simple question from a practising executive could take your stump off to eternity. In teaching such classes, the challenge was not so much about superior knowledge or being quick-witted, but of countering superior experience. While I had three years of work experience behind me, that would seldom be sufficient in dealing with vastly more experienced senior executives, especially in my early years.

One morning, G. Raghuram, my partial namesake, then-colleague, and friend, and later a transportation expert and director of IIMB in his later years, who was a budding scholar in the field of transportation, walked into my office. Raghuram was an expert with matters relating to the railways. There were very few questions about the railways in general and Indian Railways in particular that he couldn't answer with authority. His enthusiasm in matters of transportation in general was infectious. He had been asked by the institute to coordinate an EDP for CEOs of SRTCs. He had walked into my office, asking me to be a core member of his faculty team to deliver the programme.

I enthusiastically agreed, as much because Raghuram was a fun friend to work with as a latent desire to enrich my repertoire of academic diversity, as also because I was shortly coming up for promotion to full professorship and the diversity of this experience could add a brownie point or two for my forthcoming review.

But no sooner had I accepted to teach in the programme than I was deeply worried. Even stressed. After all, the programme I was to teach in was for CEOs. The CEOs would typically be senior professionals well into their forties if from the Indian Administrative Services (IAS), and into their fifties, if not from the IAS (say, from the state services or career transportation professionals outside the IAS). But regardless, they would be professionals who either had got themselves a good bird's eye view of the sector or had spent a lifetime in the sector.

In comparison, both of us in our early thirties were like babes in the woods, who hadn't cut their milk teeth. When it came to our knowledge of the road transport sector, it could be written behind a bus ticket stub. In short, we had nothing to teach them. Even Raghuram, though an expert-on-the-rise in the railways transport sector, was yet to wet his toes in the river of the road transportation.

So how were we going to handle the programme or our sessions? What would we teach? How would we teach? It is one thing to impress rookie PGPs with debits and credits and time value of money or even slightly more advanced subjects. But it is another ball game when it comes to impressing CEOs. Standing before a room full of CEOs wouldn't be a David vs Goliath contest. It would be a David vs forty Goliaths contest. We would be pulverised. IAS officers were known to be ruthless, even rude, and would not suffer inane lectures by some greenhorns telling them how to run their businesses. The situation was exacerbated because often they were not terribly enthused about attending a programme at an Indian institution, preferring as they did overseas institutions by default. They came for these MDPs either to have some relaxed time or meet some old batch-mates in Ahmedabad or because some government ministry had held a gun to their temples.

I could list several problems in teaching a class of CEOs (especially those from public sector) at the best of times:

1. They know their industry well and there is very little one can tell them that they do not already know or have been through, even if they aren't necessarily putting all that they know to use.
2. They come with the firm belief that nobody else, least of all academics, has anything to teach them.
3. And therefore, they are not easily amenable to listening to you unless you have something terribly original, captivating or earth-shattering to say.
4. They are highly hierarchy-conscious and would usually prefer to be lectured to only by those with enough grey hair, or no hair.
5. Their attention span is generally that of spoilt six-year-olds.
6. Not many of them come for such programmes because they want to. They come because the joint or additional secretaries of their departments ask them to. So it takes a lot to engage them if they are not to be sauntering out of the classroom, mid-session.

So now you know what we were up against! Functional executive programmes, like programmes in finance, accounts, statistics, economics, marketing, operations research, organisational behaviour, and such, are easier to teach in, because in them one is just teaching the theoretical aspects of a functional discipline; and there we are certainly on superior ground as compared to working executives. But a sectoral programme is different. Unless one has a sound understanding of the sector as a whole, one can make a jolly big fool of oneself in the classroom. In this particular sectoral programme, the gap between the experience of the teachers and the taught was wide enough to drive a convoy of SRTC buses through. And this was giving us some serious anxiety.

All this had me terribly worried. It wasn't as if facing the seasoned CEOs was the cause of my terror. As a matter of fact, it was not in my nature to be unduly in awe of authority. To take a minor detour, I think around 1998–99, I was moderating a session of eminent panellists in an academic conference in the high-profile Vigyan Bhavan in New Delhi. It was the last day and last session of the conference and the hall was fairly packed with delegates. The valedictory address for the conference, scheduled at 1 p.m., was to be delivered by the venerable late Shri Ram Jethmalani, at the time the union law minister. It was about 12.20 p.m., and the session was going full steam, and I could sense that it had been going exceedingly well. It was evident that the house would have innumerable questions for the panel to answer and I was sure of concluding the session well in time for the valedictory.

Just then I observed some hubbub at the door near the front row and by the manner in which an unctuous crowd was hovering around a central figure, I could make out that the chief guest for the valedictory had made an entry earlier than expected. Mr Jethmalani hadn't yet occupied his seat on the first row when one of the organisers rushed up stage towards me and whispered that the minister was half an hour early and that I should wind up the session fast.

Well, I was thoroughly irritated, and I announced on the mike, 'Just now the organisers have asked me to wind up the session promptly as the honourable minister has come in half an hour earlier than expected. Well, the speakers on the panel and the delegates have come from around the world for the theme of the conference and I have a responsibility towards them first and foremost. But ladies and gentlemen, I assure you that I would most certainly wind up the session on the dot as per the original schedule and not cut a second into the honourable minister's time; I have no doubt you are all keen to listen to him.'

The gentleman seated next to me on the podium covered the mike with his hand and whispered to me, 'Well Dr Raghunathan, I think you have just committed hara-kiri!'

I concluded the session at 12:55 precisely, and then Shri Jethmalani came up to the rostrum, walked up to me and shook my hand vigorously and said, 'Well done, Professor, well done! That should be the spirit!' and exchanged his card with me.

To get back to the original narrative, those CEOs and IAS officers were not cowing me down because of who they were. But I was mortally scared of failing before the class as a teacher. There was no way I would be a candidate for this suicidal mission, for it would be the end of my credibility as a teacher, as an academic and a professional, not counting the sheer mortification of being laughed out of a classroom.

I seriously considered withdrawing from the programme. After all our participation in any programme was a matter of our free will and choice and I had no pistol to my temple to teach in the programme. I did enough teaching elsewhere in the postgraduate, doctoral and other functional executive programmes not to be short of my required teaching load.

And yet, having committed to teach in the programme, backing out would not help build my credibility. It wasn't a real option. I would be a coward in my own eyes. Besides Raghuram was a good friend and I could hardly let him down.

Both of us spent some sleepless nights worrying and that's how we finally concocted the idea of this crazy travel, the length of the very Silk Route! We decided to travel the length and breadth of the country, across several states, to understand first hand, from a customer perspective, all about state transport services.

The benefit of such detailed state-wise intelligence that we gathered came in most handy for us in engaging with the CEOs of the RTCs. After the first session, when we casually mentioned our tour, we received the attention, respect and seriousness due to rockstars. There was little doubt that all of them put together would not have clocked in a fraction of the time and distance covered by us in buses especially for the programme.

We put our newly garnered knowledge and intelligence to good use and made significant contributions to policy, strategic and operational decisions for improving the efficiencies of their companies. We could speak with authority on the cleanliness, staff training, length of duty hours, state of the buses, luggage capacities, safety features, the state of windows (that frequently leaked when it rained) and, most importantly, we elucidated the complexities surrounding seemingly simple questions like determining a motor vehicle's age. Many of our findings found their way into suitable recommendations for improvements. In short, we had become unquestioned, undisputed and unchallenged gurus of the CEOs in the classroom. Not one soul left the classroom mid-session for a smoking break.

We finally published our findings on our long travel, sponsored by the Association of State Road Transport Undertakings, in the *Journal of Transport Management* (September 1991) in an article titled 'Passenger Transport in India - A Customers' Perspective' (cited earlier).

The 1990s remained as enjoyable as the 1980s, with varieties of challenges, including a two-year sabbatical in 1995 and 1996. 1995 was spent as a CEO of a mutual fund, floated by an Indian group in collaboration with a UK fund, while 1996 was spent as CEO, Financial Planning of a large but ailing pharmaceutical company. Both were richly rewarding experiences in two very different ways.

By the end of the millennium, I was going to be completing nearly two decades at IIMA as a professor of finance and accounting.

As an academic, while the contents of my professional life remained the same, I had written many more papers, three books and articles, and joined nearly a dozen boards, including some banks, merchant banks, regulators, stock exchanges et al. I was also a busy consultant. By the end of the millennium, I was already forty-five, and beginning to suffer from the usual mid-life crisis.

The midlife crisis creeps upon us on tiptoes, but once there, hunkers down in our psyche obstinately like the neighbourhood cat by your window, till we do something about it. If your crisis is behind you, you'll understand what I mean; and if ahead of you, well, you'll discover it in good time. Unless of course you are one of those lucky ones whose only midlife crisis is a midriff bloated with beer. My crisis was worse and crept up on me. Having taught finance for nearly two decades, I was at that stage in life when one asks oneself, 'Will I die teaching?'

IIMA, which was such an enchanting and enticing tag a couple of decades ago, was now something to be taken for granted. Questions were rising in my head. Is there life beyond IIMA? Will I survive outside this cocooned system? It's one thing to give gyaan on boards or take one-year sabbaticals; but could I survive the Indian corporate sector, cut off from the IIMA tag? Besides, the tight-fisted consulting rules at the institute—namely the rate applied per day, and the ceiling of fifty-two days in a year—were beginning to constrain one's earning potential. And I had not opted for the pension scheme at IIMA, knowing that would bind me to the institution for a very long time.

So, if I had to plan for my future, I had to enter the rough and tumble world of corporate India.

Moreover, unlike theoretical physics, pure mathematics, or for that matter, history, or philosophy, which are all subjects exclusively meant for teaching, management science is different. Management is not a pure theoretical discipline. It provides one a clear option—to teach, or to do. Some of the best students of management go on to apply the principles learnt to real life, running organisations, creating economic value, creating employment, creating new industries, even disruptive ones ... changing the world. Equally, others stay on to teach and contribute to changing the world—once removed.

Also, come to think of it, the very comfort of my situation was scary. Things were so comfortable, so secure, so satisfying that one had little reason to contemplate trying anything out of the ordinary. It was like being lulled to sleep in a safe and beautiful little boat swaying gently in the breeze on the calm and shallow waters of the neighbourhood lake on an October afternoon. One could so effortlessly give in to the inertia of it all and never experience the excitement of any risk in life. Life had turned zero-risk. So, why fix anything what ain't broke? Right? Wrong.

A zero-risk life can become boring. There is after all some fun in seeking some adventure, some excitement and some risk, even if it means risk breaking something for the adventure of fixing it. Something inside me kept nagging at me, as if saying to me, 'No, you can't die teaching!'

True, continuing as a professor at IIMA or even retiring as one was certainly an option. But given my midlife blues, the thought was becoming increasingly depressing. So, when an opportunity to rock my placid life came along, I saw it as my only chance to give myself a shake and seized the opportunity with both hands.

CHAPTER SEVEN

Creative Problem Solving—My Experiments with Uncommon Ideas

Rather than surrender to challenging circumstances, it's better to circumvent them with creative and innovative ideas ...

2001–04

'Hi Jairaj!'

'Hi there! What do I owe this pleasure to?'

'Guess what! I want to buy a fully depreciated bus from you!'

'What! Now that's an unusual call indeed.'

'Indeed.'

'But why?'

'Well, I just do!'

'OK, give me four or five weeks ...'

The opportunity that came my way towards the end of two decades at IIMA was the chance to helm a prominent private bank—the Vysya Bank in Bangalore—and I seized it. With both hands. While I had previously served on the boards of various financial institutions and banks, and even provided consultancy to a few, taking on the role of actually running a bank was an entirely different beast. It was as if I had traded in my academic robes for a captain's hat, ready to navigate uncharted waters with a mix of trepidation and exhilaration.

As I entertained the notion of transitioning from the security of a teaching career to the rough and tumble of running a bank—at the time the biggest private sector bank in India, with its network of 500 branches and a workforce of 6,000 employees—some of my well-wishers cautioned me about the risks involved, given the job security at IIMA. With a wry smile, I would gently remind them that the true risk lay not with me, but with the bank's promoters—the principal one being Grandhi Mallikarjuna Rao. After all, they were willingly entrusting their precious financial institution into the hands of a novice like myself—hands that had only dabbled in banking during board meetings, where my primary pastime was to gulp gallons of coffee. Or perhaps, on occasion, writing consulting reports for banks in which I had little personal stake. But here was a bank whose promoters clearly thought my being a newcomer to the banking sector would be my strength, as I was bound to think differently from career bankers. So if they were willing to take the risk, why wouldn't I, especially when I was restless to get my hands dirty in industry, and as an added bonus, I would be saving in two years what I had saved in academia over twenty? Well, opportunity seldom knocks twice.

I was convinced the reward was well worth the risk. And I jumped headlong into the opportunity to head the bank, which would transition into ING Vysya Bank, a foreign owned and controlled bank in the next two years. I would straddle over both versions of the bank a couple of years each, starting as the CEO-designate of the former and transitioning into the president of the latter. Yes, I was determined to try my hand at bringing a fresh dimension and perspective to banking.

It was the last Friday of January 2001 at IIMA. My preparations for the sharp transition in my career were hectically underway. At the time, I was the chair of the PGP and my term in this position was to end on 31 March 2001. But I was expected to take charge at Vysya Bank on 1 February, that is, a couple of months sooner, so that my last day at IIMA would be 29 January (a Monday), giving me a couple of days for the move to Bangalore. I was working on handing over my responsibilities to the newly identified chair of the PGP.

But providence had other ideas. On Friday, 26 January, the campus had nearly 300 students visiting from two other IIMs on account of the annual inter-IIM meet, which was being hosted that year at IIMA. It was the third and last day of the students' mega event and by that evening and next morning, most visiting students would disperse. On Monday, my responsibility would be formally over, and I would be all set to sail new seas.

It was 8.45 a.m. of the Republic Day. I had just finished my lazy breakfast and stepped out of the kitchen into the triangular green lawn at the back of our campus house with a mug of coffee in hand. It was that time of the year when the relentless assault of the Ahmedabad sun is still a couple of months away and the mild bite of the morning air touches the body and soul like a caress.

I had meant to be in my office by 9 a.m. as there was much to be done before the long weekend. Packing books and stuff in cartons to clear my office and do a million other things. Fortunately, Meena, my wife, being a professional herself, had chosen to continue in Ahmedabad (until her mid-life crisis crept up on her), and therefore had the use of the campus house a little longer. I would just pack a bag and leave, as my house in Bangalore was already fixed, fitted and furnished. Our plan was to travel back and forth every fortnight. (Meena would tell anyone who was willing to listen that the next five years that I was in Bangalore, were her best; I would reciprocate the compliment with the same fervour!)

I was in a contemplative mood as I stood on our lawn with my coffee when I heard a low rumble, gradually mounting in intensity as if a million tightly packed drums were being rolled down a rough slope, approaching slowly nearer. I thought I was suffering from vertigo. I saw the top of my neighbour's terrace wall develop an enormous crack right before my eyes, and then take a bow at a crazy angle and as if in slow motion, give way and come to rest on my garden with a crash. I was probably still contemplating if all these were correlated events, when my good wife came out of the kitchen crying, 'It's an earthquake!'

Meena had rushed out and joined me. We stood stupefied looking at the neighbour's wall on our lawn. And then we ran towards the large open common ground. A few more neighbours were also assembling there. It must all have lasted scarcely two minutes but felt like forever. And then there was a strange and eerie silence. But only briefly. Almost immediately, there arose in the air low intensity wails and shrieks, thuds and crashes from near and far, as if a particularly wicked enemy was bombarding the world, creating a subdued din of the kind one can scarcely imagine.

It was apparent that something of earth-shattering proportions had happened. Little did we realise at the time that those two minutes had just killed nearly 20,000 and injured some 1,67,000 and destroyed over 4,00,000 homes in western India. No, we knew nothing of it.

But a hundred questions were already rearing their heads in my head, all at once. At first, I was tempted to go out of the campus and take in the situation. But it would be irresponsible and foolish to crowd the streets at a time like this. The reason for my temptation wasn't idle curiosity. I felt in my bones that what we had just witnessed was no ordinary quake. If a reasonably well built and strong campus like ours had been inflicted so much punishment, the poor-quality construction of the city was probably much, much worse off.* Surface transport was likely to be seriously disrupted, telecom services out of commission, including cellular services. A look at my Nokia confirmed this.

My immediate concern revolved around the 300-odd visiting students on the campus, in addition to our own 400. Managing their logistics, such as arranging meals, transportation, and addressing parental concerns, posed a significant challenge. It was evident that Monday wouldn't mark my departure from the office, as handling the complexities of managing the visiting students and facilitating their return to their institutions required my ongoing attention and presence. Adjusting my travel plans, I postponed my joining date at the bank in Bangalore by another four or five days beyond my initial schedule. This adjustment would entail navigating through a logistical nightmare, compounded by disruptions in cell-phone services and telephone lines and anxious parents seeking information about their children. The sequence of tasks and their respective priorities remained unclear, adding to the complexity of the situation.

My next week or so would be spent in a daze. Eventually, as it usually does, life goes on, even though for thousands of citizens in Gujarat, life would never be the same again.

Amidst all this tumult, I joined my new assignment on 5 February 2001 (a Monday). That's how I came into banking.

---

* Only four years earlier, I had written an article in the local edition of *The Times of India*, an article titled 'Buildings Not Fit for Habitation' (Sept 1, 1996) stressing the point that the all-round poor-quality construction in the city was a disaster waiting to happen with the first earthquake that may come along. The article would be quoted in the house of the Legislative Assembly in the aftermath of the quake, in one of their house-discussions.

And I had to hit the tarmac running. While I knew much about banking theory, immersing myself into the operations of a bank was something else.

Seldom have clichés been cited as often as the aphorism: 'Justice not only must be done, but must also be seen to be done.' This maxim was articulated by Lord Hewart, the former lord chief justice of England, in the case of Rex v. Sussex Justices, 1924. The good lord's exact observations were, 'It is not merely of some importance but is of fundamental importance that justice should not only be done but should manifestly and undoubtedly be seen to be done.'

The truth of this maxim came to me soon after I took over at the helm of Vysya Bank.

Meena had been married to the Centre for Environment Education (CEE) for about as long as she had been married to me—about twenty years. And yet, her decision to continue in Ahmedabad while I was in Bangalore wouldn't be simple or straightforward. Here's why.

The visits to Ahmedabad presented me with a serious dilemma. Should I combine my fortnightly trips to Ahmedabad with visits to our branches and some clients and borrowers in the city? Or would it be better to make separate visits, labelling one as personal and the other as official? I needed to find the best approach to avoid any perception that even my official visits were merely an excuse to see my significant other. The last thing I wanted was to inadvertently provide subordinates and colleagues with an opportunity to make unwarranted assumptions.

The idea of paying for all my trips to Ahmedabad out of my own pocket crossed my mind as a way to pre-empt gossip. However, I realised that even if I covered the expenses myself, rumours would likely persist, because who paid for my Ahmedabad trips would not be public information.

This is when that old cliché of Lord Heward about justice came to me. After some thought, I decided to ask Meena to travel to Bangalore more frequently, reducing my visits to Ahmedabad significantly. Additionally, I delegated some of my responsibilities to our executive directors, allowing them to visit Ahmedabad in my place as needed. This arrangement continued for the next four years, as it turned out.

During my early months at the bank, fresh from the world of academia, I focused on both familiarising myself with how a bank was run and enhancing the physical appearance of its branches, which had caused me not a little angst. Vysya Bank, which was established in 1930 and had been operating for seventy years, had branches that were old, run-down, and lacked aesthetic appeal and cleanliness. In comparison to newer banks like ICICI Bank, IDBI Bank, UTI Bank and IndusInd Bank, whose branches boasted sleek and modern designs with glass and chrome, our bank's branches looked like poor relations.

It was clear that improving the infrastructure alone wouldn't be enough; a change in people's mindset was a prerequisite.

With this objective, when visiting 300-odd branches in the first few months, I took to including branches' toilets within the ambit of my inspection. I would always visit the branches unannounced and often the toilet first. In a few cases I found the toilets in such abominable state of assault to nose, eyes and mind that more than a dozen branch managers faced serious consequences. 'If you can't take care of customers' basic needs, you are not qualified to take care of their money,' was my credo. My other simple-to-understand message was, 'The front of the office and the back should be equally clean.'

It was in this phase of my preoccupation with cleanliness that one pleasant October morning of 2001, I was taking my morning walk through the humongous Cubbon Park near my apartment. I was enjoying the crisp nip in the air in the green park, when I found a man—in a bid to wash off some of his earthly sins—feeding buns and biscuits to some stray dogs, and then crushing the newspaper he was carrying them in and throwing the crumpled paper right there in the middle of the road, opposite the beautiful red 110-year old Sheshadri Iyer Memorial Hall Library, entirely ignoring a garbage can that required him to walk some thirty paces.

Something inside me snapped. I accosted the man and asked him firmly why he was littering the clean road. The man was clearly taken aback. Nobody in India is to be questioned by another citizen, however uncouth, whimsical and offensive their actions. And mostly citizens are understanding and respectful of this tradition. I had been an aberration.

Besides, I do not have the physique to follow up authentically on such aberrant interventions. The man, towering a good hand over my diminutive frame, gave my size a once-over and grasped immediately that he had nothing to fear from me if push literally came to shove. Thus reassured, he asked belligerently: '*Kyon, tumahre baap ki sadak hai kya?*' (Why, does your father own this road or what?)

And then he continued, '*Voh kachada dekho. Voh kisne fainka? Voh to maine nahi fainka? Un sabko kyon nahi roka?*' (See that garbage there? Who threw that? Certainly not me. Why didn't you stop them all (from littering)?'

Thankfully, he provided me with an opportunity to deliver a quick and snappy retort. With a sweet smile, I remarked, '*Voh kisi bewakoof ne fainka hoga. Aap to bhale aadmi lagte hain. Chaliye, ab to ise uthake udhar faink dijiye,*' I said pointing at the garbage bin. (That must have been thrown by some idiot. But you look like a gentleman. Why don't you do the honours and dispose of it properly over there?) Regrettably, he did not oblige, and I found myself picking up the trash and disposing of it myself, hoping that he might feel ever the slightest sense of shame for his actions.

While the episode ended there, it gave rise to something of more lasting value. I spent the rest of the morning taking note of the density of garbage cans in the famous Cubbon Park and found that one had to really search hard for them. The 300-odd acre park had only about thirteen trash cans! No wonder the park was fairly littered with trash.

I authorised for the bank to donate sixty trash cans, designed to be tilted on stands for easy clearing, and sent our administrative team to discuss their installation with the municipal authorities responsible for the park's maintenance. But I was surprised when my team returned with the news that the horticulture department which oversaw the park had declined our offer of installing the bins with no strings attached! Apparently, they were apprehensive that accepting the donation would attract undue media attention, suggesting that the park was poorly managed and dirty. Well, managing reality and managing perception were clearly two different things.

After some persuasion and a promise to keep the press at bay, the authorities eventually relented to our proposal. We collaborated with them, engaging around 300 employees from our Bangalore branches and 400 children from local schools, to host a 'Keep Cubbon Park Clean Awareness Day'. This event, to be held annually, took place over a weekend without media involvement. Participants were given plastic bags, gloves, caps and a poignant message, and together, we undertook a thorough one-time cleaning of the park. We also installed sixty bins, each bearing the bank's logo, throughout the park.

The 'Swachh Cubbon Park' campaign was a remarkable success, prompting us to replicate it in other cities such as Visakhapatnam, Pune and Delhi. This grassroots initiative fostered a sense of responsibility among our branch employees, igniting their commitment to upholding cleanliness within their respective branches and their surroundings. Undoubtedly, this played a pivotal role in propelling our branches to catch up with the newer, more agile banks in the race. All without any media glare.

The bank's headquarters in Bangalore's upscale Richmond Town area was beginning to show ample marks of aging and congestion. Our sights were set on erecting a new corporate building along the city's tony M.G. Road, where the bank had acquired a long-contested parcel of land. Originally secured as collateral for a loan that had soured, this valuable plot emerged from years of legal battles into our possession in 2002–03. Building the new headquarters became my passion project. The designs for the buildings had already been underway and the building was completed in a record time of ten months and the corporate office was moved smoothly to the new premises.

Once the building was nearing completion, we realised that willy-nilly, we had overlooked providing for a crèche at the design stage. So now the building was complete, without a crèche. There were many reasons why a crèche on the premises had not been thought of at the planning stage. For one, no need had ever been felt. Nor had a demand been made by the employees, probably because a great majority of them were men. Nor did banks in general make provisions for crèches in the early 2000s. Nor do many banks have crèches even today.

At the same time, the bank had been rapidly modernising in recent years. Several employees who had not invested in themselves were finding it difficult to cope with the rapid pace of developments in the bank. This had kept the productivity south and costs north. Also, as an old bank, the average age of the employees had been very high, which could become a problem when hundreds of employees retired within a narrow time window. The need for a younger, computer-literate workforce was urgent. The staff also suffered from a serious gender imbalance. But at the same time, we could not recruit more employees when we were already overstaffed.

Keeping these challenges in mind, we had designed and offered a voluntary retirement scheme (VRS) to employees. The scheme was extremely successful. Soon we were able to recruit fresher talent complementing the exiting manpower, so that many of the imbalances mentioned earlier stood largely corrected. This also meant more women had come on board. And some of them were mothers of young children and that's how the need for a crèche was felt.

So we had now resolved to have a crèche. Our only challenge was to decide where.

Our corporate building, a large six-storeyed one, standing inside large premises with considerable parking spaces on all sides, had fully used up the permitted floor space index (FSI). The ground floor was occupied by the flagship branch of the bank and an enormous lobby for customer interface, with no scope whatever for a crèche. All the other floors had offices and cubicles fully accounted for. Besides, carving out a space inside the office areas would not afford a proper atmosphere, either for the crèche, or for the kids, or for the offices.

Wider consultations suggested that not just women but also men who wanted to bring their little ones to the crèche should be able to do so. A little questionnaire circulated across the headquarters established that all that was required was space for fourteen or fifteen kids, mostly under four or five. So all we needed was some 200–250 square feet of space. But try as we may, we could not find an adequate bay to house the crèche.

Soon our administration met the municipal authorities seeking permission for extra FSI for 300 square feet for a crèche to be constructed somewhere in our premises around the building. But the request was turned down. Also, visually one could see that our building had far more open space around it within our compound than most other buildings in our vicinity, which could easily accommodate a small crèche. When this was pointed out to the authorities, we were helpfully told that a certain payment in cash to a certain official could get us the 'approval'; namely, they would look the other way and we could construct a small crèche at a specified location.

This was entirely unacceptable in principle. On numerous occasions, such as town hall meetings or other meetings, I would exhort the staff of the bank to always push back against corruption and not give in tamely. I considered this to be an important change in the mindset that had to be brought about.

We are a fatalistic people. 'But everybody is doing it!' or 'What can I alone do?' are our typical refrains whenever faced with challenges. It is no different when it comes to corruption. But everybody is corrupt! How can I alone change the system! It seldom occurs to us that it is precisely because each one of us thinks along those lines that we seldom change the ugly side of our national character, namely corruption. How do we push back against corruption?

Further, even if one wanted to be practical about it, any such course would make one a sitting duck for blackmail and further extortions from every other unctuous official who may turn up every six months pretending to be the new officer-in-charge, with oily palms extended to be greased further. Sorry. We couldn't risk any construction that was not entirely clean. Let's find another way.

But soon it was clear that there was 'no other way'.

'Then we'll have to drop the idea of a crèche,' said the administration.

But that would be inane, since we always had that option and it was a no brainer; besides, it didn't help our newly resolved objective.

Soon it was clear that the *administration* on their part had indeed found a solution, and if the *management* was rejecting it, the ball for finding a new solution lay in the management's court! Shorn of finesse, what it meant was, 'For all your big talk about not giving in to corruption, let's see what you are going to do now!' even if not in so many words.

We seemed to have hit a concrete wall. No amount of structured thinking seemed to offer a solution. When HR threw up its hands, the problem landed on my lap. And I felt stumped as no change of thinking cap seemed to be of much help. The only options seemed to be, a) bribe an official and have a crèche or b) have no crèche. What I wanted was a third option, which would give me a crèche and did not involve a bribe. Yes, we needed to push back against corruption in myriad ways.

That's when the idea occurred to me out of the blue. And that's when I decided to call K. Jairaj, at the time the vice chairman of Karnataka State Road Transport Corporation.

'Hi Jairaj!'

'Hi there! What do I owe this pleasure to?'

'Guess what! I want to buy a fully depreciated bus from you!'

'What! Now that's an unusual call indeed.'

'Indeed.'

'But why?'

'Well, I just do!'

'OK, give me four or five weeks.'

And we hung up our calls.

Sure enough, he called me when he was ready to have me haul the bus away. The depreciated bus cost ₹30,000.

I called my admin and instructed them to have the old bus taken to some metal workers. I had them remove the engine and had the scrap sold for some ₹7,000–8,000. I then asked them to have all the seats inside removed and had them sold for scrap, recovering another ₹6,000–7,000.

I now had a shell of a bus, with an entry at the front and an exit at the back. I had some metalworkers cut out a door at the rear of the bus as well.

I then asked the admin team to engage an interior restorer and work on the shell. A couple of months later, when the fancy, engine-less bus painted with gleaming, happy and colourful *Jungle Book* theme outside, and a plush interior entirely clad in soft colourful cushioning with no sharp edges, with fourteen little bunker beds up and down in seven different places arrived, we had our crèche.

The front door served as the main entry and the rear doorsteps led through steps covered with an awning, to a small plastic cubicle which served as a kitchenette for heating milk, storing some snacks, diapers, etc. The additional door cut on the absolute back of the bus similarly led to a small plastic loo. The entire contraption was neatly fenced with colourful wooden pickets in a safe corner of our parking lot, with sand carpeting the fenced area in which the bus stood. Since little children want nothing more in life than to be a driver of a bus, with the conductor probably the second-best career choice, the kids were guaranteed to have a ball.

The crèche didn't need municipal permission being on wheels and didn't need road transport permit being an engineless vehicle permanently parked in our parking lot. Just for the cash that was being demanded for turning their eye the other way, we had an entire functioning crèche that no corrupt authority could ever question.

Another instance of pushing back against corruption happened around the same period.

Clean banking encompasses far more than just maintaining clean premises. It necessitates a fundamental shift in the mindset of employees, who serve as custodians of depositors' money, towards upholding the utmost integrity, care and diligence. Therefore, effective banking initiatives must prioritise the cultivation of these values within individuals, alongside improvements in credit systems, enhanced asset-liability management, and robust back-office operations. I aimed to meet the expectations placed upon me by the promoters by bringing a fresh perspective to banking, despite, or maybe because of, not coming from a traditional banking background.

I used to make it my business at every conceivable opportunity, like town hall meetings, to exhort one and all to push back against corruption and not fall a ready victim to the influences of venality that pervaded (and pervades) the country.

And that's when, as if just to spite me, a situation arose that put me seriously to test. The bank had filed a suit long ago and won the case against a crafty defaulter. After extended litigation, an award of nearly ₹30 crore (about ₹150 crore in present-day terms) had all but turned in our favour. It only remained for the concerned judge to sign the judgment.

Our public relations officer brought me news that a court's officer had sent word that a certain judge had invited me for an informal meeting. The received wisdom was that this judge had a reputation for inviting plaintiffs who were going to be in the money for some discussions over a casual meeting. True or not, that was the received wisdom.

This was the proverbial Hobson's choice. If I accepted the dinner invite, I would be compromising the integrity, both mine and that of the bank, and diminishing the size of the bank's pie. If I refused the invite, I risked delaying or impairing the receipt of our money in any near future. The question of ethics was no longer theoretical. One was answerable to a board and shareholders and not just to one's personal value system.

This was the classic conflict of dharmas evocative of the Bhagavad Gita. But in the Gita, the conflict is resolved by deciding on one's *highest dharma* and then subsuming the lesser dharma to the higher dharma. But here, no matter what I did, I seemed to be in a pickle.

As an academic, living in a cocooned campus, one's only brush with corruption in society was usually limited to an annual affair—at the time of receiving the refund cheque from the tax authorities. They would invariably send the refund cheque a mere three days before it was to expire and then cashed in on the opportunity to revalidate the cheques—for a consideration! Fortunately, one didn't have to deal with this corruption oneself, as the chartered accountant would be at hand to do so.

Stepping outside the cosy confines of my familiar world of academia, I was suddenly responsible for making decisions that held sway over a much larger system, both directly and indirectly.

As I grappled with this newfound power, I couldn't help but sense, or imagine, the sardonic gazes and suppressed smiles of those observing my every move. It was as if they relished the prospect of a grand spectacle, knowing that regardless of my choice—giving in to bribery or or delay the receipt of money owed to the bank—they would revel in the last laugh.

The gravity of the situation weighed heavily on me. Succumbing to the pressure would only perpetuate the cynicism that had permeated our society, making bribery an even more prevalent norm.

To this day, I remain surprised at the solution that came to me—though I must confess it didn't arrive in a sudden revelation or even in the realms of my dreams; but perhaps after eliminating every other option through sheer drudgery. Yet, at the heart of my solution lay a steadfast conviction: the unwavering belief that not every human is irredeemably corrupt.

Long story short, I finally met the judge in one of the city's better-known clubs, alone. I found him sitting at a corner table. I had never had to hobnob with a judge before. Nor was this the kind of hobnobbing that one looked forward to, judge or otherwise. I was nervous.

I recognised him from my brief and the context. I put on a brave face and moved towards him like a long-lost friend, saying something like, 'Good evening, Sir! You are the very gentleman I have been wanting to meet for the last three months! But knowing how busy you are, I didn't muster the courage to ask for your time! I am gratified at this opportunity to be able to meet you at last!'

The judge was taken aback. Maybe I sounded more enthusiastic and chirpier than most would under similar circumstances.

'Ah, is that so? Why? What's it that you wanted to see me about?' he asked naturally.

'Sir, I am planning an in-house workshop on "ethical banking", and I have been looking high and low for an ideal speaker from the judiciary, which we all regard as the touchstone of integrity. You were a name recommended to me. And that's the reason I have been looking for you.'

Well, our dinner passed peacefully, with no word of any exchange of favours, and as did the judgment, and the money hit our account not long thereafter. What's more, the judge paid the bill for the snacks.

I held the conviction that India lacked a sense of public aesthetics. Hence, once the new building of the bank was complete, I made the deliberate choice to utilise the bank premises for installations that would be visually accessible to the wider public while remaining within the confines of the bank's frontage.

I had some ideas, but for reasons of probity and transparency I followed the standard protocols to facilitate the decision-making process. We invited submissions from both our architects and a renowned artist to propose installations, and I added my proposal as the third option, within a specified budget. These proposals were presented to the board for consideration, and the final selection was to be determined from among the three submissions. I felt reasonably confident that my proposal had strong prospects of being chosen, not only due to its perceived attractiveness but also because of its cost-effectiveness. As anticipated, my proposal successfully garnered the board's approval.

My proposal was to install blown-up versions of selected locks from my personal collection of old and ancient Indian padlocks. The locks would be magnified into seven four-feet bronze replicas to be installed at the front of the building, spanning the entire frontage, along the stainless-steel banister that separated our property from M.G. Road, right adjacent to the security cabin, proudly representing safety and security. Thus anyone walking or driving along the sidewalk would have a full view, and hopefully the visual pleasure, of the seven installations.

The locks bore little resemblance to traditional locks; instead, they took on diverse shapes: a standing lady, a reclining lady, the bust of a lady in prayer, a lion, a Bastar embossing depicting Indian mythology and a standing Parsee man. To execute the seven installations, three different sculptors were chosen.

The installations received critical attention in the media for a while.

It was a perfect public, and yet private, installation that significantly contributed to a key arterial road of Bangalore which otherwise has little to offer by way of communal aesthetics.

In 2014, long after my tenure at ING Vysya Bank, the bank was merged with Kotak Mahindra Bank. And then sometime in February 2023, one of the sculptures was stolen at night! Earlier, another sculpture had suffered some damage at the pedestal and consequently been removed. Because of these developments, all the remaining locks were also removed from their plinths for 'safe keeping', apparently at the behest of the police.

This saddened me no end. I felt not enough had been done by the bank's authorities to solve the mystery. After all, an installation weighing hundreds of kilograms can't just be stolen like a household article, with the security gate situated within 20 feet!

If the bank has alternate plans for the removed locks and means to take care of them by displaying them elsewhere, that would be wonderful of course. But to me it seems, even as I write these lines, there is a distinct risk of these pieces being wasted away, dissipated or eventually sold as scrap.

I therefore wrote a few emails to authorities at the highest level of the bank requesting that either these works of arts be appropriately respected and installed somewhere, or else, considering my deep and active engagement in the commissioning of these installations, I be given an opportunity to purchase them at any reasonable price the bank sets for them. I have received no response from the management of the bank so far.

And thus ended the saga of the sculptures at the end of twenty years (2003–23).

I had completed nearly four years of my five-year term at ING Vysya Bank, and it was late in 2004. But by now the bank had been taken over by the Dutch major, ING, with a majority stake. I knew that the new owners would not trust senior functionaries appointed by the previous owners, especially in a bank, and would like me replaced with a member of their own team. At the same time, my role was getting less exciting, as the policies, strategies and even operational details were being decided in Amsterdam, and India was increasingly becoming a mere grand branch operation. So I decided to move on.

CHAPTER EIGHT

A Quasi-Corporate Challenge—Thriving in the CSR Space

Management literature should replace the term 'Corporate Social Responsibility' with 'Socially Responsible Corporate'...

2005–20

... one day, during a group-level review meeting, I was asked to drop Chemical Engineering from the institute's curricula, as the admissions in this stream were declining, and we were losing money on this. I had already taken steps to reduce the discipline's capacity from sixty to thirty seats. However, I firmly declined to eliminate the discipline entirely, emphasising that engineering fields such as this were not akin to consumer goods that could be discarded due to temporary fluctuations in demand ...

During these deliberations, I underscored my extensive career as an educationist and strongly advocated for the indispensable continuation of the Chemical Engineering discipline, despite its current low demand.

A senior board member attempted to undermine my arguments asserting that they understood engineering education very well because they or their children too had or were undergoing it. In response, I countered, stating, 'Yeah, right. I frequently travel by air, and that makes me an aviation expert!'...

The law of unintended consequences takes its own course, much like a river finding its way through unforeseen bends and meanders, often shaping outcomes beyond one's initial expectations.

In late 2004, I bade farewell to ING Vysya Bank and embarked on a four-month hiatus. During this time, I delved into writing and had just finished and submitted the manuscript of *Games Indians Play* to publishers, when Mr G.M. Rao (GMR), the primary shareholder of Vysya Bank, who had been gradually selling his stake in the bank to the Dutch banking giant ING over the preceding three or four years, and was in the final stages of transferring his majority stake entirely, proposed a plan to keep me within the group's fold. He enticed me with the opportunity to lead the GMR Foundation, an organisation aimed at representing the social arm of the GMR Group.

At the time GMR Group was a tiny sapling of a presence in the infrastructure pot with ambitions to grow into a banyan tree and poised to make ripples in the space of airports, energy and highways in the years to come. Well, expected mortality of saplings is notoriously low, and I needed some convincing that this new vegetal would pan out as he envisioned, particularly as I was evaluating two other attractive options. But GMR was nothing if not a good angler, for I bit the bait and accepted his offer.

Coincidentally, by the onset of 2005, Meena was just contemplating a switch from her enduring role at CEE, an institution she had contributed to building for over two decades, and joined me in Bangalore to think about her next career move.

Learning of her intent to relocate permanently to Bangalore, Mr Rao's curiosity was piqued, and he swiftly decided to meet with her, and promptly offered her the position of second-in-command at the foundation, overseeing CSR initiatives in various locations as the group expanded. Her move to Bangalore unexpectedly sparked career opportunities which we had not anticipated!

However, a hiccup arose when Meena proclaimed emphatically that she would not be caught reporting to her own spouse—yours truly—dead or alive. Seeing potential disaster in such an arrangement. Mr Rao, never known to take no for an answer, quickly offered Meena a direct reporting line to him—a commitment he upheld for the next fifteen years—with a dotted line connect to me. This arrangement left her little room for refusal. Thus, in March 2005, she became the foundation's director of community services, while I was the CEO—an intriguing situation given neither of us foresaw working in the same organisation until hell froze over. Such is life's peculiar unpredictability.

And thus, lo and behold, our stars realigned, our paths re-converged, and our careers entwined at the GMR Foundation, later to become GMR Varalakshmi Foundation, and both of us ventured into the unknown.

We would spend our next decade and a half at the foundation. But our jobs would involve so much travel over the next few years—the secret of success of our marriage would remain unchanged!

It's easier to teach a clowder of cats to dance than establish and nurture institutions of excellence anywhere—more so in remote rural towns of India. This challenge is especially amplified in a state that likely hosts about 25 per cent of the total engineering colleges in India, which probably also means many of these institutions are merely real estate ventures masquerading as engineering colleges, preying on unsuspecting students.

Little did I know that the scene in Rajam, leave alone the educational scene, would unfold like a surprise package when I first visited to size up our institutions there!

My maiden visit was depressing. Rajam was an arid whistle-stop of a township with minimal charms to boast of, and the prospect of spending weeks after weeks in the future in that tiny township—if you could call it that—was not an idea that infused me with energy at first. But the place would gradually grow on me.

It was not an easily accessed township, not yet a municipality, with the closest airport in Vizag situated a good two and a half hours' drive away, accentuating the sense of professional isolation. The wee town housed about 25,000 inhabitants, with much of the concentrated life seemingly confined within the 100-acre campus walls of the GMR Institute of Technology (GMRIT), the flagship educational institution of the foundation.

But even the institute campus was far from being a vibrant hotspot. Life after 6 p.m. was non-existent—like a ghost town at the dead of night. The hostels had a curfew for students, and girls faced earlier curfews and limited library access compared to boys. The segregation and restricted interactions between genders were rooted in conservative regional customs and parental concerns of safety for their girl children. My many arguments with GMR on the matters of gender segregation and bias notwithstanding, I comprehended the necessity of respecting these norms to facilitate girls' access to engineering education. GMRIT couldn't defy these societal conventions without jeopardising girls' opportunities for technical education. My well-intentioned reforms had to proceed slowly and cautiously without disturbing these sensibilities, as numerous concerns demanded attention and prioritisation in the monumental endeavour ahead.

But maybe I am jumping the gun here. Let me first paint a quick portrait of how the foundation's activities stood at the time.

The foundation held oversight over a clutch of modest educational institutions situated in Rajam. Among these was the flagship, GMRIT, an engineering college with barely 1,200 students and forty-five faculty members (only three of them with PhDs). The facilities within the 100-acre campus comprised three academic blocks, four hostel blocks and nearly a dozen faculty apartments. The campus at the time was sparse of vegetation, though in later years it would bustle with greenery, with hundreds of trees already planted.

And then there were a clutch of community-based initiatives including a skill development centre, financial aid for government schools, balbadis (village pre-schools), freeships for talented children, mobile medical units and sundry community development programmes. Primarily centred in Rajam, the foundation aimed to extend similar activities to communities near all of the group's businesses. Similar endeavours had already begun in Chennai, Mangalore and one or two other areas.

These arrays of activities were amalgamated under the GMR Foundation, initially birthed as a trust, later morphing into a society, and by the time of our involvement, it had matured into a Section 25 not-for-profit company. Renamed GMR Varalakshmi Foundation soon after our involvement, in tribute to Mr Rao's wife, the foundation's scope of activities was modest.

GMR had delineated an expansive vision for the foundation's future hitched to the growth of the group in the infrastructure landscape. However, while he had absolute clarity about wanting to make a difference to lives and livelihoods, he said he relied on us to give his hazy vision a tangible shape and structure. Thankfully, the weight of our colossal task would creep upon us only gradually.

'In theory there is no difference between theory and practice. In practice there is,' said Yogi Berra. I had taught some highfalutin management theory in my academic career, but the wisdom of Yogi Berra's words dawned on me when I hit ground zero at the helm of the foundation.

We had moved from Bangalore to Hyderabad in 2006 to be closer to our activities: especially the Group's prestigious Shamshabad Airport project as well as many of the foundation's ongoing activities, including those in Rajam. We would spend the next eight years there before moving back to Bangalore.

No sooner had we taken charge that a million questions descended upon us like a cloudburst.

Which activities should the foundation embrace in its portfolio? What should be the nature of educational activities? What should we do more of or less of? How to cater to the specific needs of the vastly different geographies the group was moving into—from metros to remote rural areas, from the northeast to the deep south? Without clarity, the demands for our resources would be all over the place—whom to prioritise, whom to reject? Deciding on regions and causes is pivotal to ensure a conceptual clarity and concentrated impact. The problem with India is, if you chuck a pebble up, it falls on a worthy cause. Without such a roadmap, we wouldn't know the direction to go, and our resources would scatter like confetti at a parade.

What kind of management theory would bind all these questions within a systematic framework? After much thought and stock-taking, we decided to place the current activities in four key buckets so as not to spread ourselves too thin, and ensure impactful spending outcomes, namely: education, health, livelihoods and community development. These categories also fell well under the UN's definition of activities key to alleviating poverty.

Accordingly, we also limited our activities to areas near group project sites directly impacting local communities, and Rajam. For instance, the Hyderabad airport project in Shamshabad impacted villagers who sold their land. Those living nearby also faced disruptions of various kinds. The foundation aimed to mitigate their hardships by strengthening access to quality education and health, as well as training local youth for airport-related jobs and other opportunities that would come up in the vicinity, ensuring benefits from the presence of the airport in their proximity.

We opted for in-house management of community services, avoiding outsourcing to NGOs, to foster direct engagement with our stakeholders near our project sites. The only exception was schools; we collaborated with established managements like DAV, Chinmaya Mission and Bhartiya Vidya Bhavan, who understood school education better than us.

We concretised these ideas by running them past GMR, the family, the board, the senior management team and other key stakeholders.

In due course, over the next fifteen years, the group would come to boast about eight airports worldwide, half a dozen power plants adding up to about 8,000 megawatts, highways adding up to just under 2,000 lane kilometres, apart from being present in urban, aero businesses and sports, with its footprints growing from four odd locations to some twenty-five, spread over fourteen states.

As the group grew, so did the foundation. Its simple activities of 2004 grew significantly by 2020, to include about fourteen skilling centres, three hospitals—the biggest one being in Rajam (a 170-bed institution) and two smaller ones in two different project sites in Orissa and Kakinada and five or six mobile medical units. The engineering college would grow to be among the best and biggest in Andhra Pradesh, with 4,000 students, and 220-odd faculty; the degree college would grow to have about 2,000 students; and there would be four schools with a total student strength of about 4,000, implying a total student strength of 10,000, give or take.

The Rajam academic infrastructure would grow from a handful of buildings to six academic blocks, about 120 faculty apartments, eight hostel blocks and a sports complex.

The community service initiatives grew across some twenty-five locations, including fourteen skill development centres, farm and non-farm livelihood initiatives, multiple tent-schools, work with several hundred government schools and balbadis, creation of public toilet facilities in rural and urban areas, which were all directly managed by Meena, while I directly oversaw all educational institutions and hospitals, in addition to providing general oversight as the CEO of the foundation.

What is more, thanks largely to unremitting hard work of Meena and her close-knit team, the foundation won at least a dozen distinguished awards for high calibre community work and CSR across the length and breadth of India.

I had encountered the face of corruption when at the bank. As I observed earlier, our fatalistic nature often drives us to feel helpless with thoughts like, 'What can I alone do!' or succumbing to peer pressure with sentiments like, 'Everybody else is doing it!' But little had I believed that academic institutions would be susceptible to any serious forms of corruption. Well, I was naïve, as we shall see shortly.

I was in my office one day when the principal of GMRIT called with alarming news. The local press within Vizianagaram district was agog with a story which suggested that some GMRIT students were involved in ragging a junior, leading to police intervention on the campus.

If these reports held any truth, it was an incredibly serious matter. As the chairman of the institute, it was deeply unsettling for me, as I've always been a staunch critic of the ugly shape ragging can take, often resulting in unforeseen tragedies and lifelong trauma. The Government of India, along with the higher judiciary, has rightly and repeatedly denounced this unfortunate practice. At GMRIT, we took extensive precautions to ensure our institution remained untouched by the scourge of ragging. Implementing stringent anti-ragging measures such as distinctive uniforms for first-year students, prominently displayed warnings against ragging, we proudly maintained a pristine record entirely free from any form of such misconduct.

Further investigation revealed that four GMRIT students had rented an apartment not far from the institute. It was not uncommon for students to live on their own in pursuit of every freedom contained in the Constitution and then some, which they felt the campus hostels cramped somewhat.

In this instance, a second-year engineering student emerged from the shower in their apartment, only to have his towel playfully pulled by a third-year student, a prank typical of youths. The victim hollered, while a third roommate, also a third-year student, video-recorded the scene on his phone. The fourth roommate, whose father worked as a police constable in the local police station, held a grudge against the towel-puller and sent the video to his father to exact revenge.

The enthusiastic constable father, with plenty of free time on hand at the sleepy police station, arrived at the scene with gusto, with a colleague, Jeep, gun, and all, and kicked and dragged the perpetrator all the way to the police station for the 'crime' of having engaged in ragging of a 'junior'! An FIR was filed, naming GMRIT as a party.

The superintendent of police, warming his seat in an otherwise sedate setting, despatched a police patrol post-haste to the campus for a flash parade, if only for a bit of action. They seemed to hold the institute responsible without any investigation, blaming them for the alleged incident of ragging, even as the principal persistently objected to the police presence on the campus, explaining why it was not a ragging incident at all. It was all like a quirky scene from a cop comedy unfolding in real life!

The incident had unfolded far from the campus or its hostels, taking place in a private apartment around 7 p.m.—well beyond the institute's regular hours. Crucially, it didn't involve any freshmen or cause harm to anyone, thus diverging from typical ragging scenarios.

But then, our police is hardly renowned for implementing the laws of the land with much application of mind.

Thanks to our meticulous adoption of all requisite anti-ragging measures and records in strict accordance with established norms and regulations and then some on top, we left little option for the police but to close the case and asked for the media to carry a rebuttal to the story.

I talked about my naiveté about possible corruption in academic institutions. Only later would we realise that this extended dumb charade was likely orchestrated to extract some form of recompense from us, exposing the misaligned expectations some police officers have regarding the institutions that have the misfortune to fall under their jurisdiction. Nowhere does it seem to be truer than in India that any kind of power can instantaneously be turned into cold cash.

Netas, babus, cops, courts and we the janata deploy much of our ingenuity more towards transforming every ounce of power into lucrative fiscal opportunities rather than employing it to address humanity's genuine hardships.

Another brush I had with corruption in academia took a different shape. One afternoon, I received another call from the GMRIT principal. While our application process for accreditation had been underway, sometime in 2009–10, he had received an unexpected summons to Bangalore from the regional representative of the apex regulatory body charged with the responsibility of assessing the quality of technical and management educational institutions in the country.

This regulator wields near-absolute authority over some 8,000 engineering, technical and management colleges. Entrusted with the formidable task of planning, formulation and maintenance of norms and standards, its pivotal role extends to ensuring quality assurance through the accreditation of these educational institutions.

This body, like many regulatory bodies in India, has faced allegations of ineptitude, corruption and mediocrity. Past incidents have included graft charges against their chairman and arrest of a member secretary for allegedly accepting a bribe to grant recognition to a technical college in Andhra Pradesh.

Those were the times and that was the environment in which the principal and his team were bravely trying not just to survive but prosper by dint of hard work. But the official he was meeting had an easier solution to gain the desired accreditation.

Towards the end of his meeting, the official had slipped a small note across the table with the number '30 L' scrawled upon it. Momentarily befuddled, the principal had struggled to comprehend the meaning behind this cryptic message. Without skipping a beat, the official continued, 'Arrange that amount in cash, and we'll ensure you get to pick the inspection committee of your choice for your institution.'

Caught off guard, the principal promptly called me, and I advised him to calmly ask the corrupt official to go ahead and set up any committee of their choice for inspection and leave. Eventually, when we received our upgraded accreditation, it validated the importance of standing firm against corruption. Over the years, we embraced numerous inspection committees, progressively improving our accreditation. While this incident appeared as an extreme case of corruption, the integrity of the inspection committees, mostly composed of academics from various institutions, remained largely intact.

I had all along consistently advocated within our team the imperative of exceeding mandated accreditation standards by significant margins, ensuring that even our most ardent detractors would find it challenging to undermine our accomplishments. It's a fact that unscrupulous regulators tend to exploit loopholes when you barely meet the minimum requirements, not when you soar far beyond them. To achieve this objective, the principal had spearheaded an array of initiatives focused on enhancing GMRIT's academic rigour, administrative efficiency and elevating its infrastructure to a superior level through months of diligent effort.

This is a common misconception in the minds of many, including those in the business world, that the corporate social responsibility of a business entity ends with it running a robust charitable foundation involved in benevolent or community development initiatives. It does not.

In truth, philanthropy aimed at contributing to civil society represents just a fraction of the broader spectrum encompassed by CSR. As the three words—corporate social responsibility—suggest, CSR embodies the socially responsible conduct of a corporate towards their stakeholders. Perhaps management literature should replace the term 'corporate social responsibility' with 'socially responsible corporates' to drive the point home.

Now, a corporate entity has as many stakeholders as a millipede has legs, towards all of whom it is answerable in myriad ways: employees (ensuring fairness, gender parity, work–life balance, a safe environment, upskilling, etc.); customers (product/service quality, after-sales service, fairness, fair pricing, etc.); suppliers (timely payments, development, fair trade, etc.); government (tax compliance, governance, adherence to regulations, etc.); environment (climate change, pollution reduction, conservation, renewable energy and sustainability); and of course governance (set of transparent principles, practices, and processes by which a company is directed and controlled, with accountability and fairness). And anyway, serving the stakeholders or the community is more than just spending money—it's about embedding their rights and aspirations in every business decision.

For a cynic, expecting ethical conduct from a corporation might seem like expecting the devil to act divine, but ethics, values and corporate codes are pivotal in CSR. It's merely robbing Peter to pay Paul when a corporate house engages in some social work but underpays its factory workers or engages in other unfair practices. Similarly, when an airline exploits a situation like a cloudburst in Leh to engage in price gouging, it contradicts the principles of CSR. Violations such as unfair competition, price manipulation, environmental harm, tax evasion, unjust land acquisition or delaying payments to small suppliers all go against the spirit of CSR. A socially responsible corporation consistently confronts these ethical dilemmas.

Meena and I were acutely aware that our responsibilities in the group extended well beyond the mere management of foundation activities. Our role demanded the intricate task of trying to embed these values into the business core of the group. In our capacities as heads of the foundation and CSR activities, as members on various boards and committees within the group, we sought not just to sow seeds but to cultivate enduring roots of these principles within the corporate framework.

We aimed to lay down foundations of CSR values deep enough in the group that would endure long after our time.

Our participation in board and other meetings would often be tempestuous, thanks to Meena and I being prone to speaking our minds—we came from academic and NGO backgrounds where hierarchies were paid scant regard. The clash between the demands of the business world and our commitment to intellectual independence, as well as the community and environmental point of view was a recurring saga, one that frequently led to our entertaining tug of war with the business leaders.

In the business world, success is a make-or-break affair amidst its unique demands. Yet, our roles required us to view these pressures as a litmus test of the group's commitment to societal values. Upholding principles and values mean little if we're unwilling to pay the cost in economic terms, or enduring delays or sacrificing cherished values. These scenarios often coloured our 'lively' meetings.

Often top executives, in professional and family businesses alike, have a predilection for lending receptive ears to gossipmongers, toadies and scamps. It's important for professionals to resist this tendency as much within themselves as in their superiors. I personally had to encounter and confront this challenge first-hand.

One afternoon I received an anonymous email forwarded by the chairman, Mr G.M. Rao, which vaguely accused a certain supervisor at Rajam of some thievery involving pilfering of some inventory, with no specifics: exactly like this sentence itself. The chairman wanted the matter investigated.

Now, I must state that the problem of anonymous notes and whispers to the chairman was a Rajam specialty. Rajam was a hotspot that fairly bristled with his extended circle of family and friends forming a tapestry woven over decades. They had a keen knack for exploiting this one weakness of the chairman's bubbly penchant for readily lending his willing ear to any passing rumours, which they used to settle scores with one another.

Back to the anonymous note, it came as a bit of surprise, considering we probably had more checks and balances in our stores (and elsewhere) than possible permutations of a Rubik's cube—internal audits, inventory audits, reviews, surprise inspections, gate passes for stores, gate passes for the campus and the list could go on. And we also had robust whistle-blower mechanisms overseen by an independent entity. But alas!

I asked to be left with the matter, stating I would take a call as I saw necessary. But the chairman was explicit that I investigate.

I tried to push back with the arguments that without any specifics—the timing of the purported theft, the items allegedly missing or the modus operandi deployed—the launching of an open-ended investigation into the red herring would transform the management into modern-day Sherlock Holmes hunting for elusive clues and cast aspersion upon everyone employed in the stores as potential suspects.

True, there are many who vouch by the mantra of 'Trust but Verify'. However, in my view, this maxim is comparable to trusting your spouse while simultaneously having a detective tail them all day. With a meticulous whistle-blower policy in effect—demanding some specific evidence to support an accusation rather than a vague and unsubstantiated claim—I found it an anathema to allow an anonymous note to override institutional processes.

In conclusion, I resolved the issue by conducting an analysis that looked into the variance between book stocks and physical stocks over the past five years. This assessment revealed an accumulated discrepancy totalling approximately ₹3,000, which was hardly indicative of any pilferage. Emphasising the extravagant cost involved in initiating a special audit, installing additional cameras or initiating any form of investigative pursuit, I underscored that these expenses would far exceed the identified discrepancy, not counting the loss of morale among the employees.

It is not uncommon in the workplace to encounter conflicts where organisational interests may diverge from individual perspectives. In such instances, the Bhagavad Gita advocates prioritising the higher dharma as a guiding principle. I encountered such a dilemma when I got a phone call from the chairman.

'Raghu, I have a request. There is a second-year student (he gave me the name) in GMRIT who happens to be the grandson of a close friend of mine, who is an important minister in the state. Apparently, he is falling a little short of the required attendance in classes and his examination ticket has been withheld. My friend has requested to make an exception this one time and to release his exam ticket so that he saves a year. I have confirmed to him that we will do so. Please ensure that this is done.'

I found the request troubling. In my view, decisions regarding a student's excused absence from classes should ideally align with academic protocols and processes. The chairman and I had often discussed that it might have been more appropriate if the chairman could simply inform those seeking favours that he would bring the matter to my attention or Meena's (in the case of giving donations), so that we could take a considered call. We could think through the issue, review its suitability against the policy, and take into account special circumstances, if any. Moreover, the responsibility of unpleasant decisions and communicating them could be left to us, and the chairman himself saved from this. This approach would also have made any subsequent change in decision-making less challenging.

GMR acknowledged our perspective but often forgot to do this in the heat of the moment! With regard to donations, he could never refuse, given his immense generosity and soft heart that made it impossible for him to say no to anyone in need.

In this case, he believed that granting a 'small' favour to a prominent politician might hold practical value, especially given the business group's close collaboration with the state government in the infrastructure domain.

I sought a day's time to gather the necessary information and provide an appropriate update. The institute maintained certain flexibility regarding attendance, particularly for health-related reasons. Moreover, there was a policy in place to notify and prompt students and their families in advance about attendance deficiencies. If any reminders were missed and a student had a marginal attendance deficit, they had a stronger case for requesting some leniency.

In the event, it transpired that the student's attendance stood at around 57 per cent, significantly lower than the university's required minimum of 80 per cent (and our internal ask of 90 per cent). There were no documented leave applications or records of medical emergencies to justify the shortfall. Despite the institute's efforts, which included two verbal reminders and three text messages sent to the student's parents about the impending attendance issue, there had been no response. Besides, there were four other cases of attendance shortfall, all of them with smaller margins than this particular student. If we chose to regularise the attendance in this specific case, what precedent would it set for other similar cases? Many colleges were known to be lax in such matters, but I had been steadfast in upholding academic discipline.

I reported the situation to the chairman, who graciously agreed to reverse his decision and explained the situation to his friend. That was the advantage of working with a man who always saw the other point of view and perspective and gracious in acknowledging a mistake.

The distinctly different backgrounds and cultures of academia and business frequently result in a lack of seamless integration between the two worlds. This disparity is often why individuals within the predominantly urban corporate sector, including senior executives, tend to underestimate the complexities involved in transforming a small rural educational institution into a high-octane establishment. It's essential to recognise that such an endeavour is a long-term process; decisions cannot rely solely on short-term cost-benefit analyses, which are common in many corporate settings.

A demonstration of this disparity came to my notice starkly, when one day, during a group-level review meeting, I was asked to drop chemical engineering from the institute's curricula, as the admissions in this stream were declining, and we were losing money.

I had already taken steps to reduce the discipline's capacity from sixty to thirty seats. However, I firmly declined to eliminate the discipline entirely, emphasising that engineering fields such as this were not akin to consumer goods that could be discarded due to temporary fluctuations in demand. Furthermore, the current demand for seats in any discipline couldn't accurately predict industry requirements four years later when the students would graduate. In my view, a comprehensive engineering college needed a robust presence across all engineering disciplines, supporting both teaching and research.

Additionally, these academic decisions were the responsibility of our eminent GMRIT board, which had endorsed the continuation of chemical engineering. I stressed that such decisions couldn't be solely driven by short-term commercial considerations.

During these deliberations, I underscored my extensive career as an educationist and strongly advocated for the indispensable continuation of the discipline, despite its current low demand. I even went to the extent of politely telling the chairman with all due respect, that while he was indeed a great infrastructure builder of the country, when it came to academia, it would be fair to say that I probably understood the world of education better than him. A senior board member attempted to undermine my arguments asserting that they understood engineering education very well because they or their children too had undergone or were undergoing it. In response, I countered, stating, 'Yeah, right. I frequently travel by air, and that makes me an aviation expert!'

My actions and decisions at the engineering college were deeply rooted in my extensive background, spanning over two decades, with two distinguished institutions, IIMC and IIMA. Leveraging my learning and experiences, I was committed to imbuing GMRIT with technological proficiency and transforming it into a genuinely competent and respected institution.

I had brought my experience to bear from my early days at the foundation when I had conducted my first review of the flagship

GMRIT. I had been astounded to see that the total number of PhDs in the faculty was three, two of them in behavioural sciences. And precisely the same number of publications! And none in any peer-reviewed journal of any repute either!

Our intake from the state's engineering college entrance exams was mediocre. Participation in academic events by both faculty and students were as rare as oxygen at 35,000 feet. The more I delved, the clearer it became that the institute's academic standards fell far below acceptable levels.

Consequently, I decided to start at the very top, and formed an impressive board comprising some eminent and serious figures from higher academia, scientific institutions and industry. This was to set high standards for academic and institutional governance, which in turn could guide the future actions of the institution suitably in all spheres. Concurrently, we initiated a dual-track strategy, targeting systematic improvements in both faculty expertise and student quality.

While enhancing the quality of our faculty was an urgent imperative, the exercise would have been sterile without empowering them more. One of the things that had struck me was that a common faculty lounge provided the sole refuge for the faculty to take a break from their classes, and there existed no private space for them to engage in focused work in any modicum of privacy. Thus, in the following couple of years, we went on a limb to ensure that every faculty member received their own air-conditioned cabin—a space conducive to their productivity and privacy.

We had launched a drive to equip each faculty member with laptops incentivising their acquisition through appropriate financial assistance. In due course, we had ensured that all faculty workstations were furnished with institute computers.

Financial incentives were introduced for publication of research papers, to foster a culture that would motivate faculty to research and put pen to paper, that is, try to publish. Incentives were also extended to encourage faculty members to seek and secure research grants. New faculty members joining at the entry level were required to enrol for a PhD upon joining, and their progress was meticulously monitored, including their publication commitments. Senior faculty recruits were expected to hold a PhD degree and boast a commendable publishing record.

Laboratories were reorganised and upgraded within a new unified laboratory block, aligning the facilities in a more logical and functional manner, and thus freeing more classroom space in academic blocks. Furthermore, endeavours were made to sponsor faculty participation in seminars and conferences, both nationally and internationally, encouraging their scholarly engagements. Salary structures were rationalised to retain talented faculty, incorporating suitable incentives to recognise good performance. The criteria for evaluating performance underwent a comprehensive review, fostering an environment that nurtured excellence.

Diverse incentive programmes were implemented to attract higher-calibre students and offer them a more nurturing environment within the institute. Emphasising an integral component of the curriculum, extensive focus was placed on student projects and internships. Moreover, top professionals from the hospitality sector were invited to impart lessons to students on grooming, personal hygiene, and attire etiquette.

To tighten academic rigour, attendance requirements had undergone a rigourous revamp. Efforts were also made to rectify the gender imbalance. As for the degree of freedom to move about freely on campus, for both girls and boys the library timings were aligned significantly, keeping the timing for girls just an hour short of the timing for boys (to pacify parental sentiments), and shifting a section of the library to the girls' hostel block to make up for the minor imbalance. Special classes became the norm—preparing students for the daunting recruitment processes through simulated interviews and other such rigourous endeavours. And then there were the tailored sessions aimed at grooming students for specific job profiles, elevating their prospects of securing coveted positions. Extracurricular activities received significant encouragement and were generously incentivised. We urged students to present papers at student seminars and engage in spirited competitions with other colleges in the state.

Witnessing top corporations actively recruiting our graduates in abundance and observing entire families from humble beginnings experiencing substantial advancements in their futures was profoundly gratifying. At IIMA, whether or not I taught a finance course, a student could potentially become the RBI governor or SEBI chairperson; at GMRIT the gratification was that one's efforts had a definite impact on the lives of thousands of students.

In September 2022, a few years after I had retired from GMR Group, and when GMRIT was ranked the second-best engineering college in the state of Andhra and the degree college on the campus among the top fifteen in the state, GMR most graciously sent me a message thanking both Meena and me for the strong base we had laid at the foundation.

'Cleanliness and order are not matters of instinct; they are matters of education, and like most great things, you must cultivate them,' observed Benjamin Disraeli, a sentiment that resonated abundantly when I assumed leadership over two factories of GMR Industries Ltd (GIDL).

One day GMR called me on the phone, and proposed that I assume the role of managing director of GIDL in addition to overseeing the foundation. Initially, I wasn't particularly enthusiastic about delving into the business domain, firmly committed as I was to the foundation's initiatives. However, around that time, ethanol—a by-product of sugar production—was gaining substantial attention in the media as a potentially eco-friendlier fuel for the automotive industry. The idea of blending ethanol, say 10 or 20 per cent, with conventional fossil fuel to significantly diminish carbon emissions piqued my interest, prompting me to explore its potential by embracing this additional responsibility.

GIDL had two main factories—a mid-sized sugar factory and an iron ore factory falling under the ambit of GIDL, both in the vicinity of Rajam. Upon my initial visit to both these factories, I must confess my heart sank, and not just a little.

The iron ore factory resembled a fictitious town from a novel where everything was black! A pervasive coat of black soot coated every nook and cranny—offices, guesthouses and everything in between. The grounds were an absolute nightmare, with a thick layer of coal dust that masked any distinguishable features. The workers themselves, all sporting equally soot-covered countenances, resembled so many black ghosts. The factory lacked proper facilities for the workers to have a hygienic meal or even take a moment for themselves to answer nature's call. It felt as though I had stepped into a factory straight out of the Victorian London of Dickensian novels.

Upon questioning the distressing state of affairs, I was earnestly assured that this was the standard look for all iron ore factories. Apparently, this unavoidable scenario resulted from the copious amounts of coal burning required for iron ore processing—a justification that left me slightly befuddled.

The sugar factory, while not quite as bad, nevertheless lacked the charm of paradise. Every surface, inside and out, was sticky with sugarcane residue. Broken glass panes and dangling wires posed serious accident hazards, and the site lacked essential safety measures such as guardrails. In fact, not long before, there had been a fatal accident of a worker. Once again, I was assured that as sugar factories went, ours was among the better ones.

The fact that I had never before seen an iron ore factory or even a sugar factory up close turned out to be a blessing in disguise, as I had no benchmarks to compare our factories with. This allowed me to focus solely on the glaring unacceptability of their absolute state.

As the cleaning operations got underway, it dawned on me that conducting a one-time clean-up of the factories was the simpler task. The real challenge lay in instilling a culture of cleanliness and orderliness among the management, staff and workers of the two factories. Many of them were convinced that iron ore or sugar factories could not be anything other than what they were. My task was to shift their mindset and internalise a way of thinking otherwise.

During my consulting days at IIMA, I had visited some impeccably clean factories of the TVS Group where one could eat off the shop floor, even if they were not quite iron ore or sugar factories. Those visits had reinforced my view that a factory did not have to be dirty or disorderly. Moreover, images of foreign sugar and iron ore factories I found in some international industrial journals had little resemblance to ours. I decided to set them as our goalposts.

While we had to immerse ourselves in the economics of the two factories, to me, the mission of cleaning up the factories was equally crucial. We approached the task with a resolute sense of urgency, like a military operation. Thankfully, I had a team that was ready to step up to the challenge.

We revamped the workspaces in the iron ore factory to confine coal dust to specific areas. Our top priority was establishing a hygienic canteen equipped with powerful blowers at the entrance to prevent coal dust from infiltrating, along with a spacious toilet complex and ample wash areas for post-work showers. These essentials were frequently overlooked in factories located in underdeveloped regions of India.

In just a few months, the factory underwent a remarkable transformation, instilling a sense of pride in every worker. We displayed various slogans promoting cleanliness throughout the premises. I personally took the initiative to identify dirt and clutter that often went unnoticed by others. By demonstrating how to clean specific areas first-hand and getting my hands dirty, I made a significant impact on the employees, motivating them to maintain the factory's cleanliness standards diligently.

Simultaneously we had been working on the sugar factory, which was scrubbed until it shone, and the last traces of stickiness gone. Machines were cleaned of all traces of grease. Every machine and handrail received a fresh coat of paint. Every glass pane was reinstalled. Wires were drawn taut. Naked bulbs were shaded. Safety guardrails were installed as necessary. Pigeon-deterring spikes were installed. Whew!

After about six months, the two factories gleamed like precious jewels and remained consistently well-maintained thereafter. What is more, the productivity at the two factories started showing a distinct uptick, not that investment in clean toilets and dust-free work environment needs to be justified by higher productivity.

Simultaneously, I was looking at the economics of ethanol more closely, for that had been my primary motivation to take up this assignment. My investigations revealed that Indian productivity of sugarcane cultivation was significantly lower than that of Brazil, the largest sugarcane producer in the world. Also, Brazil's cost of production was less than half of India's. The reasons were not far to seek.

In the sprawling agricultural landscape of Brazil, land ownership spanned vast expanses, with average land holdings extending into thousands of acres. In stark contrast, India painted a different picture, with an average land holding per farmer of 1.6 acres, or thereabouts.

The potential for industrial-scale farming in India, unlike Brazil, was also impeded by the ubiquitous two-foot-high bunds that separated each field, hindering the possibility of large-scale mechanised farming. While mechanised farming required a certain optimal gap between plants to maximise yield and drive the harvesters into the fields, it clashed with traditional planting methods that believed that canes needed to be planted as close to each other as possible for maximal yield.

Moreover, the logistical infrastructure required for consolidating scattered ethanol production on both regional and national scales was notably lacking. As a result, while ethanol theoretically held promise for reducing carbon emissions, the harsh reality was that the Indian cost of ethanol production was prohibitively high for both domestic and international markets. Additionally, the infrastructure for distributing ethanol across the country, or even regionally to petrol pumps, was sorely inadequate. Regrettably, this reality has seen little improvement even today.

For these reasons, my dalliance with ethanol gradually lost its lustre, prompting me to gracefully bow out and pivot back to my full-time role at the foundation.

Lo and behold, happily, two or three years down the road when these two factories were sold, the buyers were struck by how well-kept and clean the factories looked. That fact itself was able to command some premium.

Opportunities knock one's doors at random and can often be serendipitous in nature. To me this happened sometime in the first quarter of 2008, when GMR called me to his office with a compelling proposition. Once I was in, he articulated his desire to bring a prestigious American business school to the Indian educational landscape. Despite our ongoing involvement in various educational initiatives, GMR expressed an earnest aspiration to make a substantial contribution to our nation's educational sphere.

This institution was part of his vision which entailed constructing a significant campus in Hyderabad around the group's airport in Shamshabad. The overarching plan was to identify leading institutions within specific hubs like education, health, entertainment and manufacturing. Attracting top brands to each hub would stimulate investments, fostering the growth of an aerotropolis—a dynamic urban zone around the airport, similar to cities thriving along rivers or highways. This was the essence of his envisioned blueprint. Alongside a senior colleague, we were given full autonomy to convert the plan for a business school into reality. Seeking guidance from McKinsey & Co., we set out to forge connections with top American business schools to identify a suitable partner, and we organised meetings with their deans to explore potential collaborations.

To me this was manna sent from the heavens! While I thoroughly enjoyed developing the various educational institutions under my charge, what GMR had just asked of me was a different level of institution building altogether.

In our initial efforts, we reached out to renowned institutions like Harvard, MIT, Columbia, NYU and Boston University. However, our attempts didn't gain significant traction. It seemed that for these American institutions, their focus in Asia was mainly on Singapore, Hong Kong and Shanghai. India wasn't yet on their radar despite the allure of a well-equipped campus awaiting their occupancy.

Amidst these ongoing discussions, catastrophe struck in the form of the sub-prime mortgage crisis, unleashing a domino effect that rippled into a global financial meltdown. Both in tangible and psychological terms, the progress on this front was abruptly halted, unable to proceed further.

The law of unintended conssequences can take the most unexpected paths. An unforeseen development occurred as a parallel consequence of one of my books. As an author, one hopes that their books will be read, but who could have anticipated that writing a book would set off an entirely unanticipated chain of events?

One fine morning, I was pleasantly surprised to see an email from Joseph Caron, the then-Canadian high commissioner to India. Mr Caron, a scholarly gentleman with an illustrious background having served as the Canadian ambassador to China and Japan, possessed a profound affinity for the Orient. He had chanced upon my book *Games Indians Play* and found its framework of game theory to depict the unseemly side of Indians rather interesting. He was inviting me for a chat over dinner the next time he was in Hyderabad, or I was in Delhi. Little did I imagine that this casual invitation would burgeon into a lasting friendship, one that endures to this day.

Around 2008, during our first of many dinners, I shared with him our struggle with US business school collaborations. He suggested exploring top Canadian business schools due to their cost-effectiveness and comparable quality. He offered to link me with influential schools and even connected me with the dean of Schulich School of Business, York University, Toronto, who was shortly visiting India, paving the way for a possible partnership.

I went back to my senior colleague and GMR with a new proposal, albeit a Canadian one and got their go-ahead before meeting Dean Dezso Horvath of Schulich School of Business. Dr Horvath was a matter-of-fact workaholic and a scholar of the old school—the kind of a serious don with whom one could barely take the liberty of cracking a joke. He was visiting India intending to find partners to set up a presence in Bangalore.

Between Dr Horvath, my colleague and me, we made several forays to Delhi and met with the HRD minister (education being under the HRD Ministry) to get a formal government approval for Schulich's presence in India. This was because the UGC and AICTE norms at the time did not permit foreign educational institutions to operate in India. The bill for foreign universities to operate in India had been perennially pending with the parliament. More than once, the affable minister told us, '*Aap aiye aur apna school chalayiye. Aapko koi takleef* *nahi hogi. Bill jaldi pass hojayega.** *Aap fikr mat keejiye. Yeh India hai. Yahaan aise he chalta hai!*' (You come and run your school. You will not face any problems. The bill will soon be passed. You don't worry. This is India. Things happen like this only!)

However, all universities in Canada are government-owned and as a matter of policy, they do not enter any collaborations with foreign entities unless the government regulations are laid down in black and white.

We got out of this cul-de-sac after much toing and froing, when fortuitously I found a provision under the AICTE that permitted dual MBA programmes for foreign institutions in tandem with an existing Indian institution, provided the first year of the programme was held in India, with the students going to the foreign entity for their second year. And then the degree could be granted by the foreign entity alone. That the Canadian government would also allow the graduates to work in Canada for three years was an unexpected sop. This was laid down in black and white and Dean Horvath agreed to follow this route, paving the way for a GMR School of Business, floated exclusively for this arrangement, partnering with Schulich.

Now both sides had pitches to make. We advocated for Hyderabad as the ideal location for their school while they vouched for Schulich in Bangalore. After presenting our vision for a campus near the Hyderabad aerotropolis and committing 20 acres of land, backed by Joseph Caron's support, they embraced our proposal. With minimal fuss, we sealed the deal by signing a memorandum of understanding to proceed with the school concept.

Dr Horvath, who had been the dean of Schulich for over three decades, was a delight to work with as he was for the most part extremely rational in his interactions and a pleasant gentleman in every

* The draft Foreign Universities Bill, to permit foreign universities to operate in India, would be passed only in 2023.

aspect. He became another good friend as our interactions increased over the years.

And then the global financial crisis hit the world, not without some fallout effects in India as well. This also coincided with Indian energy sector facing challenges, leaving many infrastructure companies burdened with high levels of debt. Consequently, GMR Group had to curtail their plans for a 15–20-acre campus development. However, pivoting swiftly, GMR offered a building adjoining the airport to Schulich. Consequently, in 2013, this building became the operational campus of Schulich School of Business in India.

Dean Horvath constituted an eminent advisory board comprising industry stalwarts for Schulich India, which included Mr Ratan Tata. The periodic interactions with Mr Tata, his innate simplicity and humaneness, and the many insights I got of his thinking over a few years, including his take on why Nano didn't succeed in the Indian market and so forth, have been part of my cherished memories.

Dr Horvath proposed to me to also helm the India campus as its director, a role GMR graciously allowed me alongside my position as the CEO of the foundation. This dual responsibility persisted smoothly until 2018, when after discussions with GMR, I retired from my foundation role at sixty-four. Seeking the liberty of a senior citizen, I aimed to dedicate more time to writing and my hobby of collecting locks, among other pursuits mentioned in Chapter 9.

However, Dr Horvath wanted me to continue as the director of Schulich School of Business, India campus, my retirement from GMR Foundation notwithstanding. I agreed and continued till 2020 to play this role.

CHAPTER NINE

Hobbies—Homo Sapiens, Homo Hobbicus

Hobbies are a key to being happier humans ...

1984–continuing

I am often asked which of the locks in my collection is my favourite. That is like being asked which of one's children is one's best-loved! Nevertheless, let me describe a few which are fascinating in some ways.

Consider some of the locks in my collection. You can clearly see the only keyhole on the lock, which of course is the correct keyhole (it's not a pseudo or dummy keyhole, for instance). The lock works with a single key, which you hold in your hand. And yet, it could take you forever to figure how to insert the key into the keyhole. These are topographically designed locks such that the key, even the correct one, cannot be inserted without prior knowledge. Similarly, consider this combination lock of the Mughal era. The lock comprises five or six tumblers (discs), each with five or so Arabic letters. Many random combinations of the discs produce one or the other āyāt (verse) from the Quran, but one specific āyāt opens the lock. Or the lock that rings a jingling bell when opened, so that it can't be picked easily on the quiet when you are dozing. Now how do you decide which one is your favourite?...

It was the late spring of 1984. Meena, my bride of just three weeks, and I were checking out of one of the green wooden cottages of the J&K Tourism Development Corporation in Gulmarg, aka 'Meadow of Flowers', a popular holiday retreat nestled west of Srinagar. We had just given the cosy little cottage a thorough once-over, lest we should have left behind a toothbrush or a comb—chargers weren't in yet, mind you. The inspection complete, as we stepped out into the deck, the caretaker took out from his loose shirt pocket a fist-sized lump of dark metal with a curious protrusion on its side. It turned out to be a padlock with a key sitting snug in the keyhole, which instead of being on the front, was on the side of the lock. When he shot the latch in place and inserted the shackle of the strange-looking lock into the staple, instead of giving it a simple turn, he gave the key quite a few turns as if he were winding a grandfather clock. He elaborately unscrewed the key out of the keyhole, leaving the padlock hanging on the hatch like a forgotten earring. The brief show was fascinating, at least to me.

I eagerly asked him for the key to take a close look. He handed me a tubular little stick, worn smooth with constant use, with a ring-like head which could easily pass for a toy whistle. But as I peeked inside the hollow of the smooth tubular exterior, I could see cork-screw threads. I had never seen a lock or a key remotely resembling what I saw now. This was no ordinary lock and key, certainly nothing like the run-of-the-mill yellow Navtals, the chubby Godrejs, or the metallic Tigers which I had seen most of my life. No, this was not one of your ordinary keys—all cut from the same cloth—with a bow or a narrow hole for a keychain on one end of the shaft and a bit resembling uneven teeth on the other. This key had character in its simplicity.

My curiosity was piqued, and I couldn't resist asking the caretaker to demonstrate how the lock worked all over again. He seemed amused by my fascination, but indulged me, nonetheless. Who would have thought that one could enjoy the working of a simple lock and key so much!

Always interested in things mechanical, the lock caught my fancy, and I couldn't resist the urge to buy it from the caretaker. But then the usual worries set in—would it be impolite to make such an ask? Would he take offense? Or would he quote an exorbitant price—in which case, what about our honeymoon budget, which was already stretched parchment thin from all the shopping we had done for papier-mâché boxes, beads, bells and walnut wood décor items? My new wife had already been giving me quizzical looks about my spending and I didn't want to push my luck too far. And yet, the fascination with the lock was such that I was ready to throw caution to the winds and take the attitude of 'in for a penny, in for a pound', and ask him the question; in any case where was the downside in asking?

As a rookie assistant professor, I earned a salary that would have given a monk in a monastery an inferiority complex. What's more, she knew it all too well. We may have been only just married, but we had known each other some six months now. She has just completed her master's and was yet to start looking for a job. She knew too that nearly 40 per cent of my hermit's salary went towards housing.

A new spouse myself, I had little idea of budgets and didn't even know how I was supposed to respond to my brand-new wife's restraining hand. But my internal struggles were brief. I reminded myself that nothing ventured, nothing gained.

And then I saw the little tourist shop near the Reception and Tourism Office of the cottages, and a bright idea popped in my head, and I asked the caretaker point-blank, '*Suniye, agar mein aap ko ek naya Navtal lock isi size me kharid doon, to aap mujhe uske badley mein yeh wala purana lock de dengey?*' (Listen, if I buy you a new Navtal lock in the same size as this one, will you swap this one in exchange?)

The old man gazed at me dubiously, unsure he had heard me right. So I repeated myself, this time a little more deliberately. The man beamed, his expression clearly announcing he knew a fool when he saw one, and said, '*Kyon nahi? Aap hamey naya tala dengey to hum aap ko purana tala keyon nahi dengey*?' (Why not? If you buy me a new lock, why won't I give you the old one?), clearly implying the question was superfluous, or even dumb. '*Chaliye, udhar dukaan hai ...*' (Let's go, the shop is there ...) and saying this, he picked our bags and marched towards the shop, his body language explicit that he intended to hold me to my word.

Now, strangely relieved, I followed, with my wife hurrying behind me, to the little shop which sold the usual knick-knacks of tourist interest, including little padlocks. I bought him a gleaming new Navtal and he gladly handed me his old lock. I restrained my impulse to hug him. This was the first of a win-win deal for me if ever there was one, and we parted, each imagining himself the better for the deal.

One honeymoon may have just ended, but I was entirely innocent of the fact that another one had just started!

What was I going to do with the lock, asked my good wife. 'Well, for one, it could serve me as a paperweight in my office. Or, if just left it on our coffee table, it could also be an interesting conversation piece. Besides, wouldn't it be a lifelong memento to our honeymoon, to lock away our memories for good? And what about the sheer mystery value the old lock holds? And what if someday, it fetches us a few thousand rupees for its antique value? It is an investment ...' I held forth. I didn't know what to make of Meena's enigmatic smile.

I spent a bit of time playing with the lock, screwing and unscrewing the key in and out, feeling in my palms the weight of my Lock No. 1, whose beautiful uniform patina, shiny from constant use, suggested that it was at least eighty or ninety years old, if not older.

A few of months rolled by and it was December 1984. I had a heavy load of my third term teaching coming up, and we needed a million things for the new home. A lot of our furniture had been damaged in transit while moving from Ambala to Hyderabad and since then, our home was furnished very minimally. The situation was beginning to overwhelm me, and it seemed a Herculean task to furnish a home adequately without breaking a bank. We scoured second-hand shops, garage sales and other cheap locales. Every penny was counted, and every purchase scrutinised for its value and longevity. We learnt that sometimes the things that matter most can only be bought with money!

In the two years that I had already lived in Ahmedabad before I was married, I had heard of a certain flea-market called the Aitwari—meaning a Sunday market—held on the eastern bank of River Sabarmati. The market was known to offer a wide variety of products at very reasonable prices, especially second-hand furniture, metalware, and other bric-a-brac. I had also learnt that bargaining was the only way to close a deal in Aitwari, and never to start the offer at more than 50 per cent of the asking price. I finally decided to pay a visit.

And thus began my weekly forays to the Sunday market, towards which end I put my seventeen-year-old, second-hand Vespa to good use. As I entered the flea-market, I had to pass through a whole row of road-side eateries, sweet-meat and savoury shops.

Expectedly, the market was a bedlam of a souk of scraps that had over two dozen sections earmarked for trading in new as well as used goods, all of them having one fact in common—they were the cheapest money could buy. There were the sections dedicated to food items;

clothing; an extensive wooden section devoted not only to furniture, but also dismantled doors, windows, swings and even old bullock-cart wheels; assorted ironware ranging from the useful to total junk sold by weight; automobile parts; books ... you name a category of things, and you could find it there on the dry river bed stretching into a few acres.

It soon dawned on me that if you had a keen eye, a bit of patience and a wee bit of cash, you could not only accumulate some basic furniture pieces for a song, and have them restored for a whistle, but even look like an antique collector in the bargain. In any case, what is an antique but another man's discard?

I was soon the envy of my friends, who would take a wistful look at my restored furniture (some of which is with me even today), and even try making some trips of their own to the Aitwari with a view to pick up a table or a cupboard, only to return overwhelmed by the chaos prevailing there. But that's not how it works with a flea market. You simply cannot have something specific in mind and hope to find it at the bazaar when you make a trip. It is hardly a supermarket, a super marketplace though it may have been. You hung around the bazaar some *x* number of times before you found a random item *y* of your choice or liking. In other words, you had to enjoy scouting the market for its own sake, expecting to find nothing of value in any one trip.

It was during one foray sometime after our Kashmir trip, rummaging around a steel scrap dealer's ware at the market, that I saw a strange object which resembled ancient weaponry. The dealer informed me it was an old lock. The device was a nasty piece of work, over a foot long, old and rusting—the tetanus content of which could kill one probably as fatally as a blow from its heft could. When I inquired exactly how the lock worked, the dealer shrugged and pointed me to an old locksmith's stall, informing me the man could fit a key to the lock.

While the metal scrap was meant to be sold by weight, my keen interest promptly stirred the dealer's wily side into quoting a price way higher than that the lump of rotting metal warranted. Talk of prices driven by demand and supply! The locksmith inspected the lock with a seasoned eye and assured me that he could fit a key into the old lock, and I could leave the device with him and pick it up along with the key the following Sunday. Once I was convinced that the cost of making the key could not quite bankrupt me, and that the locksmith held a regular stall at that very spot every Sunday, my decision was made. It may be said however that the purchase of this second lock had little to do with my acquisition of the first one in Gulmarg. The two were truly random and independent events.

I was in for a surprise the following week as I collected the lock and the key. What the locksmith handed me by way of the key was a foot-long iron bar of sorts with a couple of grooves at the bit end. My second lesson in the workings of locks unfolded.

The key was inserted inside the long tubular lock at one end and pushed hard, so that the two grooves at the end of the keys compressed a couple of tong-like springs attached to the shackle of the lock to be pushed out and released the shackle. I understood that these locks were probably in use in rural hinterlands of Western India, that is Gujarat or Rajasthan and may be even the eastern fringes of present-day Pakistan and could be anywhere around 80–120 years old or more, going by the amount of rust and the condition of the lock. But there was, and is, no reliable way to estimate the exact age of the thing.

After a thorough cleaning and oiling, the lock found its new purpose adorning the centre table in our drawing room, anchoring a stack of newspapers and magazines. As a makeshift paperweight, it became a fascinating conversation starter, adding a unique touch to our decor.

It was 1986 now. Things were beginning to look up. The promotion in the year before to associate professor had coincided with the end of my long wait for campus-housing, and some minor consulting assignments had injected some buoyancy to my meagre salary. Meena was beginning to do well in her job too.

We hadn't taken a vacation since the last one to Kashmir two years ago. And so we were planning our first ever vacation down south. We are both Tamilians but had never spent any time beyond childhood vacations down south. After a few iterations, we zeroed on to a ten-day trip to Kodaikanal. Our Kashmir holiday had taught us to look for Tourism Development Corporation (TDC) cottages as good value for money and sure enough Tamil Nadu TDC did not disappoint. We booked a cottage for eight days and flew Indian Airlines (as it was then) to Madras (as it was then) and took the overnight train Pandian Express to Kodaikanal Road (also Kodi Road). Here our Ambassador car with an add-on air conditioner (courtesy of a dear friend) picked us up.

We drove straight to Kodaikanal. But exactly one and a half days into the Kodi-cottage, we realised that we are both terrible holidaymakers; and maybe Kodi had only so much on offer to occupy us. There was only so much paddling you could do in the lake, only so many walks you could take and only so many drives you could indulge in. The three books we each had carried were nearly done. So what were we to do for the next six days?

This was our first exploration of the region as adults, and for all we knew, maybe our last opportunity for another long spell before we would breathe the air this far down south of India.

So, we decided to overcome our common aversion to soiling our soles as in trekking, to stir up our souls and worked out an itinerary to visit the awe-inspiring shrines of Madurai (Meenakshi temple), Tiruchy (Rock-fort temple), Tanjore (Brihadeeswara temple), Kumbakonam (Kasi Viswanathar, Adi Kumbeswara Swami and Upplillappan temples) and Chidambaram (Nataraja temple).

And thus commenced our first real exploration of our roots, via a series of temples. We knew little about most of the resident deities of the temples, but we knew that the architecture of these temples was good enough to live or die for. By the time we were done with the first two temples, our jaws were already dropping down to our chests and we had many more to go.

As Trichy was part of our itinerary on account of its famous Rock-fort temple, we had resolved to take a minor diversion from there to my ancestral village called Angarai, adjacent to the little town of Lalgudi—of the violinist Lalgudi Jayaraman fame. As we were about to swerve off the main road into the *agraharam* of Angarai, I was excited with anticipation as my faint memories of childhood were triggered, having visited the village a couple of times during the 1962 Indo-China War and then again the 1965 Indo-Pak War. But the excitement turned into disappointment as we entered the agraharam. Many of the beautiful old, tiled houses had been brought down in favour of gaudily painted 'modern' structures. The bullock-carts had been replaced by cycle rickshaws, auto-rickshaws and Maruti 800s. Sadly, the village had lost its idyllic character. And that's when I recognised my maternal grandfather's house, where my mother with my siblings and me had hibernated as the wars waged up north and families were evacuated from the border areas.

Fortunately, this house remained unchanged, even if it was fairly run-down for want of maintenance. My uncles had sold it long ago and moved on to cities. But our arrival in the shining Ambassador had in any case brought out several *mamis* to the street bare feet, drilling us down with their unabashedly curious looks. Our interest in that particular house didn't go unnoticed. Our Tamil with a strong northern flavour had immediately slotted us as a pair of curiosities. Questions flew. Names were mentioned. Memories jogged. A couple of very old ladies distinctly remembered my grandparents and even my mother, whom they referred to as 'as that chit of a girl, Amba'. We were soon ushered into the house—in the nooks and crannies of which I had played as a child—with the warmth typical of our country folks.

The archetypal house of the region—as it resided in my memory—was narrow in the front, but nearly 200 feet deep. The house was divided into three segments, the first for the living quarters, the second for a semi-open kitchen, the third for livestock, and the fourth for the ancient latrine, now replaced with a modern toilet.

It was just as I was returning from the fourth to the third segment that I noticed the old padlock dangling from the door's chain latch. It looked beautiful in its ancient design and patina, and nothing like the locks one encountered every day. I asked the host if the lock worked. I was told it has been hanging there ever since they bought the house and to the best of their belief, it came from the times of my grandparents and that nobody had ever bothered to look for the key. I was wondering if it was worth the trouble to ask for the lock as a keepsake, given that it didn't even work, even if my interest in the lock was obvious. Just as we were emerging into the second segment, someone came up with the padlock in hand, telling me they had given it a tug with little hope it would open, and the shackle had just come ajar. Clearly, the mechanism had given up long ago. But I was told graciously that if I would like it as a memento from my ancestral home, it was mine for keeps. I jumped at the offer with profuse gratitude, and we took leave.

The gears in my head engaged with a near-audible click. This was my third lock, and what made it even more exciting was that all these three locks performed the same function, but barely resembled each other. I couldn't wait to return to Ahmedabad and seize the first opportunity to visit the locksmith in the Aitwari to have a key fitted for this new (or should I call it old) lock.

I had always been fond of things old, things mechanical and things one can potter with. It's as if the three locks in my possession had unlocked some hidden desire in me, as they met those criteria! I was no longer scouting the Aitwari for furniture as much as before. Slowly and steadily, my forays to the Sabarmati-bed became more frequent. I was drawn to the riverbed almost every Sunday morning, scouting the length and breadth of the market for old locks. There were plenty to be found, if one was willing to look hard enough. My collection of locks started swelling steadily, slowly at first and once I had understood them better and learnt where to look, a little faster. I had already started detecting plenty of interesting variations in the dozen odd locks I had collected since my first three.

However, it soon became obvious that not all old locks were interesting. Many of them, including the second lock that I bought here, had hundreds of rotting clones, which somewhat dampened the satisfaction index of that lock in my collection—the one with a rod of a key which the flea-market locksmith had made me. Clearly what I thought was a rather unusual lock wasn't so unusual after all, because even in those times, they were made by the thousands for the westwards trade and plenty of them have survived in rural Gujarat and Rajasthan. And then there were crates full of key-less old lever-locks of the usual variety, of little novelty value, at least to my eyes.

So I refrained from making any purchases on many of my trips. And yet, I didn't mind the unfruitful visits. Having once worked for a mining company, I found something similar between mining for precious metals and collectibles. Neither is likely to occur in abundance or in large lumps of concentrations. Both mining and rummaging for collectibles amidst junk involve plodding through loads of overburden before you hit pay-dirt. And yes, both involve enormous hard work, patience, and about the same degree of motivation that a serious gold prospector betrays.

There is a parallel too between a collector and a birdwatcher. As one can appreciate, one who does not enjoy the laborious process of spotting a new avian species can never make a good and successful bird watcher. It's the same with a hobbyist or a collector. The fun and satisfaction derived by a hobbyist spans the entire process of the activity, not just the object collected.

In all these activities, patience is the key. Neither Rome, nor a collection, expertise or any skill associated with a hobby, is built in a day. Patience, fortitude and loving all aspects of a hobby for its own sake are the key.

There is the element of that famous quote from the Gita, namely:

karmanye vadhikaras te
ma phalesu kadachana
ma karma-phala-heturbhur
ma te sango'stv akarmani

The Sanskrit translates to: you have a right only to perform your prescribed actions, but you are not automatically entitled to the fruits of those actions ... Let not the fruits of action be your motive, nor let your attachment be to inaction.

For a collector, this translates itself to, 'You have a right only to the actions of a diligent search, but you are not automatically entitled to any fruits or finds. Do not imagine that just because you have been searching hard, you must automatically be rewarded with the nuggets of your choice, and never fall out of love with the very process of the search.'

This may exactly be the reason why a true hobby is akin to a spiritual experience. Even if finding what you are seeking is not easy, the happiness resulting from the attainment of what is sought, when it happens, can be very intense. And if the attainment is serendipitous, the resulting ecstasy is even more heightened.

Of course, much of what I'm sharing here is in hindsight. When my hobby first began to take shape, I did it all unknowingly, spontaneously, and impulsively. The act of visiting flea markets, sifting through boxes filled with weathered locks, and engaging in negotiations over prices were all enjoyable experiences. Discovering a lock that captured my fascination, whether for its uniqueness, special features or intricate mechanisms, brought me immense joy, even if it meant paying a premium price.

Even in the early stages of my burgeoning interest in locks, I was beginning to grasp the importance of not appearing too eager when negotiating for a lock that caught my eye. After a few instances of being outsmarted by shrewd dealers, I quickly learnt that the best bargains were often secured when I was genuinely prepared to walk away from something I truly desired. Additionally, I adopted a strategy of dressing somewhat tackily for these excursions, opting for crumpled white pyjamas, and equally crumpled kurtas, and leather slippers. In this attire, I aimed to blend in with the weekend market crowd, suspecting that those dressed more formally might be charged higher prices. However, this tactic became somewhat unnecessary over time, as my face became familiar to most relevant vendors. Furthermore, my inability to speak Gujarati marked me as an outsider, making me an easy target. At the same time, the vendors faced little demand from other buyers interested in rotting locks, resulting in a relatively unbiased market, if you catch my drift.

As I was beginning to be recognised, one of traders, Rajendra Bhai Talawala, as he introduced himself, accosted me, and asked bluntly whether I bought locks for trading! I said no, I was not a trader, and that I was a teacher, but a collector of locks. One day, taking me aside, he showed me a bagful of amazing locks. But so were the prices he quoted. I was a greenhorn, and he could see me bite the hook, and I ended up buying a few lovely locks for an arm and a leg. Of course, I did not tell Meena about how much I paid for any of my locks. I usually told her a sum less than half of what I may have paid. She pretended to believe me. Rajendra Bhai remained a companion in my quest for locks for many years, though I did not forever remain so gullible and learnt to get slightly better bargains.

What is fascinating about hobbies is this: however narrow the field of the hobby, it invariably opens an entire new world. It was no different with my locks. Weeks turned to months, months to years and years to decades, and my collection continued to grow. It is close to four decades now, and my fascination has not flagged.

I discovered that there were locks in use that required three, four or even five keys to open. What purpose did they serve? Well, if several brothers or friends who didn't entirely trust each other were to open a shop or a cash safe, all of them had to be present with their respective keys to open the lock. There were locks that required one key to open the lock and the other to close it! Why would anyone need such a lock? Well, 200 years ago, they didn't have automatically locking doors as we have today. But if you wanted a handyman to complete the work, lock the door with his key, put it under the foot-mat and leave, you could return home using your other key, with the same algorithm repeated next morning. I found locks where you could not see the keyhole, or the keyhole that you saw was a fake one. There were several hidden tricks to reach the keyhole before you could get started on inserting the key, meaning, the locks combined hard keys with soft knowledge of tricks which worked in combination. There were locks where you had the key and could see the keyhole but could not insert the key into the keyhole, unless you knew how! There was this lock that rang a bell as you turned the key, so one couldn't pick the lock on the quiet. There was another that would lock from one side, but open from the other side of the lock, reducing the probability of being picked down to one-half. One of the locks I bought weighed nearly 30 kg, and another only about 3.5 grams! There were locks of steel, brass, copper or simply mixed metals. There were locks from Rajasthan, Gujarat, Ladakh, Nepal, UP (especially Aligarh), Kerala and a few odd ones from the regions of Pakistan, Iran and China, though I collect mainly Indian locks, for to me, they represent out heritage.

One can only marvel at the creativity, ingenuity and craftsmanship of the lock-makers. And get an insight into the world which needed such locks.

As the collection grew, so did the need to store them carefully, maintain them meticulously and showcase them aesthetically. Today, the collection consists of about 700 locks, with the oldest north of about 500 years. I am looking forward to documenting them carefully and hope to create a physical or a virtual museum someday.

I am often asked which of the locks is my favourite. That is like being asked which one's best loved child is! But let me describe a few which are fascinating in some ways.

Consider some of the locks in my collection. You can clearly see the only keyhole on the lock, which of course is the correct keyhole. It's not a pseudo or dummy keyhole, for instance. The lock works with a single key, which you hold in your hand. And yet, it could take you forever to figure how to insert the key into the keyhole. These are topographically designed locks such that the key, even the correct one, cannot be inserted without a great deal of labour. Now imagine the complexity of fitting a key if one didn't have the original! Similarly, consider this combination lock of the Mughal era. The lock comprises five or six tumblers (discs), each with five or so Arabic scripts. Many random combinations of the discs produce one or the other āyāt (verse) from the Quran, but one specific āyāt opens the lock. Now how do you decide which one is your favourite?

When I started collecting locks forty years ago, I had no idea why I was collecting them; what would happen with the collection, what I would do with them ... nothing. I just collected for a lark. And then in due course things happened. The collection in the late eighties or early nineties was televised in Surabhi, a well-known show that documented something unusual every time, curated by the pleasant duo of the tranquil Siddharth Kak and vivacious Renuka Shahane. It began to be written about and in due course there were very few magazines or newspapers or even television channels that had not covered the collection. At one time, the Limca Book of Records approached me and included the collection in one of their editions. The collection is the subject of conversation and curiosity for all visitors to our house, and helped me make friends, even from as far away as Israel, Ukraine and Germany. Whenever I go to a new place, I look for locks, lock bazaars, lock collectors and museums with locks, even if I essentially collect only Indian locks. I have researched what has been written about locks across the world, which I am afraid doesn't amount to much, because there is relatively little on the history of locks, even if coffee table books with pictures abound. On Indian locks specifically, very little again. I have even written a book called *Locks, Mahabharata and Mathematics—An Exploration of Unexpected Parallels*, in which I tell several stories from the Mahabharata and explore some parallel of those stories with some of the locks in my collection, and then what both the stories and the locks have in common with some mathematical principles. I have given innumerable talks on my locks in a variety of forums. The Bangalore International Centre even made a half-hour film on the collection in 2022.

I consider myself a successful hobbyist. Spending countless hours collecting locks has brought me immense pleasure. Moreover, I believe I'm making a small contribution to conserving and raising awareness about an obscure Indian craft tradition. In doing so, I pay homage to the ingenious craftsmanship of artisans across centuries. Despite the collection gaining some attention through articles and television features, my primary motivation has always been pure love for the hobby itself.

Now in the autumn of my life, as I contemplate documenting my collection with videography to capture the workings of some of the more complex trick locks, which, should I pass away today, may forever remain unopened.

But, guess what? There is no recognised term for the hobby of collecting locks, like collecting stamps is called philately, or collecting coins is called numismatics. Nor is there a system for cataloguing or coding the locks based on their characteristics. Why? Perhaps because the hobby hasn't had that much traction yet among the small world of collectors.

There are some half a dozen lock collectors' associations in the US and Europe combined, but to my knowledge none seem to have suggested a term for the hobby of collecting locks or cataloguing or a coding system for locks so that a lock could be reasonably identified by their codes.

Well, I am trying to set that right, by proposing an eleven-digit coding system for padlocks, with each digit representing one or the other attribute of a lock, except for the country code which takes up the first three digits. Digits 4, 5, 6, 7, 8, 9, 10, and 11 respectively represent appearance, material, dimension, weight, mechanism, tricks, number of keys and vintage. The twelfth digit is optional, and denotes either a padlock or an in-built door lock. I hope it catches on, preferably as Raghu's Coding System for Padlocks!

And yes, I have also proposed a term for the hobby of collecting locks. After toying with many options such as, seraphilia, cerrarphilia, claustrophilum, cleidophilia, seralogy, I rejected them all, as they sounded more like a disease (as in haemophilia), or a homeopathic medicine (as in podophyllum), or a blood condition (as in haematopathology), and such.

I have finally zeroed in on *philoseralogy*. Philoseralogy combines elements from Greek and Latin and may be interpreted as a term representing the love and passion for study of locks. The term is formed by merging 'philo' and 'logy' derived from the Greek 'philia' and 'logos' meaning 'study of' or 'science of', sandwiching the two with the Latin term 'sera', which means a lock. Hence in my lexicon, a 'philoseralogist' would be the practitioner of philoseralogy, or one who collects locks for a hobby. And what's more, it sounds scientific enough!

However, as with any newly coined term, its adoption and recognition within the lock-collecting community would depend on its resonance and acceptance among enthusiasts, which I hope it does.

We may end this chapter with an extra dimension that I associate with hobbies. I begin with the question, 'What makes humans special?'

'Our ability to ask such ridiculously complicated questions,' may be a tempting answer. After all, that's a question that philosophers, sociologists, anthropologists and even economists, have been asking for ages.

Answers vary of course. They include abilities like self-reflection, laughter, tool-usage, language-based communication, abstract thinking, etcetera, etcetera. But then there are just as many arguments countering these views, demonstrating how numerous animals also demonstrate these characteristics.

Let me add two distinct differentiators of my own which are definitely not found among animals. One, cooked food. Two, and a more nuanced differentiator, if you rule out what the wag said about being human—namely being able to identify the boxes that have parts of a bus in a 3x3 grid—which consumes my fascination, and is the theme of this chapter, is the human propensity to practise a hobby—pursuit of something for its own sake, for divertissement, for pleasure, for filling up leisure time, for a lark. In short, for the heck of it. One pursues a hobby because it is there to be pursued, as George Mallory may have put it.

Many humans collect assorted bric-a-brac—from dusty old typewriters to decrepit old clocks—as a hobby. Surely animals don't go about collecting miscellaneous hoojamaflips?

Ah, but they do! Don't many birds collect and display an assortment of brightly coloured thingamajigs—pebbles, shells, discarded plastic toys, coins, spoons, colourful glass pieces, your aunt's brooch, spectacles—you name it—in and around their nests, much like you and I clutter our homes with all sorts of 'collectibles'?

But scholars tell us that the birds collect those baubles—not for the heck of it as a hobbyist would—but for a very specific purpose, namely, to attract mates of the opposite sex, in an elaborate ritual in which suitors are won or lost.

With humans on the other hand, collecting trinkets as a hobby is intended to be a labour of love—and strictly so. Of course, one may purchase expensive baubles to impress or attract a more worthy mate, not unlike some birds. But those collections do not count as a hobby. Collecting for hobby is just that—collecting for hobby. For no reason than that it pleases you to collect; that it gives you pleasure to collect; that it is your passion to collect. Whatever else it is, a proxy for attracting mates it is not. Meena can testify to that, even if she has come to terms with my hobby!

And thusly I rest my case, as to why a hobby, alongside cooking, is one of the two discriminators of humans from animals, and why it is desirable or even important that we all cultivate hobbies that would become a dimension of our personalities.

CHAPTER TEN

Fighting the Good Fight—A Dash of Consumer Activism

Once again, 'If there is no downside, go for it' is a valuable lesson, anywhere, anytime, and every time ...

1975–continuing

'Dear Mr Governor,

We know you must be a very busy man these days. What with coping with inflation, fuel prices, fiscal deficit, interest rates, monetary policy, and what have you. But Sir, believe it or not, we the common people, must face the brunt of all the above and then some. This letter to you is about one such issue, which affects our lives significantly, namely housing. In virtually any list of significant human needs, shelter always ranks up there among the most basic needs. Now what can RBI have to do with shelter? I will explain shortly ...

It's unfortunate but true that many corporations genuinely believe that their rhetoric about good corporate governance and their actual practices are like two different chapters in two different books. Prioritising the needs and concerns of their customers—the most important stakeholders of any firm, one would believe—is often conspicuously absent. It's only when customers make a big fuss or wield significant influence that their complaints are taken seriously. This leaves many consumers who lack such power or influence to fend for themselves, especially when our legal system is notoriously slow and ineffective in resolving conflicts.

However, we cannot let this discourage us from standing up for our rights and demanding accountability from these corporations. We must fuse a common cause and use whatever means legitimately available to us, whether it's through media, social media campaigns, public protests, or other forms of activism, to make sure our voices are heard. Or simply by haranguing the concerned with letters, emails and what have you. We must not let our government and legal system off the hook either, and do what we can to ensure that they do everything in their power to protect the rights of consumers. Imagine the pressure on the errant corporates if every consumer did this.

We in India offer an enormous market to corporates. But sadly, our clout when it comes to consumer rights is not proportionate to our strength as consumers. That's why we each need to stand up and put up a fight against corporates who take us for granted and wage the battle until justice is served. In short, we must grow into a society of aware consumers. After all, we fight back against a corporate house, institution or system only after we have been wronged already. So what can be the downside? Things can only get better from there, right? Albeit not without a dash of one's time and grit, we must admit.

In the end, it's up to us to be persistent and determined in the face of corporate negligence and apathy. We cannot let ourselves forget that our power lies in our numbers and our willingness to speak out for what is right.

Since my formative years, I have always gravitated towards the underdog. When I perceive unjust or unfair treatment in an institution, I take it personally and show the tenacity of a bulldog until the situation is rectified. If I find myself unable to rectify the situation, I'm not hesitant to walk away. This tendency first manifested itself during my time at INS Venduruthy, and then at Western Coalfields, and also during the doctoral admissions issue at IIMC. For me, these battles, whether with institutions or as a consumer, serve as a way to keep my life exhilarating and my adrenaline flowing! There's nothing quite like the thrill of standing up for what's right and steadfastly refusing to yield to arbitrary authority.

When you are seriously wronged as a consumer, and you're up against a corporate behemoth, they often say it's a futile fight, as the odds are stacked against you—it's a Chihuahua versus Great Dane fight. But don't they also say, it's not so much the size of the dog in the fight, but the size of the fight in the dog that counts? From my own personal experience, I know that it is possible to win these fights, even when the odds are stacked against you. It takes courage, determination and an enormous amount of perseverance, but most importantly, it takes a valid and legitimate case.

I have found that these battles need to be approached with a sense of adventure and as a quest, much like the Knights of the Round Table. And indeed, these are knightly adventures, because not only is one fighting for oneself, but in the hope that one's victory will result in systemic changes, and that one can be a voice for the silent majority. If enough of us do that, corporates will think twice before taking us consumers for granted.

Here are some of the times I did precisely that and went toe-to-toe with the big boys: Rolex, HDFC Life, Mercedes Benz and even against the housing sector itself. These companies or sectors may be larger than life, but that was the fun of taking them on. One may not have won all the fights a hundred per cent, but one did make dents.

Rolex: The Tale of the Rotten Watch

My first trip to Italy was for a nine-month stint at S.D.A. Bocconi University in Milan, thanks to the European Foundation for Management Development (EFMD). I was there to research, not teach, but the finance department asked me to teach a short course in finance. I decided to cover some unconventional topics from finance literature and the response was most encouraging.

In fact, the course was so well received that I went back year after year for the next 25 years to teach not only that course but also others. Typically, I would spend several weeks at a time conducting classes, either during my summer break or when I had a hiatus from teaching at IIMA, and later availing my annual leave during my corporate career.

At IIMA, since I was technically representing the institute, they had a policy in place to split the remuneration I received from these assignments. It was a win-win situation—I got to explore the beautiful country of Italy and teach a completely different set of students often representing twenty different countries, and in a different academic system, while the institute got a share of the honoraria.

But let's jump back to 1992, when this part of the story is set. This was my third or fourth visit to Bocconi and I had made some great friends there—some of whom remain dear to me even today. My wife, Meena, would often join me on these trips and we always brought along some traditional Indian gifts for our Milanese friends. India was still a mystery enough for Europeans to wonder if we went to work on elephant backs!

In 1992, my Milanese friends had a surprise for me as my birthday fell during my visit. They gave me an amazing gift—a steel Rolex Oyster Perpetual watch. As the Italians are known for their generous and warm-hearted nature, I accepted the gracious gift with gratitude. The watch came in a beautiful green leather box, complete with all the necessary certificates, including a warranty card listing service centres all over the world, including one in Bombay. The service centre listed on the card was a small watch repair shop on M.G. Road in the Flora Fountain area.

To my friends' delight, I wore the Rolex proudly through the rest of my visit. When I returned to India, fortunately, the Indian customs was relaxed, and I faced no questions at all about the steel Rolex watch I was wearing. When they asked me if I had anything to declare, I truthfully told them, spreading my arms, 'Nothing beyond what I am wearing, apart from some chocolates.' So, I was home safe.

However, the joy of donning the Rolex was short-lived, as a couple of years later, in 1995, while I was in Chennai on a sabbatical with a mutual fund, the crown of the watch unexpectedly detached from its mechanism and fell into my fingers as I was winding the watch. To my dismay, the protrusion on the crown that connected with the watch's innards appeared to be corroded with rust. I mean, seriously? A Rolex giving up on me after just two years? It was heartbreaking.

Academics like me in India didn't stumble upon Rolexes everyday. Moreover, it was a gift from my dear friends, and had huge sentimental value. It was a double whammy.

Fortunately, I had with me all the necessary paperwork—warranty, authenticity certificate and service centre directory. Besides, my friends had bought the watch at Milan's top Rolex showroom on Piazza del Duomo, whose legitimacy could not be questioned. So I wasn't about to let the watch rust away without a fight.

Clueless on the best way forward on how to fix my Rolex, considering the watch was already out of warranty and I certainly didn't want the neighbourhood watch repairer to touch it, I decided to pay a visit to the Bombay service centre listed by Rolex, during one of my trips to the city. But was I in for another shock! The service centre gave me a flat-out 'nope', claiming that they were not a registered service centre for Rolex. Apparently, they couldn't be since they didn't have an import license for any spare parts. For good measure, the owner even showed me some envelopes with postage stamps on them, containing plain sheets of paper enfolding ultra-thin parts of Rolex watches sent over from Geneva. 'This is how we import our parts,' he added truthfully. I couldn't decide whether to laugh or pull my hair.

As if things couldn't get any worse, the service centre informed me that since my watch was no longer under warranty, they would charge me around ₹5,000 just to take a peek inside and diagnose the issue. And that was not all—only after the initial examination would they give me an estimate for any further repairs needed. They asked me to come back a few hours later to check on the progress.

As I returned to the service centre, the chief technician greeted me with a glass full of spirit (as he told me). Suspended limply in it was my poor Rolex, stripped down to its bare bones, no longer looking very prissy. It was quite a sight to behold the watch's inner workings exposed like that. But what was truly gut-wrenching was witnessing the many rusted parts falling apart before my eyes. The technician explained that water had seeped inside where the crown met the casing, causing the corrosion. 'Whatever happened to stainless steel?' was my first reaction. He estimated that the cost of parts needed to fix the watch would be around ₹25,000. However, he couldn't guarantee that it would necessarily work even after the repair. He could only promise to do his best.

Well, well, well! If ever one had a white elephant for a pet! I reluctantly paid the ₹5,000, asked them to reassemble the innards back into the casing. I packed up the sad remains of my short-lived Rolex and left the service centre. But not before I had it in writing from them that they were *not* a registered service centre for Rolex.

Back in Chennai, I immediately shot off a fax to the Embassy of Switzerland in New Delhi, addressed to the ambassador. It went something like this: 'Dear Sir, when my friends gifted me a Rolex, we believed we were buying a piece of Switzerland's finest craftsmanship. But alas, we have been sorely disappointed. The watch has failed after only a couple of years, and the service centre listed by Rolex in Bombay turned out to be *not* an authorised service centre at all! Could you please write to Rolex in Geneva and ask them to set matters right? I know you can't do much, but your word may carry some weight with Rolex.'

Well, I wasn't exactly expecting the Swiss embassy to magically fix my watch, but I thought it was worth a shot. I followed my usual rule: 'No downside? Go for it!' I mean, why give up on a Rolex without some drama?

To my surprise, the embassy promptly wrote back, giving me the contact details of the CEO of Rolex. Who knew complaining to an embassy could be so productive? This is a pattern I have found—help and support can and do come from the most unexpected quarters, if the cause is genuine. It could be as trivial as sharing contact details, or people giving a name or contact, or even joining fights enthusiastically.

Anyway, I quickly fired off a fax to the CEO of Rolex, giving him the lowdown on my shoddy Rolex. Now all I had to do was wait and see if I would get a reply, or if my fax was just going to end up in the trash where my watch seemed to be headed.

I got a response. It was the classic blame game! 'It's not us, it's you. You must have left the hatch of the watch wide open, allowing water and sweat to seep in' was the tone. But they offered to fix the watch for a fee; not free!

I was livid! So I decided to give them a taste of their own medicine by faxing them an ad from *TIME* magazine, featuring a Rolex Oyster Perpetua submerged in a glass of water. I also reminded the CEO that I had a PhD and was a CEO myself, so were they seriously suggesting that I didn't know how to properly close the crown after winding a watch? After a few more exchanges, I even threw in a sly threat to write to *TIME* magazine enclosing their listing of the Bombay service centre, and the latter's written assurance that they were not.

At last Rolex blinked and agreed to replace the faulty watch with a new one, but only in Geneva.

Luckily, I was going to Milan for my annual teaching gig, and as a double dip of luck, my airline allowed for one stopover in Europe. So I took a stopover in Geneva and made my way to the Rolex factory. It was as easy as pie! I didn't even have to go through security checks, they already had my details at the reception, and I just swapped the rusted watch for a brand spanking new one. That was back in 1995, and to this day, that watch runs like a charm.

HDFC Life: A 'Savings Assured Plan' Sans Either Savings or Assurance

In 2004–05, my private banker's relationship manager (RM) approached me to discuss my portfolio. Upon reviewing it, he seemed surprised, as if he had anticipated finding a wide array of insurance products but was left askance to discover none. I clarified to him that I held the belief that insurance was only essential for individuals who would face significant financial hardship in the event of a tragedy. Given that both my wife and I possessed reasonable independent incomes and some assets, we felt no compulsion to include insurance in our portfolio. Personally, I've never been fond of dwelling on hypothetical scenarios, but I'm fairly confident that my cats wouldn't be left destitute if something were to happen to me. The same goes for Meena.

Nevertheless, the RM delicately proposed that as I was 'getting up there in years', (I was nearing the big 5-0), it might be wise to contemplate incorporating an insurance-linked savings plan into my portfolio. Personally, I had never held a favourable view towards such plans. Any insurance plan entails paying a premium to offset the slight probability of a substantial loss. Consequently, insurance-linked savings products tend to offer lower returns compared to regular savings products, as the returns must account for the insurance premium, thereby diminishing the savings component.

But since both my wife and I were now financially secure, I figured there was no harm in adding a savings-linked insurance product to my portfolio. After all, a little extra protection couldn't have too much of a downside. So, I turned to the affable RM and asked him to suggest some suitable options.

I could fairly see the excitement on his face as he pulled out his folder of insurance plans. It was as if he was presenting me with the Holy Grail of finance. Eventually, he produced a glossy brochure of 'Savings Assurance Plan' of HDFC Life.

I had just pulled out of a meeting and was in a hurry to get back in, so I hastily agreed to go with the product without giving it much thought. I mean, both HDFC Life and my private bankers were highly respected corporates, so what could possibly go wrong? I had a private banker for a reason, right? So, it was only right that I let them earn their commissions. So I went with the flow.

With the decision made, I reached for my chequebook and wrote out a cheque for the first year's premium of ₹5.5 lakhs. The RM assured me that the related papers would be sent to me in due course. So I left it at that and went back to my meeting.

Fast forward six years to around 2009–10. I had purchased a house—in which I live now—in Bangalore, for which I had taken a modest bridge loan from a bank. As one who treats a loan hanging over my head like a Damocles sword, I was eager to pay it off as soon as possible.

And then I recalled that I had this Savings Assurance Plan of HDFC Life, into which I had been depositing ₹5.5 lakhs every year for five years now, with the sixth annual installment shortly due. Happily, the policy's three-year lock-in period was over, and I could now redeem the plan to extinguish this loan.

So I asked the local HDFC Life manager to give me the-then redemption value of my Savings Assurance Plan into which I had poured in ₹27.5 lakhs in principal over the last five years. I was expecting the redemption value to be higher than the principal of course, but to my surprise, I was told that the redemption value was about ₹22.5 lakhs! It was as if the plan had been playing a diminishing act with my hard-earned money for the past six years. I mean, this was supposed to be a 'Savings Assurance Plan' from the trusted HDFC family. Shouldn't it have at least 'assured' me that my principal was safe, or 'assured' me a minimum return?* It seemed like the only thing it had assured was the loss of my principal!

* A word of clarification. Products like 'Savings Assurance Plan' fall under the category of unit linked investment plans (ULIPs). These products typically lop off the entire commission due to them over the duration of the premium paid, say ten years, up front. For example, assuming an average commission of say 3 per cent (in practice, they are progressive, that is, starting with a larger per centage in the first year and then gradually

As the saying goes, 'when in doubt, read the manual'—and so I dug out and dusted off the papers related to the Savings Assurance Plan that had been buried in my cabinets for years. As I delved into the fine print, I could feel my blood pressure rising. And let me tell you, the more I read, the less assured I felt about this so-called *Savings Assurance Plan*.

According to this policy, 'In case of death during the first year from the date of commencement of the policy, a basic benefit of 80 per cent of the premiums received will be paid to the nominee of the life assured and in case of death after the first year, the amount payable on death will be the 'lesser of', *yes, the lesser of*, the sum assured (maturity benefit, which if I recall right, was ₹45 lakhs)—plus any attaching bonuses; or the total of the premiums paid plus interest, at 6 per cent per annum compounded, on each premium from the premium due date to the date of death.'**

Now does that pop your eyes out? It certainly did mine! I mean this was supposedly an 'insurance-linked-savings' product from a top insurance company, duly approved by the Insurance Regulatory Development Authority (IRDA)! What was shocking and scandalous was the 'lesser of' clause, in small print. What it means is that invariably, in case of death after the first year, the beneficiary can only hope to receive the lower of ₹45 lakhs plus bonuses, or whatever the policyholder had invested plus 6 per cent. And they called it 'Death Benefit'! What impertinence, when in comparison the policyholders could have earned 6 per cent return or higher (depending upon the

---

reducing in subsequent years), they charge the ten years' cumulative commission of 30 per cent up front from one's principal, so that if you invest ₹100, only 70 of the that is actually invested. That's why even after five years of paying an annuity, the terminal value at the end of five or six years remains below the principal value. The terminal value will exceed the principal only if you remain invested for much longer. As a rule, it is best to avoid investing in ULIP like schemes.

** What happens in case of death after the first ten years? Well, the product had a different catch, which we shall disregard for our purposes here.

tenure) in a simple fixed deposit (FD) in a bank. So where was the 'insurance' element in the product?

Clearly, the policy was a bad cake with no icing. A real shocker. And scandalous, like catching your favourite sporting hero for sexual harassment. This so-called 'insurance-linked savings' product was basically just a black hole for one's hard-earned money, with no actual insurance component whatsoever, nor any assurance either pertaining to one's capital or to the return. To add insult to injury, one couldn't even borrow against it like one can with a friendly neighbourhood bank FD, and worse, it had a three-year holding period (during which period one couldn't redeem the policy)! I mean, what kind of non-insurance product offers less return, less flexibility and less convenience than a simple fixed deposit? Like selling a car with no engine and calling it a 'driving assurance plan'! And yet, they still had the nerve to take a 20 per cent cut if one died in the first year.

Well, one can hardly deny that the product was very 'cleverly' structured—for the insurance company, that is. To the buyer, it served a stale sandwich for the price of a gourmet meal.

Now all this raises two important questions. One pertains to the matter of governance in an insurance company belonging to a celebrated group like the HDFC, which prides itself for the quality of its corporate governance. This company was selling an 'insurance' product, which was a wolf in sheep's clothing. It makes you wonder how the insurance company got away with it, and how their sense of integrity permitted floating the product in the first place.

The second question relates to the IRDA itself. How did the insurance regulator approve such a product in the first place? According to their website, the IRDA's objectives include 'protect the investor's interest; promote orderly growth of insurance industry in the country; devise control activities needed for smooth functioning of the insurance companies including investment of funds and solvency requirements to be maintained by insurance companies; and adjudicate on disputes, among others.' It is difficult to understand how approving the product mentioned above, with zero insurance element, aligned with any of these objectives. Clearly, the regulatory body needed to review their product approval process and ensure that they were indeed serving the best interests of the investors.

I was so disturbed by the product that I decided to dig my heels in and fight. Not only was there no downside to this fight, but there was also a significant upside to it. And there was a big downside to not-fighting, as in losing a shark's bite sized chunk of my invested principal.

So I decided to call up the top dog himself, the managing director of HDFC Life. But CEOs of large corporates in India are not easily approached. Undeterred, I persisted in my efforts and managed to get through to the big honcho of HDFC Life. Despite not being the original CEO who had introduced the product, he was reasonable enough to step up to the plate and engaged in a conversation with me. I questioned him, like a journalist would, on how the product qualified as an insurance plan, given that in case of death, it simply returned my money at 6 per cent interest or the maturity value plus bonuses, whichever was lower!

Despite his attempts to deflect the conversation towards IRDA's clearance of the product, I persisted in my questioning. I made it clear that my concern was not at this stage about IRDA's approval, but rather about the lack of insurance element in the product, asking pointedly once again, 'Just show me where the insurance element in the product is? To me, it seems like a shoddy imitation of a regular fixed deposit, only worse.'

The long and short of it was that the MD assured me that one of their RMs would contact me within a couple of days, and 'sort out the matter'.

Lo and behold, the next day, a suave young man in a bright tie met me in my office and said, his face beaming, 'Sir, we have discussed your case internally. And as a special case, we are happy to give you 4 per cent return on the five years of premium paid by you. I hope that would conclude the issue satisfactorily.'

'Four per cent? Did you say 4 per cent? How very kind of you, sir! Do you think you're doing me a favour?' I asked sardonically, my voice dripping with anger. 'You are offering me a measly 4 per cent return on a so-called insurance-linked savings product with zero insurance content? And that too 'as a special case'! If that's the best you can do, I'll have to take this up with your MD once more.'

The RM returned after consulting with his superiors the next day and asked me, 'What's the interest rate you're expecting?' I replied, 'Well, the average interest rate in 2004–05 was about 6 per cent, so that's the least I expect.'

After a few more rounds of back-and-forth, the RM returned to me with a grin and announced that his management had approved my request as a 'special case' (again) and that I would receive the cheque in two days. It's a good thing I wasn't holding my breath; else, I might have turned blue waiting for that cheque to arrive!

I had meticulously calculated the final value of my annual premiums using the trusty Excel sheet. But to my dismay, when I finally received the cheque, it was for a smaller sum! When I raised the issue, the RM seemed shocked and claimed, 'But sir, our calculations are all done by computers! Surely there can't be any mistake!'

I was losing my patience. I asked the RM to meet me once again, only to find that they had calculated the interest on my five years of annuities paid using simple interest instead of compound interest. It felt like I was caught in a never-ending game of Tom and Jerry. I couldn't believe that anyone in their right mind would use simple interest in this day and age. Or was the idea of time value of money or compound interest, which was taught in Class 8 in every school, novel to HDFC Life?

After some more back and forth, I finally managed to get the correct amount. I had to fight the battle over several days to assure myself that my principal and returns stayed assured. But during all this time, there was no admission from their side that there was something wrong with their product. They had fixed my problem only as a 'special case'.

The incident tossed up a bunch of vexing questions. While I managed to put things right for myself, what about the average Joe or Jane out there who may be less financially savvy than me? How many of them would have the knowledge and wherewithal to call out a large corporation when they are being taken for a ride? After all, that vile product was still out there systematically sucking away people's savings.

I couldn't ignore the larger issue at hand and move on. This is exactly what large corporations hope for—to exert their dominance over consumers who lack financial expertise or social influence, and to silence the most troublesome consumers capable of making a nuisance of themselves, by addressing their concerns at an individual level and that too only when absolutely necessary. Clearly, something needed fixing.

With the above in mind, I wrote a detailed letter and an email to the non-executive chairman of HDFC Life suggesting a recall of the product in the best traditions of a group with a reputation of good corporate governance. I emphasised that recalling a defective product was a symbol of good governance, practised willingly by many corporations globally, and as a reputed leader in the industry, if the house of HDFC counted themselves among them, they had a responsibility to uphold these principles.

When my communications to HDFC Life's chairman went unanswered, I decided to take matters into my own hands and write articles for the press. I wrote three articles in all, two in *The Economic Times* and one in *Moneylife*. My first two articles, published in August and September 2011, aimed to expose the deceptive product by its name, 'Savings Assurance Plan'. I also called out the insurance regulator, IRDA, for sleeping on the job. I mean, come on, guys! Wake up and at least smell the coffee!

After my article in *The Economic Times*, the IRDA reached out to me, asking for further details on the product. I didn't know if I should be amused or aghast. If the IRDA had cleared the product, shouldn't they have had all the necessary details? But apparently, their database was in a clutter, and they needed my help with this product. At least that's what I was told.

In response to the media articles, I started getting emails from the public which were deeply disturbing. One elderly lady, aged eighty-three, wrote to me saying she had paid ₹4,000 per annum for ten years under the HDFC Savings Assurance Plan, and that she was only getting a maturity amount of ₹32,446; 'I wonder if I made the right decision ...' she mused.

So, let's get this straight: HDFC Life sold the 'Savings Assurance Plan' to a lady when she was seventy-three, who was now stuck with a policy that would have paid her 20 per cent less than her principal, had she died in the first year, the probability of which for a seventy-three-year-old wasn't negligible! Besides, her principal wouldn't even grow for the next several years, if she wanted the plan redeemed, for say medical reasons. Selling such a product to a septuagenarian is like robbing a baby of candy. And let's not even get started on the fact that technically 'life insurance products' were not even supposed to be sold to people over seventy! So, was it HDFC Life's way of acknowledging that it was peddling a non-insurance product after all?

In my article for *Moneylife*, I shared the emails I received from these victims and questioned whether it was ethical for bank managers to sell complex products to vulnerable groups such as senior citizens, teachers, clerks and housewives, or for that matter to anybody. I emphasised the urgent need for SEBI to regulate investment advisors and prevent such exploitation.*

Well, finally IRDA woke up from their torpor and admitted that the product was dodgier than a ₹3,000 bill. They told me they had withdrawn the product, but only prospectively.

But what about the poor saps who still had their hard-earned money invested in the dodgy Savings Assurance Plan? IRDA conveniently ignored that question, leaving the victims high and dry. And as for HDFC Life, to my knowledge, they never did the decent thing and recall the crummy product, leaving their clients suckered.

The bottom line is that when governance, regulation and redressal are all weak, it becomes imperative for us to exercise greater caution—placing a heightened emphasis on the adage *caveat emptor*, particularly in our investment decisions, especially when purchasing insurance products. Unfortunately, none of our regulators, credit rating agencies or financial institutions, including banks, are truly up to par.

* This kind of cross-selling of financial products by bank managers were continuing at the time of writing these lines. For example, see 'Sebi probes MFs owned by banks amid allegations of mis-selling', *The Economic Times*, 6 September 2022.

Who says sleeping giants cannot be woken up? The IRDA did wake up, and they did take some corrective measures, even if they didn't go all the way! For once, I could see the power of media in action!

Home Builders: One-Sided Contracts

I was looking to buy a house in a gated community in Hyderabad in 2007. I had paid the initial signing up advance of ₹10 lakhs, and was about to sign the pre-sale agreement, when at a whim, I decided to carefully read the contract and its many clauses in fine print. What I read gave me goose pimples! The contract read like a joke, except that if I signed it, the joke would be on me. I asked for my advance back from the builder as I wasn't prepared to sign this one-sided contract. At this point I also realised that the homebuyers, even when aware of such clauses, had no recourse or alternative as nearly all builder contracts followed a similar vein.

These contracts place the homebuyer at a grave risk of being stranded, as the builder diverts their life's savings to fund other projects, contractors, sub-contractors and suppliers. And we have all seen scams along these lines.

And that's when I wrote the following 'Open letter to the RBI Governor RBI: Homebuyers need help', as an op-ed in *Livemint* (and later as a personal one-to-one letter):

> Dear Mr Governor,
>
> We know you must be a very busy man these days. What with coping with inflation, fuel prices, fiscal deficit, interest rates, and what have you. But Sir, believe it or not, we the common people, must face the brunt of all the above and then some. This letter to you is about one such issue, which affects our lives

significantly, namely housing. In virtually any list of significant human needs, shelter always ranks up there among the most basic needs. Now what can RBI have to do with shelter? I will explain shortly.

We are queasy giving our suits for dry-cleaning, when we read the print on the back side of the receipt, because it appears so one-sided. But Sir, have you ever read—we mean really read—the contracts the builders hand out to the ordinary house buyers to sign for a transaction worth lakhs and even crores? We would be happy to send you a typical contract if you so wish.

We are all reasonable people and understand the real world and expect these contracts to be one-sided. But how one-sided really? Something like this: while the buyer will have to pay a penal interest of 18 per cent per annum for a delay of even 15 days on his instalments to the builder, the builder has no such obligation for delaying the completion of the work by any length. The instalments may be demanded every three months or upon each stage of completion, whichever is earlier, upon threat of penal interest. This means, even if the builder has not completed a stage of construction, he can still demand the instalment and if we do not pay up, slap penal interest as per the contract. He is not obliged to complete any of the promised facilities that he is supposed to provide at the time of handing over the house or even any time thereafter. It depends upon his goodwill to do so. They cannot be contractually demanded, though we are obliged to pay for them. We, the property buyers, have no say in the quality of construction promised. The buyers cannot have any claim to warranty on defective construction even for one full season. And we aren't yet talking of all the small print, under which the builder may encroach upon the buyer's property, privacy, or peace at will. And the most unfortunate thing is that most buyers do not (and others cannot) even read what they are signing on, thinking the process to be a mere formality. In any case they have no choice. They either sign up, or they do not get to buy a house. Or they pay up tens of lakhs or even a few crores—often their entire life's savings—and then suffer inordinate delays or shoddy construction when the builders haven't been outright crooks.

In other countries, Builders Association prescribes standard proformas of contracts which are a little more balanced to reasonably protect the interests of homebuyers. In India we have no such luck. In fact, the Builder's Association of India, New Delhi, set up in 1941, has even confirmed the fact. Now Sir, you can imagine the plight of the homebuyers in a country, where legal system at best limps? Now if the buyer is further weighed down with such contracts, what are his chances for a fair deal?

You may still be wondering where you come into all this. Well, right here. Sir, as you know, banks are the major funders of housing loans in this country. Often, the agreements with the builder are linked to the loan contracts, so that the loan disbursals directly go to the builder and so forth. Now supposing every bank were to require that all payments to the builders by the property buyers will be made through an escrow account held by the bank providing the housing loan. The builder in turn will get a bridge loan from the bank for completing the project. The bank could also hold a limited power of attorney from the house buyer (borrower) to ensure that the builders have met all their obligations and once so satisfied, clears the escrow. Even if the borrower must pay a small charge for the bank's service, this charge is mitigated by the fact that his money in the escrow account earns in the meanwhile. The builder's cost of borrowing is minimal since it is protected by the escrow. In any case, even that minimal cost can be passed on to the buyers against this hugely enhanced security for the homebuyers, who are otherwise at the mercy of the one-sided contracts of the often-unscrupulous builders. The bank could in such a case can also insist on a proforma contract document along the lines of the more developed countries, thus offering further protection to the homebuyers-cum-borrowers. In fact, such a service may encourage home loans and minimise cash transactions so prevalent in the building industry.

Of course, an enlightened bank, or a bank working towards ethical banking, could do this proactively. But perhaps, there is bound to be that first mover inertia for a bank to initiate such a move, because the builders may discourage their buyers from borrowing from such a bank.

Sir, this is where you come in. Could the RBI, as a regulator and supervisor of the financial system, promoting fair practices in banks, ask all the scheduled banks to route their housing loans through an escrow mechanism? If every bank were required to follow such a practice, surely it will raise the standards of the building industry, through greater transparency and accountability and protect the homebuyers from unscrupulous builders, wouldn't it?

We do hope as an enlightened governor of the RBI, you will see merit in our suggestion.'

Three weeks prior, on 31 May 2008, I had already published another op-ed in *The Economic Times*, titled 'Dealing with One Sided Contracts'. Not done yet, I would continue my crusade in my *The Times of India* blog with a post titled 'Outraged (Why the RBI was wrong), May 18, 2010'.

Considering how big a chunk of a middle-class family's savings the purchase of a house took away, I was on a mission to hold those in power accountable and fight for what was right. Through my writing, I wanted to speak truth to power and demand change.

I did not stop with an open letter to the RBI governor. Even though the governor acknowledged it and forwarded my letter to his deputy governor for action, I knew I had a long road ahead. The deputy governor passed the letter on to her general manager, who did call me once, but failed to take any meaningful action thereafter. But I wasn't prepared to be deterred by a mere brush-off. I refused to let their inaction discourage me and continued to advocate for change.

And just to make sure my message was heard loud and clear, I sent letters to the finance minister and the finance secretary (no downside, remember?). Of course, there was no response, but so what! I knew that the cause was too important to let go of, and I continued to push for change and call for a regulator to protect the interests of homebuyers.

For good measure, I also wrote to the chairmen of HUDCO, HDFC and National Housing Bank et al., to hammer home my case.

I also decided to reach out to the Builder's Association of India (BAI) in New Delhi. I pointed out to them the enlightened practices of other similar associations worldwide. Take for example Australia, where there are not one, not two, but three associations of builders, each providing standard contract proformas to potential buyers for various kinds of purchases. These proformas are so well-drafted that any deviation from them would be risky for either party, unless attended to by good lawyers. Sure, these contracts still lean in favour of the builders, but definitely less than the Leaning Towers of Pisa that ours in India resembled! By using these standard contracts, buyers could mitigate risks and have a smoother experience.

My letter to the BAI, which had been around since 1941, evoked an eye-popping response. According to them, 'BAI looks after [only the] common problems of its members' and of course buyers aren't their members! Their response went on as a consolation: 'The prospective buyer has got to carefully study the terms and then enter into contract. If you feel that you have been wronged by a certain builder, you can avail the facility of legal process.' An oxymoron, clearly, when you couldn't even buy a house without signing those one-sided contracts first.

In my articles and letters, what I tried to drive home the point that the risks involved for house buyers are colossal and often unknown. When builders divert homebuyers' funds, it puts the common man at grave risk. In case of a financial crunch, which is not uncommon, the buyer is the one left holding the bag. And again, such scandals have happened on a large scale where builders have taken full instalments from homebuyers with merely a fraction of the projects complete! Banks have been found to be complicit in many such cases.

In retrospect, I like to think that my persistent efforts through those letters and articles may have played a small part in bringing about some change. Slowly but surely, the gears of the government system turned. While I cannot say for certain whether my contributions did add a drop in the ocean of government thinking, the establishment of the Real Estate Regulations and Development (RERA) Act in 2016 seems to suggest that many forces came into play and progress did happen. However, the road to protecting the rights of homebuyers is still a long one. As recently as November 2022, according to press reports, RERA was rocked by a scandal exposed by Sandeep Patil—a whistle-blower—at grave risk to his life.*

---

* See, for example, Pradeep Gupta, 'Whistleblower who exposed RERA scam recorded his statement before court', *The Times of India*, 22 November 2022, https://timesofindia.indiatimes.com/city/thane/whistleblower-who-exposed-rera-scam-recorded-his-statement-before-court/articleshow/95678991.cms.

While the actual intent of setting up RERA was to enhance transparency and accountability within India's real estate sector, it faces several limitations. These include jurisdictional disparities, inconsistency in regulations, enforcement challenges, delays in resolving disputes, ambiguity regarding ongoing projects, insufficient control over financial matters, reliance on self-reporting, inadequate coverage of commercial real estate, low awareness and limited penalties, all of which hinder its effectiveness.

As I said earlier in the chapter, it is now up to us to hold RERA and other regulators to account, for them to earn their keep.

Mercedes Benz: A False Promise

I always nursed the childhood dream of owning a Mercedes, but my wallet kept me in check. It wasn't until much later in life, when I had one foot in retirement, that I finally decided to give in to my dream and purchased a brand-new Mercedes. Of course, it wasn't the top-of-the-line model with all the bells and whistles, but one which fitted nicely within the budgetary constraints my good wife imposed upon my indulgence. Thank goodness for her financial wisdom, or else I might have ended up buying a fancy car and living in it!

I bought a nice deep blue car, sticking no plastic Ganesha on the dashboard for safety! After all this was supposed to be a super safe car. I had noticed while browsing through the pre-sale brochure idly that the model I had bought was supposed to have a safety feature called Pre-Safe. The brochure informed the reader that 'in certain hazardous conditions', Pre-Safe takes pre-emptive measures to protect the vehicle's occupants. Reading the brochure further, I learnt that in case of an accident, the Pre-Safe feature of my Mercedes was supposed to kick in and take necessary precautions. As per the brochure, depending on the type and severity of the impact, the following measures would kick in, namely: the hazard warning lamps would activate; the emergency lighting would turn on; the vehicle doors would unlock; the front windows would lower; the engine would switch off and the fuel supply would be cut off.

All this looked mighty impressive, but I couldn't help but wonder how helpful Pre-Safe would be if the car was already totalled, and whether the company should not add a feature where the car transforms into a lifeboat and sails us to safety in case of floods!

It's always nice to get a validation that you are about to make a smart purchase. Especially when it comes to safety features that could potentially save your life. It's like finding a ₹2,000 bill in your pocket that you didn't know you had. Except, in this case, it's a bunch of safety measures that you hope you'll never have to use but are glad to know are there just in case.

A month after I had bought the car, one day I had my nose inside the owner's manual, and I couldn't help but notice a recurring theme: 'certain features may only be available for certain models'. Well, isn't that just peachy? I guess I'll just have to settle for the less fancy version of my car, as long as it had its Pre-Safe, I thought.

However, on the Pre-Safe feature itself, the manual left me hanging. It didn't specify if the feature was exclusive to certain models or applicable to all. Nor whether it applied to the models sold in India. It was like reading a mystery novel without a clear ending. But given the lack of any disclaimers or restrictions, I assumed that it must be available for all models.

After some investigative work, my research suggested that the model I had purchased in India probably did not come with the promised safety feature, despite what the pre-sale brochure had indicated. When I confronted the dealer seeking confirmation of my hypothesis, they seemed more evasive than a politician after elections.

Dissatisfied with the dealer's wishy-washy response, I took my enquiry directly to the company, and emailed them. I wanted a clear answer: 'Does my car have it or not? And if not, where in the manual does it say, "Not for India, mate!"?'

Soon after sending my query, I received a response from one of their customer relationship managers, acknowledging my email and promising a 'satisfactory solution', while also asking for some time to investigate the matter.

Soon after, the dealer started bombarding me with calls asking me exactly what I wanted. I reiterated that I was waiting for a response from Mercedes Benz regarding my query and that my next steps would depend on the answer I got.

However, I didn't receive any email response from Daimler for ten days, while the dealers and Daimler's customer connect manager kept calling me asking me how best to resolve the matter.

In phone conversations, both the dealers and Daimler's customer connect managers admitted that there had been a mistake and the sales brochure was not meant for India. They acknowledged that a disclaimer should have been included to state that the model sold in India did not have the Pre-Safe feature. However, they would not provide any written confirmation of this admission.

At this point, I decided to take matters into my own hands and wrote to the managing director of Daimler, India, on 29 June. I politely suggested that Mercedes Benz could proactively recall the models sold under wrongful information and fix the feature for all buyers. To underscore my point, I reminded them that Apple and Microsoft often reward those who find bugs in their systems and apps. While I didn't expect a reward, I believed ensuring that my car was fitted with the Pre-Safe feature would be a good start. After all, I was the one who had discovered the 'bug' in their manual and brought it to their attention in India.

After several discussions back and forth, the Daimler representatives explained that introducing the Pre-Safe feature through software alone was not possible, as it also required hardware changes that Indian versions did not have. They kept asking me for suggestions on how we could reach a mutually acceptable resolution.

Now it was my turn to play ball. I put my thinking cap on. Living in a country where enforcing even airtight contracts in courts was like herding cats, I knew that even if I won in the consumer court, Daimler could drag it on for decades in the higher courts and bleed me dry. Did I have the stamina for a prolonged legal battle? As a senior citizen, all I wanted was to cruise in my new car in peace.

After some deliberation, we came to an agreement that I would receive a refund of the approximately ₹3 lakhs I had paid for servicing and warranty for three and five years, respectively. Essentially, my car's servicing and warranty for the duration would be free. However, I stipulated that the pre-sale brochure either needed to be amended or discontinued altogether.

It seems like Daimler has learnt its lesson and has now taken measures to ensure that such a miscommunication does not happen again. It's good to know that they have taken the necessary steps to prevent any future misunderstandings. With the withdrawal of the pre-sale brochures from all their dealers, they can avoid any confusion and provide clear and accurate information to their customers through their online brochures.

After all, we are all consumers and have the power to make a difference and create positive change in the world. By standing up against being cheated and fighting for what we believe in, we can make some impact and inspire others to do the same. Each of us may be comfortable using different weapons—from using social media to going to consumer court, to publishing research papers. But we all do have our own weapons, and each has its place.

So, let's keep fighting, keep pushing, and keep standing up for what's right!

CHAPTER ELEVEN

The Evolution of an Author—The Art of Authorship

Success is a hard long road. No short cuts ...

2005–continuing

Do I consider myself a successful author?

Hmm, let's see. For the first half of my life, I was a full-time academic. The 3 Rs—Reading, 'Riting and Researching were the core of my bread and butter, leaving my eyes, fingers and brain numb, and so I spent those years honing the craft. The writing was further sharpened over decades of penning columns in various national dailies and magazines. All this training and thousands of hours spent on the 3 Rs—I must have crossed the 10,000-hour rule of Malcolm Gladwell a while ago—gave me a sound grounding for the second half of my life, when I ceased being a full-time academic. My development as an author in the public domain gave me a great deal of satisfaction. That some of the books sold well was a bonus.

So, now to answer the question, whether I am a successful author...

What are the essential skills required to be an author?

Exquisite writing skills? A strong vocabulary? Immense imagination? Audience connect? Clarity of thought? A good plot? Ability to research? Extensive reading and retention? Good marketing?

Well, I think while you do need to have at least two or three of these attributes to make the cut as an author, the single most important attribute is: 'none of the above'! It is something far less abstruse and far more elusive—it is discipline or persistence! If you haven't spent years glued to your desk, with unvarying regularity, every single day, for hours on end, furiously typing or writing away, then you might as well forget about becoming a successful author. I have heard many an aspiring writer, after they have written the first fifty pages of their book, say that they are not inspired to go on, that they have exhausted their store of narratives, or that they have hit a 'writer's block'. 'Writer's block!' Before they have written their first book! To me, that is an affected term for procrastination!

But if you do manage that discipline and develop the resolve to sit down and write every day, day after day, for months, then more often than not, something magical will happen. Ideas will dance before your eyes, words will cascade freely from your fingertips, sentences will twirl in your imagination and before you know it, you will have a theme that hangs together! Sure, it might take a little while for the creative juices to run from the tap, but if you stick with it just that bit longer, the magic will invariably grow wings and your book will unfold itself. So forget about inborn talent and creativity; just embrace the art of sitting, for in its humble repose lies the gateway to the realms of authorship!

Yes, becoming a successful author parallels the delicate art of weaving intertwining threads of persistence, perseverance and unwavering dedication. It's about forsaking life's little pleasures—forgoing that fun evening with friends to battle with an obstinate page which simply refuses to dance with our thoughts; embracing the dawn of a Sunday with determination to grapple with an idea that seemed within reach in the haze of half-sleep but now slips away like fine sand, rising from bed with the resolve to untangle the intricate web of a wayward plot, rather than take that drive to the golf course. But the true essence lies within the realm of discipline, which requires not only unremitting commitment, but also the relinquishing of fleeting gratifications as a habit.

Becoming an author requires a significant investment of time, steadfast focus and relentless dedication. It's a journey that frequently calls for sacrifices, delicately balancing personal relationships, financial stability and the familiar solace of our comfort zones.

The writer's life can be solitary, requiring extended periods of introspection with thoughts and words. This can sometimes make it difficult to maintain the lively social connections that enrich our lives. Additionally, writers must be prepared to face harsh criticism and rejection of their work, which can be disheartening and demoralising.

In short, a career in writing is an audacious undertaking, fraught with considerable risk, as authors frequently encounter turbulent waters where financial stability is elusive. To sustain their passion and hone their craft, they may need to embark upon other jobs or gigs, to make ends meet. It is a delicate tango between one's inner need to write and the more practical need to survive. But sacrifices and challenges notwithstanding, writers are driven by their passion for storytelling and the desire to create compelling, meaningful work that resonates with readers.

Indeed, one of the joys of being an author lies in the abundance of books that must surround their lives, and the act of reading itself. After all, if you don't read, you can't write. Besides, as the sage once proclaimed, the line between those who do not read and those who cannot read is gossamer thin. And therefore, those who do not read, by extension, also cannot write.

Certainly, when we speak of reading, we're not referring to perusing social media posts or WhatsApp forwards. We're talking about books—thoughtfully crafted works that serve as nourishment for a writer's soul. Books that refine our ideas, sharpen our language, polish our style, and influence our approach to writing.

Assuming you have written your magnum opus, or at least, say, 40–50 per cent of it, how do you get to finding yourself a good publisher?

You start with researching and shortlisting the right kind of publishers for you. This may mean identifying publishers who specialise in your genre or style and have a distinguished reputation and a history of publishing works that align with your intended book.

A reputed publisher for a book is the equivalent of publishing an academic paper in a peer-reviewed journal of high quality. It serves as a distinguished seal of approval, bestowed by a specialist of publishing who possesses a boundless wealth of reading experiences, surpassing what most of us could hope for in a lifetime.

If a publisher takes on your manuscript, it's akin to a certification affirming the worth and marketability of your work. It signifies that someone out there not only believes in the potential of your book but also envisions the possibility of it becoming a profitable venture, benefiting both you and them. It is akin to being awarded a resplendent golden star for your work, granted by a panel of experts who hold the power to shape your writing aspirations.

Striving to secure a reputable publisher isn't unlike trying to get into an IIT or IIM. You know the odds are stacked against you, but you're determined to give it a shot anyway; your very best shot, that is.

Good publishers can add a ton of value to your work. They don't just publish your book—they'll often provide valuable editing and copyediting support to help shape your manuscript in the best light possible.

And then, there's the matter of distribution networks. A good publisher will have all the connections necessary to get your book into bookstores, libraries, airports and online retailers around the world. They can even lend a bit of marketing support to help get the word out about your book—though, let's be honest, most publishers typically reserve their full efforts and spend on marketing only for their biggest stars—say, a generic Salman Rushdie, Arundhati Roy or Amitav Ghosh.

Now, before you start submitting your work hither and thither, you need to make sure you've got your ducks in a row. You'll want to have at least four or five chapters (if not the whole book) completed before you even start looking for a publisher. All well edited, worked and reworked till your fingers and brains go numb. After all, you don't want to get your hopes high only to realise that you can't deliver the goods. Nor would a halfway decent publisher even look at your manuscript until then.

Once you have shortlisted your list of publishers, it is time to craft a compelling submission letter, paying meticulous heed to the submission guidelines of the publishers (you can usually find it on their websites). The submission letter should professionally introduce your manuscript to the editor with enticing allure. It should contain a synopsis that encapsulates the essence of your work. Whether the publisher explicitly demands it or not (and most do), it helps to include a comprehensive proposal that showcases the artistic merit, topicality of the subject, the intended readership and commercial viability of your work.

And then the wait for a response begins—if you even get a response at all, that is. You should be prepared to wait anywhere from three to four months just to get a simple acknowledgment after submitting your manuscript. It's like waiting for the Hogwarts acceptance letter when you are just a Muggle. So there's nothing to it but persevere with fortitude and patience.

And truth be told, if you are a first-time author in India, finding a good publisher who will accept your work can be a daunting task. Unlike in other countries, literary agents aren't really a thing here yet. And beware—blind submissions rarely get a response. So, your best bet, and not much of a bet at that, is to submit your manuscript through the publisher's online portal.

And let's face it; the odds really aren't in your favour. Those handful of big-name publishing houses probably only publish one out of every 100 to 150 manuscripts they receive from aspiring authors. You are a needle waiting to be discovered in a largish haystack!

So you must be prepared for potential rejections. It is best to take them as signals for further polishing your work. Maintain your resolute spirit, continue submitting to well-suited publishers or agents, and hold steadfast in your belief in your work. Don't lose faith in yourself. Just in case it helps, if your manuscript is rejected, remember, you are in the company of Agatha Christie, J.K. Rowling, James Joyce, Isaac Asimov, Dr Seuss, Pearl Buck, William Faulkner, Rudyard Kipling—just a few whose manuscripts were repeatedly rejected.

If you're lucky and good enough to make it through the hoops, get accepted and get assigned an editor, then you're in for the high of a lifetime. They'll guide you through the arduous process of getting your book ready for publication. And by 'arduous process', I mean it could take anywhere from eighteen to twenty-four months before your book is finally ready to see the light of day.

So, if you're thinking about becoming an author, just remember—patience, perseverance and resilience are the three keys to hold at all times.

What does an author's economics look like?

Well, for starters, getting an advance for your first book is about as likely as spotting a unicorn riding a rainbow, unless you are Barack Obama or Shah Rukh Khan, that is. And when it comes to royalties, you're looking at a measly 7.5 per cent for paperbacks and 10 per cent for hardcovers. In fact, 90 per cent of books sell less than 3,000 copies, with 75 per cent of those sales happening in the first year. So if your book is priced at a reasonable ₹400 per copy, that's only ₹30 in royalties per copy sold. Congratulations, you just earned a whopping ₹90,000 for a couple of years of hard work and another year or two of waiting. Even if you manage to sell 5,000 copies, which is considered good in India, that's only ₹1.5 lakhs. Halfway successful artists make much more than that for similar hours of work.

What's more, as a first-time author, you see the first colour of your money only about two years down the road. So, unless you're willing to live on instant noodles and tap water for the next few years, you might want to think twice before quitting your day job. But then again, there have been exceptions!

Reprints are as rare as principled politicians, and revised editions are even rarer. Unless your book is selling big, needs a facelift or a brain transplant, don't expect a revised edition anytime soon.

And don't go updating your LinkedIn profile to 'Author' just because you have one or two books under your belt. You need a whole series of them before you can claim that title. And if your debut book flops like a fish out of water, you're in for a rough ride for the subsequent ones.

So yes; it's a tough world out there for aspiring authors, but with a bit of grit and determination (and a whole lot of luck), you might just be able to make it.

Is self-publishing a good option?

Well, self-publishing is all the rage these days, leaving traditional publishers feeling a bit green around the gills. But for authors, self-publishing seems like an attractive alternative. With royalty per centages reaching a sky-high 75 per cent, it's like hitting the literary jackpot. And the best part? You get to set the price yourself! The turnaround time from submission to publication is faster than your friendly neighbourhood pizza delivery guy. Sure, you might largely be left to your own devices when it comes to editing and copy-editing, but who cares when you can have your book on the virtual shelves as soon as yesterday? And let's not forget the best part—no unsold books cluttering up your basement! Just print on demand, edit errors in real time and save the trees. It certainly seems like a win-win situation.

While the benefits of self-publishing may be appealing, it's important not to overlook the challenges of marketing and distribution. It can feel like trying to sell sand in the Sahara Desert, with average sales figures in this segment hovering around only 250 copies per year. Although the royalty percentage may be higher, the significantly lower sales numbers mean limited financial gains and a narrower reach for your message.

Moreover, self-publishing often lacks the external validation and meticulous editorial scrutiny provided by traditional publishers. While virtual publishers may offer editorial services, they may not match the care and rigour of established publishing houses. Securing reviews in print media for self-published works can be challenging, particularly in regions like India where book reviews are scarce, regardless of the publisher's reputation.

Additionally, self-published authors typically incur upfront costs to the virtual publisher, further diminishing their bottom line. The prospect of seeing self-published works on the shelves of bookstores or airports is slim.

In essence, while advocates of self-publication—ranging from those offering self-publishing courses, independent book publishers, freelance publishing professionals, select literary agents and proponents of publishing democracy—may often strongly push for self-publishing, the true fulfilment and recognition of publishing often stem from working with a reputable publisher.

What follows once the book hits the bookstores?

You thought that getting your book published by a top publisher was the hard part? That's cute. The real fun starts when your book hits the market and suddenly you find you're the one in charge of marketing. You become your own town-crier or bellman, and publicist. You'll do anything to grab a little bit of attention for your book.

When you don't find your book in the papers, you turn to Google and start typing 'goodreads' with trembling fingers, hoping, and praying that your book has made the cut.

And of course, there are those bookshops and airports. You find yourself hovering around, looking for your book like a kid searching for her missing toy. And when (and if) you finally spot a copy or two, you feel like you've hit the jackpot. You may even find yourself slyly shifting your book to a more prominent position if you find it tucked away deep behind other books. No airport signings for you, my friend. Not yet at least.

As an avid reader, you've always detested those pesky typos that make you cringe. So when you stumble upon a glaring error in your own published book, it's akin to a punch in the gut. And then, horror of horrors, you spot more of them, like those flying termites swarming off the ground after rain. You bring it up with the copyeditor, and they respond with a meagre apology and a promise to correct them in the next reprint (if there is ever one). But until then you're convinced that every single reader will flip to that exact page with the giant typo. Even if there is a reprint, you can't help but fret that the corrections you painstakingly sent may be overlooked or mishandled. While this is your one book, for the publisher, it's one among the hundreds they churn out each year. Suddenly, your editor has done the disappearing act! Oh, the joys of post-publishing life!

OK, so you have published your first book. Now what?

Indeed, writing one's first book successfully is like making that first million, which is rather tough. Thereafter the subsequent books and millions follow a little more easily!

And then, the next one gets even easier, and the next one easier still, assuming you remain committed to getting those next ones. That said, a debut book is also like crossing the first ten-mile marker of running a marathon. The journey ahead may still be arduous, but the initial hurdle has been surmounted, and the path forward seems less daunting.

But setbacks, like clouds, can come in various shapes and sizes. And when they do, take heart and don't give up! Remember again that rejections and setbacks are an author's frequent companions. Even J.K. Rowling had to send her manuscript to twelve publishers before finally getting a yes! So, keep writing and don't let rejection bring you down. Your success story could be just around the corner.

Do authors plan out their entire plot or story before putting pen to paper, or does the plot take shape as they write?

While some individuals may have a clear plan from the outset, many of us navigate the writing process with uncertainty. Personally, my books tend to evolve organically as I progress. While I may begin with a vague concept, it's not unusual for the manuscript to take unexpected turns midway. This unpredictability also applies to fiction writing, where publishers may request alterations to characters, plot or endings. However, such editorial involvement is less frequent in specialised works. Personally, I've learnt to trust the expertise of my editors and publishers; after all, they possess extensive knowledge of the literary world, and I'm simply along for the journey.

What constitutes a successful book?

Perceptions of a successful book can vary considerably based on individual objectives and aspirations. For some, the sheer fact of having their book published by a reputed publisher might constitute a fulfilling accomplishment. Alternatively, authors may gauge success by achieving bestseller status, amassing high sales figures, garnering substantial revenue, significant advances or receiving glowing reviews. Others might view success as reaching a specific target audience, earning commendable critical appraisals, or bolstering their personal or professional reputation. Winning or being shortlisted for awards could signify success for some, while for others, it might entail sparking widespread discussions and significantly influencing society in a particular direction. Ultimately, success in the realm of literature presents itself in multifaceted ways, and it is up to the author to define what they aim to accomplish with their book.

I regard a successful book as one that brings joy to the author throughout the writing process, while being skilfully crafted with a well-thought-out plot or theme, backed by necessary research. The book's worth is authenticated by being accepted by a reputable publisher, receiving favourable reviews from esteemed critics, being discussed by intelligent readers, making a difference somewhere, somehow, and earning the author respect from peers and other thinking individuals. If it sells over seven to eight thousand copies, that's a remarkable feat, and anything beyond that is cause for celebration. Moreover, if a book manages to avoid numerous typos, goes through reprints, or has a prolonged shelf life, that's the cherry on top. For an average author, such success is nothing short of extraordinary.

It's crucial to remember that authors like J.K. Rowling, Agatha Christie or Isaac Asimov are akin to the Djokovics, Nadals or Federers of the tennis world. While not everyone on the tennis circuit ascends to those heights, many manage to carve out respectable careers nevertheless with their levels of play.

How do authors get ideas for their books?

Writing books is like curating thoughts. To be an author, one must cultivate the hobby, whether consciously or unconsciously, of absorbing the vastness of our surroundings in all its aspects. This entails being an astute observer of the world, a dedicated reader of contemporary works, and possessing a genuine curiosity for a multitude of subjects. As for me, I prefer to embark on a voyage within my own memories. Though it may seem sub-optimal and somewhat unstructured, this is how my ideas come to life. Relying on one's memory may sound challenging, but it isn't. Engaging in reading, introspection and discourse across diverse subjects, be it through books, articles or podcasts, either individually or with friends and scholars, often results in an intensified expansion of knowledge, firmly ingrained in one's mental realm. In my case, the dimension of being a former teacher adds to this equation, while the dimension of being a columnist has further enriched my perspective.

As one reads more and more, ideas find solid ground and become deeply ingrained, requiring minimal conscious record-keeping. As an idea takes root in the mind, an internal guide instinctively directs one towards relevant sources of additional information, recollections of previous readings, or the individuals who imparted such knowledge. And in the present age, we have an ocean of information available through platforms like Google or Google Scholar or ChatGPT or Gemini to aid and explore these ideas further.

Let me share an example of how I crystallised the idea for my book *The Good Indian's Guide to Queue Jumping*. I had always watched at the airports, with half fascination and half irritation, how it is in our national character to jump queues. We sit quietly on our haunches over a two-and-a-half-hour flight and then try to shave off 2.3 seconds overtaking the guy in the row ahead of us while disembarking. Or how completely unfazed we are placing our bag ahead of the one standing in front of us at the security check. I also remembered reading some news reports and articles about some smart souls using the wheelchair at the airports to jump the long queues at security checks, or about some innovative methods deployed by some to jump online queues when you are put on hold with music! Or how we simply cannot follow lines in a lane of cars ...

Are Indians unique in this national pastime of queue jumping? How do other nationalities fare when it came to queue jumping? How do people react to queue jumpers? How often are queue jumpers successful? What would be the best strategy to jump a physical queue? What formal research in the area of say, social norms, crowd dynamics, fairness and equity, punishment, cross-cultural perspectives and technological solutions had been carried out in the field of queue jumping? How effectively could the results of such research be applied in real life? A lot of questions came to my mind ... wait a minute ... was there a book here, a tongue-in-cheek book, or a satirical take on our queue-jumping trait, screaming to take shape? So I went to Google and Google Scholar to find some answers and before long, I had enough material for a small book—*The Good Indian's Guide to Queue Jumping*.

Do I consider myself a successful author?

Hmm, let's see. For the first half of my professional life, I was a full time academic. The 3 Rs—Reading, 'Riting and Researching were the core of my bread butter, and breath. Writing cases and academic articles was part of the job description. The writing was further sharpened over decades through penning columns in national dailies and magazines. By the 1990s, I had also authored or co-authored at least three books covering various fields of finance.

All this training and thousands of hours invested in the three R's likely surpassed Malcolm Gladwell's 10,000-hour rule long ago. It provided me sound grounding for the second half of my life, when I ceased being a full time academic. My development as an author in the public domain started in 2005 and gave me immense satisfaction. That I was able to publish over a dozen books with some of India's best publishing houses thereafter must count for something. That some of them even sold well was a bonus. It assures me that there's at least someone out there—a book cognoscenti—who values my writing.

Be that as it may, I prefer to think of myself as a satisfied author. I take some pride in the fact that my books are not mere regurgitation of existing material, but an amalgamation of my experiences, research, perspectives and imagination. They may not be seriously scholarly works, but rather fun and informative reads that hopefully encourage readers to look at familiar subjects in a new light, and mostly in the Indian context.

Over the years I have received my share of emails and phone calls from readers of books and columns! Many of them have shared how they enjoyed this or that of my books or learnt about this or that aspect of a subject, or how they did something similar to what I had done in this or that context, or how something I had written made them think hard or even change their ways. One promoter of a Bangalore-based NGO (The Ugly Indian) dedicated to cleaning up Indian streets once reached out to me stating how *Games Indians Play* had served as an inspiration for their work. These messages are an author's reward in themselves! Not that I haven't been ever trolled for some of my writings! But fortunately—or is unfortunately the word?—these have never been cerebral criticisms to make me lose my sleep.

But of course, I am far from a being a widely recognised or celebrated author. No one, beyond my immediate circle of friends, professional acquaintances, and perhaps some of my former students, may recognise me in a mall. So the notion of my 'success' as an author is open to interpretation. But I can assert with confidence that I am a contented author, satisfied with the books I have written, and excited about the ones I am yet to write.

As I mentioned earlier, while most authors secretly hope for their books to become runaway successes, the reality is that for most average authors like me, hitting the 5,000-copy mark is reason enough to pop the champagne. As for me, while authorship may not have translated into millions of dollars, that's perfectly acceptable. Writing has always been more of a labour of love for me, more of a hobby, than a wealth-creating endeavour, which means I can let the publishers worry about the profits, while I focus on the pure joy translating my thoughts into words on paper.

Fortuitously, all my books have received positive reviews from well-regarded publications, both domestic and international. While a handful of snarky reviews have inevitably surfaced, I simply choose to disregard them and continue my writing journey.

One of the pleasures of being a moderately successful author is getting invited to a variety of events—book clubs, universities, colleges and even clubs like the Rotarians (who knew they were into books!), even if the likes of Jaipur Literature Festival (JLF) or even the 'lesser' fests have steadfastly ignored me like the third place in the decimal. I always enjoy these gatherings—after all, what's better than getting to talk about your own work and have people actually listen!

The high points of these speaking engagements were undoubtedly when I spoke at the TEDx based on my book *Games Indians Play*, and later at the New York City Club of Harvard following a good review of one of my books in the *New York Journal of Books*, or gave a talk on the 'Art of Authorship' in downtown Toronto. And in recent years, my modest standing as an author has also given me the confidence to take on the role of Chair at the Bangalore Business Literature Festival.

So, then again, am I a satisfied author? Short answer? Absolutely. But ...

Let's face it, my life story is more on the 'meh' side, which is the verbal equivalent of a shrug—nothing to write home about. I spent a good chunk of time as an academic, but never quite reached Nobel Prize potential. Yes, I was a corporate CEO, but hardly a serious threat to a Sundar Pichai or Satya Nadella. And while I've been a decent columnist for years, I have been no Stephen King or Art Buchwald. As for my writing career, I've published over a dozen books in the popular domain with the best publishers in India, but let's just say I'm unlikely to cut it to a Booker or a Pulitzer anytime soon. As a matter of fact, if you Google for Bangalore-based authors, you are unlikely to find my name there!

In our minds, there often lingers the question of SFBP versus BFLP—that is, whether it's better to be a Small Fish in a Big Pond or a Big Fish in a Little Pond. While it may seem desirable to be a big fish in a big pond (BFBP), not all of us possess the exceptional talent of a Djokovic, Nadal or Federer in our respective fields, prompting this contemplation. As for me, I identify myself as a MFMP, or a mid-sized fish in a mid-sized pond (keeping in mind that pond sizes themselves are relative). This tag suits me just fine, as I came to terms early in life with the realisation that I lacked any extraordinary gifts; rather, I was quite average in every aspect. Therefore, maximising my average potential largely involved competing against myself, pushing myself to work hard and improve upon my previous efforts, with little focus on competing with others. Perhaps my sole above-average trait lies in being above average at more things than many.

But yes, I can brew a mean cup of coffee.

Whether I qualify as a successful author is subjective and dependent on the evaluator or the criteria used for assessment. However, one thing is certain: I am unequivocally a contented and fulfilled author.

Before I sign off, I must confess that even while I may describe myself as a moderately successful author, I attribute much of my modest triumphs to the fickle nature of lady luck. When my debut book, *Games Indians Play* (*GIP*), was published in 2006, I was fortunate enough to have already authored three or four books in finance of academic nature and had honed my craft as a columnist and possessed a respectable academic pedigree. Thus, it would be remiss of me to claim complete anonymity at that juncture. So, one could argue that my path to publication in the public domain was smoother than that of an average first-time author.

Soon after the publication of *GIP*, my editor moved to another reputed publishing house; a random happenstance. Encouraged by the success of *GIP*, when I submitted my next manuscript *Don't Sprint the Marathon* to him, he deemed it worthy of publication, and the book fared well in sales, albeit not quite reaching the levels of *Games Indians Play*.

With two successful books in a row, my third and fourth books would have had to be terribly bad not to be accepted for publication! And without the third and fourth, certainly not the fifth and sixth, and thus all the way to the eleventh and twelfth. And that's where steadfast focus, staying power and discipline to write day after day after day, alongside a full-time job, kicks in. These attributes have to be a way of life, not a flavour of the season.

However, the most significant stroke of luck in my life has been my wife, Meena. An accomplished author in her own right, and a long-standing development sector professional, Meena possesses a keen eye for editing, a passion that matches mine for mangoes. She became my primary editor, scrutinising each of my books—except perhaps the first two, when we lived in two different cities—half a dozen times, with a fine-toothed comb before sending them off to the publishers. She has also been responsible for the titles of over half my books!

As you can see, I have been singularly blessed with good fortune in myriad ways. One can't help but wonder what can be accomplished if lady luck decides to look the other way!

Acknowledgments

This book has taken the longest in coming to fruition, when compared to my other books. Though each chapter told an absorbing story in its own right—if I do say so myself—a persistent question loomed over me like a veil: How did they all connect? Was the intention for the book to be an autobiography or a memoir? Or was it motivational, or self-help, with an underlying message?

The first question seemed laughable—who would be interested in the biography or memoirs of someone relatively unknown like myself? On the second point however, whether the chapters even had a unifying theme for readers to take away, I thought the answer was in the affirmative. Each chapter conveyed the underlying message that approaching daily challenges as if they were adventures, with oneself as the protagonist, can make them more manageable and even enjoyable. And then there was the subtler message in each chapter which I have tried to capture in the epigraph at the top of each. Most chapters also conveyed the idea that it usually paid off to go for an opportunity, especially when there was no downside to it. The book therefore could be seen as motivational, as it encourages readers to adopt a certain mindset towards life's tribulations. Should I pitch it as a motivational book then?

However, I was hesitant to categorise or slot the book specifically as memoirs or motivational, as I wanted it to be more than just a specific category. Yet, publishers often expect books to fit into a certain category, making it a challenge for authors. I can relate to this need for clear categorisation, having experienced first-hand the frustration with my book *Games Indians Play*, which is about India and Indians, often placed (or misplaced?) in the sports section of bookshops!

Identifying the appropriate audience for the book was another obstacle, but I believe I have struck a balanced tone that ought to suit both young and adult readers, both professionals and students. It does provide insights into India spanning half a century—India of the seventies, eighties, nineties and the first two decades of this century—which may have some context-value and novelty-value for youngsters, and nostalgia-value for oldsters.

Even now, I find myself uncertain about the categorisation of my book—should it be classified as self-help, motivational or leadership literature? Hence, my profound gratitude to Karthika, Gautam Padmanabhan and Westland for graciously accepting to publish my work, allowing me to rely on their expertise in determining the most fitting niche for the book. I offer heartfelt appreciation to Aurodeep Mukherjee, my editor, whose profoundly constructive and critical insights I wholeheartedly embraced during the finalisation of the manuscript.

Throughout the writing journey of this book, I had the privilege of sharing early drafts of numerous chapters with a select group of my close friends and confidantes: Suresh Krishna, Subroto Bagchi, Capt. Mohanram of the Indian Navy, Rear Admiral Sanatan Kulshrestha (my batchmate during my officer cadet days at INS Venduruthy), K. Jairaj, Ravi Chellam and Raghuram. Their insightful feedback and constructive critiques have been of immeasurable worth, significantly influencing the evolution of this book into its final iteration. I extend my heartfelt appreciation to each of them for their invaluable contributions.

And then, there is my very dear younger sister, Shyama—a scholar I respect deeply—who brought her immense powers of critiquing and editing into the manuscript, as only a fond sister can, making it more fluid and more error free. I am indebted to her.

My gratitude also goes to the endorsers of my book, who graciously and readily agreed to review the manuscript and provide their insights on the book for the back cover and front pages of the book.

To Saroj, I am grateful for the affectionate and dutiful care and concern that he always shows for my welfare and even comfort, 24x7. Without his support, my task of writing this book would have been twice as challenging.

To finally, Meena, my best friend and wife, I owe double my gratitude as always for her tireless editing of version after version of my manuscripts.